*Un*schooled

Raising Curious,
Well-Educated Children
Outside the
Conventional
Classroom

Kerry McDonald

Foreword by Peter Gray, PhD

**CHICAGO
REVIEW
PRESS**

First edition
Published by Chicago Review Press Incorporated
814 North Franklin Street
Chicago, Illinois 60610
ISBN 978-1-64160-063-7

Library of Congress Cataloging-in-Publication Data
Is available from the Library of Congress.

Cover design: Preston Pisellini
Cover photograph: Fat Camera/iStock/Getty Images
Interior design: Nord Compo

Printed in the United States of America
5 4 3 2 1

To Molly, Jack, Abby, and Sam, who teach me how to learn.

Author's Note

UNSCHOOLING IS SIMPLY LIVING, and allowing your children to live, without the specter of conventional schooling and school-like thinking. It is the act of fusing living and learning, of seeing them as one and the same. There is no one way to be an unschooler, no singular path of facilitating self-directed education. There is you, your children, your family, your community—your life. You will define and practice unschooling in your own way. I hope that the thoughts in these pages give you some ideas and suggestions, but your unschooling adventure is uniquely yours.

This book represents my personal views and experiences related to unschooling and self-directed education. It does not reflect the beliefs of all unschoolers or any particular self-directed learning organization. There are many thoughtful people who have been on the unschooling path for a long time and have valuable insights to share. In these pages, I have tried to highlight some of them; others are mentioned in the Additional Resources section at the end.

All of the names and details in this book are real. No one asked to be anonymous, and all were eager to share their perspectives on unschooling. This book focuses mostly on unschooling in the United States, but many of its concepts can be applied more globally. I do not intend this book to provide legal guidance for complying with local homeschooling regulations and alternative education requirements. For more information about the topics discussed in this book, please visit www.unschooledbook.com.

Contents

Foreword

BEFORE YOU ENTER FURTHER INTO this wonderful book by Kerry McDonald, it would serve you well to think broadly about the meaning of *education*. Too often, in everyday language, we equate education with *schooling*. We ask someone "How much education have you had?," and we expect them to tell us about the number of years they spent in school or their highest diploma. But any serious consideration of education requires us to think of it as something much bigger than and quite different from schooling and as something impossible to quantify.

In the long run of human history, schooling as we conceive of it today is new. It's been common for only about 150 years. It arose at a time in history when people believed that the most important lesson for children to learn is obedience and that there is some finite set of facts (or what were deemed to be facts) that must be drilled into everyone's head. Schools were designed for obedience training and drill, and they persist today primarily toward those ends, regardless of what school administrators, teachers, parents, and students themselves might want the ends to be.

The structural elements of schools—the confinement of students into age-segregated classrooms, the top-down hierarchy of authority, the required curricula, and the uniform systems of testing and grading—all dictate that obedience and memorization are the primary ends. As long as students obey by doing what the teacher tells them to do and memorize what the teacher tells them to memorize, they will pass. The only way to fail is to disobey. Many if not most people today recognize that schools aren't serving well the real needs of individuals or society. They fail to cultivate the initiative, creativity, critical thinking, love of learning, and social-emotional skills that are so valuable for success and happiness in today's world. Yet we foolishly try to fix the problem by doing more of what isn't working—requiring that young people spend ever more hours per day, days per year, and years of their life in school.

Education is something quite different from schooling, and it has been part and parcel of our human nature for as long as we have been humans. We might define education broadly as *the sum of everything a person learns that enables that person to live a satisfying and meaningful life.* This includes the kinds of things that people everywhere more or less need to learn, such as how to walk upright, how to speak their native language, how to get along with others, how to regulate their emotions, how to make plans and follow through on them, and how to think critically and make good decisions. It also includes some culture-specific skills, such as in our culture how to read, how to calculate with numbers, how to use computers, maybe how to drive a car—the things that most people feel they need to know in order to live the kind of life they want to live in the culture in which they are growing up. But much of education, for any individual, entails sets of skills and knowledge that may differ sharply from person to person, even within a given culture. As each person's concept of "a satisfying and meaningful life" is unique, each person's education is unique. Society benefits from such diversity.

Most of education, thus defined, is necessarily self directed. It derives from the self-chosen activities and life experiences of the person becoming educated. It requires an active, questioning mind-set, not the passive, obedient mind-set of schooling. As schooling has continued to occupy ever more of young people's lives, an increasing number of families have come to realize that it leaves too little time for self-directed education. Therefore, an increasing number of families are taking their children out of standard schools, out of any kind of imposed curriculum, and providing them, instead, with the time, freedom, empowerment, and resources needed to take charge of their own education.

It turns out that children are brilliant at directing their own education when we give them the opportunity to do so. This should not be surprising. Throughout human history, up until very recently, children were nearly always in charge of their own education. We would not have survived as a species if they weren't good at it. Natural selection has shaped children's curiosity, playfulness, sociability, willfulness, and innate desire to do well in the world in ways that serve beautifully the purpose of education.

Many of the families who opt out of coercive schooling become legally homeschoolers, but instead of doing school at home they enable the children to pursue their own interests. These are the families that generally call themselves *unschoolers*. Others enroll their children in settings that are legally schools but are structured in such a way that children are free to pursue their own interests. Such schools are often called *free schools* or *democratic schools*. Increasingly, families who have taken either of these routes are using the term *self-directed education* to describe their practice, and I am delighted to see that Kerry McDonald has used this term throughout this book. The term unites the families who have opted for different ways of supporting their children's self-education, and it helps us see that all of these families are part of one big, worldwide movement aimed at allowing children to live and learn in the joyful, natural ways that they are designed to live and learn.

As this book makes so clear, the choice of self-directed education is not an abrogation of responsibility on the part of families but an embracing of responsibility. In such families, the initiative and direction for education come from within the child, but parents and other adults help by providing the environmental contexts and security that children need to optimize their abilities to educate themselves.

This book is the best introduction to the world of self-directed education that I have yet seen. Kerry McDonald is the mother of four children who are in charge of their own education. The book benefits from her family's experiences, but it is far more than a personal account. This is a thoroughly researched, well-documented work that describes the full range of ways by which families and, increasingly, society as a whole are helping to facilitate children's abilities to educate themselves.

You will read here of home-based unschooling, world schooling, several varieties of free or democratic schools, and various types of learning centers and other community resources that enable children to pursue their own interests. As the author shows us repeatedly, there is no single right way to facilitate self-directed education for children, but the key to all of the ways lies in trust of, and support for, each child's own desires. And now, dig in and enjoy this book!

—Peter Gray, PhD
Research Professor, Department of Psychology, Boston College

Introduction

"It is, in fact, nothing short of a miracle that the modern methods of instruction have not yet entirely strangled the holy curiosity of inquiry; for this delicate little plant, aside from stimulation, stands mainly in need of freedom; without this it goes to wrack and ruin without fail. It is a very grave mistake to think that the enjoyment of seeing and searching can be promoted by means of coercion and a sense of duty."

—Albert Einstein[1]

THE SEASHELLS AT THEIR TOES sparkled in the strong June sun. My four children were ankle-deep in ocean water, shrieking with excitement each time they spotted a hermit crab or a sea star or a snail as the tide retreated. We were at "rocky beach," my kids' made-up name for that stretch of coastline near Cape Cod, Massachusetts. It is a favorite family spot, a place we spend hours together in the warmer months marveling at the critters living precariously along the shore. The beach was quiet that weekday but for the crashing waves and seagull squawks. It's a good half-mile wooded walk to the public beach from the parking lot in this state-managed nature preserve. The short hike and the rocky coast keep the number of beachgoers to a minimum even at summer's peak.

On that late spring morning, the beach was nearly empty for the first hour of our visit. I relaxed in the sunshine while my kids played. Then, a busload of middle school students from the town's public school arrived, worksheets and pencils in hand. I overheard the teacher, a pleasant, middle-aged man, giving instructions. The students, he said, were to explore the immediate beach area searching for the items listed on the worksheet. When those items were found, students were asked to write their observations and cross the item off the list.

I watched the students scatter with joyful enthusiasm, delighted to be at the beach on a warm day on the brink of summer. While my children continued their exploration and discovery of the tidal creatures, shouting now and then when they spotted something new or fascinating, the students consulted their worksheets. I sat on a rock noticing these two groups: the schooled children with their worksheets and instructions and inevitable assessment, and the unschooled children with the wide-open beach and all its treasures as their natural learning space.

One of the students ran past me toward a classmate shouting that she had found something really interesting along the beach, a critter of some sort. "Hey, look at this!" the girl exclaimed. "Isn't it so cool?" The friend inspected the critter and then glanced at the paper she was holding. "It's not on the worksheet," she replied matter-of-factly and turned to walk away. Her enthusiasm deflated, the girl dropped the creature and caught up to her classmate to find the next item on the list.

Children are natural learners. They are born with the drive to explore and synthesize their world. Their childhood curiosity and exuberance lead them to learn and discover, to make connections and deepen their knowledge, so that they may gain essential skills. This inclination to learn, along with a passion for discovery, does not magically disappear at a certain age. Our industrial model of schooling systematically diminishes a child's natural curiosity and ability to self educate. Educators have long known this to be true. In his 1967 bestselling book, *How Children Learn*, teacher and social reformer John Holt writes:

> In short, children have a style of learning that fits their condition, and which they use naturally and well until we train them out of it. We like to say that we send children to school to teach

them to think. What we do, all too often, is to teach them to think badly, to give up a natural and powerful way of thinking in favor of a method that does not work well for them and that we rarely use ourselves.[2]

For the girl at the beach, her enthusiasm and curiosity were driving her to seek and discover. Like the unschooled kids nearby, she was drawn to explore the beach without regard to an arbitrary assignment. How long will it be before, like her friend, her natural learning instincts are extinguished?

I was born in 1977, the year Holt launched the first newsletter for homeschooling families, *Growing Without Schooling*. At the time, Holt was an unofficial leader of the fledgling homeschooling movement, supporting parents eager to remove their children from school even before the practice was legally recognized in all US states by 1993. He also coined the term *unschooling* in the 1970s and sought to distinguish education from schooling. Schooling is one method of education, but it is not the only one. There are many ways to learn without being schooled. Holt believed strongly in the self-educative capacity of all people, including young people. As a classroom teacher in private schools in both Colorado and Massachusetts, he witnessed firsthand the ways in which institutional schooling, even at purportedly "good" schools, inhibits the natural process of learning.

Holt was especially concerned about the myriad ways that schooling suppresses a child's natural learning tendencies by forcing the child, through curriculum and instruction, to learn what the teacher wants her to know. He believed that parents and educators should support a child's natural learning, not control it. Rather than simply replicate the curriculum and assessment expectations of the schooling they chose to leave, parents should detach altogether from a schooled mind-set. The deepest, most meaningful, most enduring learning is the kind of learning that is self determined. Something piques our interest in a particular subject or skill and we take the necessary steps to learn more, to do more.

Like most people, I was schooled to believe that learning is something that happens to us, something passive and rote. A teacher teaches us, or tells us what we need to read or do in order to know, and then we learn. But as I watched my own children, I realized this wasn't true. They learned to smile, to sit, to roll, to crawl, to walk, and then to run without any direct instruction. They learned to talk not by sitting in a classroom being taught how to talk but by being surrounded by people who talked and who encouraged them to try. Mostly, though, they learned all of these things naturally, following their own human desire to investigate, interact with, and understand their environment. Boston College psychology professor and self-directed education advocate Dr. Peter Gray studies natural learning tendencies and the ways these impulses can be eroded through schooling. He writes in his book, *Free to Learn*:

> Children come into the world burning to learn and genetically programmed with extraordinary capacities for learning. They are little learning machines. Within their first four years or so they absorb an unfathomable amount of information and skills without any instruction. . . . Nature does not turn off this enormous desire and capacity to learn when children turn five or six. We turn it off with our coercive system of schooling.[3]

As I observed the ways in which my young children mastered new skills, I also realized how different their timetables were. My older son, Jack, rolled earlier and sat up later than his big sister, Molly; she crawled "early" but talked "late." I began to appreciate the vast differences in human development and wondered why we expect certain things at certain times in certain ways from children. As Molly and Jack grew and two more children, Abby and Sam, followed them, I realized that these normal human variances were even more pronounced than I originally thought. Jack was running at ten months. Molly didn't walk until she was almost a year and a half, when she suddenly ran down the hallway in our city condo. Sam rolled over at just one month old. Abby talked in full sentences before she was a year. Sam was much later. Molly taught herself to read at age four. Jack taught himself to read at seven. Jack taught himself to swim at age four; Abby taught herself at six. Children's natural developmental timetables are incredibly varied and distinct. How could an age-segregated, one-size-fits-all system of mass schooling possibly appreciate and accommodate the vast diversity of the human experience?

As schooling becomes even more standardized and test-driven than when we were kids, and the academic pressures on children mount, more parents are questioning this cookie-cutter approach to education. They may be witnessing in their own homes and neighborhoods the striking correlation between decreasing childhood free play and increasing mental health disorders in young people. They may be dismayed by schooled expectations that now push kindergarteners to read, and they may be concerned that as instruction ousts play—and recess diminishes—more young children are being diagnosed with attention disorders and put on potent psychotropic medications because they can't sit still and focus—at five. These parents may see how their children's creativity has waned and their enthusiasm for learning has dwindled, replaced by extrinsic motivations and a determination to simply make it through the day without bullying or condescension. Learning for the sake of learning disappears.

When children go to school, their natural learning stops. They become conditioned to learn in a top-down, static, conforming style that crushes their natural creativity. The teacher, regardless of how benevolent he or she may be, tells the child what to know, what to think, what to do. The child's own opinions, interests, and unique developmental timetables are meaningless within the schooled context. Disconnected from their natural creative tendencies, their ability to self educate weakens. As they conform to the expectations of forced schooling, they stop seeking to learn and instead wait to be taught. Ivan Illich writes in *Deschooling Society*: "School makes alienation preparatory to life, thus depriving education of reality and work of creativity. School prepares for the institutionalization of life by teaching the need to be taught."[4]

Today, many parents and educators are rejecting the myth that people need to be schooled in order to learn. They are replacing an outdated, Industrial Age schooling model of education with a new learning one fit for the Imagination Age—the new era beyond the information age when creativity and ingenuity will be our key cultural and economic drivers. While homeschooling, unschooling, and free schooling may provide the initial blueprint for alternatives to school, today many new prototypes for learning without schooling are popping up across the country, from self-directed learning centers and unschooling collectives, to innovative summer camps, after-school programs, teen immersion and apprenticeship models—and even to traditional public schools that are reinventing themselves to put young people in charge of their own learning.

One thing these parents and educators share is a deep understanding that learning anything is most effective, most fulfilling, when it is self directed: when the freedom to learn is provided, when the resources are available, when the time and space for learning are offered, and when knowledgeable and supportive facilitators are available to help if needed. These are the fundamental tenets espoused by Holt: "My concern is not to improve 'education' but to do away with it, to end the ugly and antihuman business of people-shaping and let people shape themselves."[5] Now, parents and educators are taking John Holt's words to heart and are creating alternatives to school that help young people to shape themselves.

In the following pages, I share the stories of these insightful and intentional parents and educators, as well as unschooling alumni. My hope is that through their experiences and enterprises, you may find encouragement and inspiration for letting go of a schooled mind-set in favor of an unschooled one. First, it's helpful to understand the many often hidden and subconscious ways we associate learning with schooling. The early chapters reveal the ways in which schooling and education have become entangled and how we may begin to separate them by better understanding the ways in which children naturally learn. The later chapters dig deeper into the learning models that currently exist to support natural learning without schooling, and the new ones that could be scaled and expanded. The book concludes with a glimpse into the future, picturing how things might look if we as a society shed our schooled view of the world and instead imagined learning and living in entirely new ways.

Forced schooling is a cultural relic, reminiscent of a bygone age. Stuck preparing young people to do the jobs now done by robots, mass schooling ignores the cultural and economic realities of a new human era. Instead of robots, we need inventive thinkers, curious seekers, and passionate doers. Inventiveness, curiosity, and passion are all characteristics that young children naturally exude. We don't need to train them for the jobs of the future; we just need to stop training these inborn characteristics out of them. We need to give them the freedom and opportunity to pursue their passions, follow their curiosity, and invent creative solutions to complex problems. Given the vast amount of information available to us, the creative skills necessary to process it all, and the seemingly insurmountable challenges our planet now faces, we desperately need to embrace a new paradigm of education. We need to let go of the notion of *schooling*—something someone does to someone else—and instead reclaim *learning*—something humans naturally do. Only then will we have educated citizens with the agency and skills to live a good life and preserve a good planet in a new age of innovation, information, and imagination.

1

Playing School

"What does education often do? It makes a straight-cut ditch of a free, meandering brook."

—Henry David Thoreau[1]

"IF YOU DON'T STOP TALKING, I'll throw you out the window!" my first-grade teacher shouted at me. My small, six-year-old body froze. I swore she was serious and shut my mouth. I waited in terror until the final school bell rang. Then I leaped onto the school bus and ran home as fast as I could from the bus stop to the comfort of my mother's arms.

"Oh, she didn't really mean it," my mother explained, trying to soothe my shaken nerves. "She just wanted you to listen and pay attention and not chitchat. She would never really throw you out the window. It was just an expression."

Hyperbole though it may have been, I was wounded. At that moment, the reality of schooling became clear. Those previous play-filled days of part-time preschool, the innocence of morning kindergarten to gain *social skills* and *academic readiness* were a setup. They didn't really want us to be social and ready; they wanted us to learn quickly how to sit down, stay quiet, follow orders, and conform. They wanted us to lose ourselves—to lose our natural childhood exuberance—in the name of education. It was for our own good, they told us. Resistance was futile.

So I learned. I learned quickly to lick my wounds and get good at playing the game of school. I realized that to succeed at this game I needed to become adept at obedience. I did what the teacher told me to do. I raised my hand, followed instructions, colored in the lines. I stopped talking. I listened, memorized, and regurgitated to the satisfaction of the teacher and the test. I was a good girl. I also already knew how to read which, once past the window incident, made me a teacher's pet—someone she could send off to the corner to do advanced worksheets while she labored away with the "slow kids" and yelled at the troublemakers. By the end of first grade, I had this school thing down flat. Heck, I even *liked* it.

From then on, it was very clear to me what I needed to do to gain the teacher's affections, to get the GOOD JOB! sticker, to collect the As and accolades, to win. I learned the rules. Game on. As Robert Fried writes in *The Game of School*: "The Game begins when we focus on getting through the school day rather than actually *learning*."[2]

As so often happens when we reach adulthood, and especially parenthood, we realize how much we don't know. I realized that I might have been successfully *schooled*, but I didn't feel well *educated*. When I reflect on the approximately fifteen thousand hours I spent in K–12 public school, I think of what a waste of time most of those hours were. What else could I have been learning in those hours? How much more genuine could those hours have been if I wasn't spending so much time playing the game, but actually exploring, reading, doing?

As Americans, we seem genuinely willing to embrace—even fight for—freedom for most people on our planet. Yet, we place children in increasingly restrictive learning environments, at ever-earlier ages and for much longer portions of their day and year than at any other time in our history. We place the vast majority of children in schooling environments that are much more controlling and unpleasant and unhealthy than we grown-ups would accept in our own lives and workplaces. We allow children's bodies and thoughts to be managed by others, and we dismiss institutional side effects, like bullying, obesity, anxiety and depression, a decline in gross motor skills, and a rise in ADHD and other mental health disorders. Actions that would be criminal offenses in our adult workplaces are tolerated and expected in our children's schooling.

It is no wonder that under these oppressive institutional conditions—characteristic of the rise of the Industrial Age—most children have the life force drained out of them. The parent of even the most inquisitive toddler witnesses the steady erosion of his natural curiosity and wonder as the child moves through his schooling. This is axiomatic, as American schooling was designed to strip the joy of natural learning—of following the human will to explore and discover—in favor of conformity and compliance. On the subject of forced schooling, acclaimed *War on Kids* documentary filmmaker Cevin Soling writes: "Learned helplessness is a vital feature and takes place very early when children discover that they will never be permitted to follow their passions. Every aspect of student life is controlled, including their surroundings, what they can do, how they can act, and what and how they may think."[3]

Most of us think that declining childhood creativity is just a natural consequence of growing up. Yet young people who have never been schooled, or who learn in self-directed education environments, consistently demonstrate that humans' curiosity and capacity to learn and synthesize do not diminish with age. The industrial schooling framework dulls them, but creativity and a zest for knowledge can be retained and reignited within a natural learning environment.

I recently asked followers of my *Whole Family Learning* blog's Facebook page to reflect on their own K–12 schooling and share a word or phrase that sums it up. The responses were disheartening: boring, waste of time, low self-worth, pressure, anxiety, prison, opportunity cost, bullies, stress, shame, wasted opportunities, torture, hide, one-dimensional, hell, long, repetition, scary, inauthentic, abusive, authoritarianism, tedious, forced, glad it's over. Would you add anything to this list? While certainly not an unbiased sample, these responses reinforce the sentiments and findings of many students, educators, and policymakers. As Noam Chomsky says, "The education system is supposed to train people to be obedient, conformist, not think too much, do what you're told, stay passive."[4]

For many young people this "system of indoctrination of the young,"[5] as Chomsky calls mass education, leads to deep and penetrating wounds, as their spirit dims in the name of conformity. Those of us who do well in the mass schooling model are the ones most capable of quickly burying

our wounds and learning to conform. We accept the confusion of schooling with learning, and dutifully obey. For many children, the harm of
compulsory schooling is obvious. Many are at a disadvantage right out
of the gate, and those disadvantages are amplified and embedded as their
schooling continues. Others are bullied, labeled, tracked, or medicated.

But beyond these obvious harms are the subtler ones. Most schooled
children, myself included, become conditioned to value and seek extrinsic rewards and superficial achievements. We don't see value in our
work or ourselves unless someone else affirms it. We lose creativity and
individuality as we conform to arbitrary curriculum demands, teacher
expectations, and institutional mores. In Kirsten Olson's book *Wounded
by School*, educator Parker Palmer discusses "the hidden and long-lasting
wounds that result from the structural violence inherent in the ways
we organize and evaluate learning, wounds that range from 'I found
out that I have no gift of creativity,' or 'I learned that I'm no good at
sports,' to 'They drained off my self-confidence,' 'I emerged feeling stu-
pid,' or 'They put me in the losers' line and I've been there ever since.'
Equally sad and profoundly ironic is the wound that may be the most
widespread of all: the eagerness to learn that we all bring into the world
as infants is often diminished and even destroyed by our schooling."[6]

So while it may seem that some of us made it through mass schooling unscathed—and even on top—I believe that few, if any of us, really
do. We don't know how else we might have spent those fifteen thousand
hours: to follow our curiosities, to reveal our interests, to pursue our
passions, to read, and read, and read some more. We don't know how
well-educated we could have become in our youth if we hadn't spent
so much time sitting, memorizing, repeating, forgetting, and otherwise
playing school. How might your life be different now if you were granted
the freedom to pursue your passions as a child, rather than spend so
many hours following someone else's schooled agenda?

Of course, as a first grader, and throughout my years in K–12 public
schooling in a predominantly white working-class suburb of Boston, I
didn't realize it was a game. I just knew that it was school. It wasn't until
years later when I uncovered that school, as we know it, is a relatively
recent social construct. For most of human history, and most of our time

in the New World, formal schooling didn't exist for most people. And yet, we survived and thrived, passed on our knowledge and skills to the next generation, and became highly literate and numerate. Education as synonymous with schooling is a fairly new idea.

Narrowing Education to Schooling

When the Pilgrims arrived in what is now Plymouth, Massachusetts, in 1620, they brought with them a sense of duty to educate children to be literate and numerate. The clear understanding was that parents had the moral and civic obligation to educate their children, and there was an implicit belief within the community that clergymen and elders would ensure that children were educated. For the Pilgrims, family was sovereign. As historian Milton Gaither writes: "It is common knowledge that many British settlers moved to New England to build a holy commonwealth, a 'city on a hill' that would shine its light on the darkness of British decadence. But what is less well known is that the masonry being used to build this holy city was the family. The Pilgrims and many others came to the New World to build a family state."[7]

Just over two decades after the Pilgrims' arrival, Massachusetts Bay Colony legislators passed the colonies' first compulsory education statute. The General School Law of 1642 required families to ensure the "good education" of their children. The law strayed from English precedent by shifting education oversight from clergy to selectmen. This early law emphasized a developing state interest in compulsory *education*, but it was not yet narrowly focused on *schooling*, and parents remained responsible for their children's education.[8] Education was separate and distinct from schooling.

Five years later, in 1647, Massachusetts Bay passed its second compulsory education law, the "Old Deluder Satan" bill. It said that children should be educated enough to read the Bible and understand how to avoid evil and vice. This second and more consequential law required towns with fifty or more families to hire a teacher, and towns with one hundred or more families to open and operate a grammar school. These schools were not compulsory in the sense that schooling is today; rather, it was the town that was compelled by the state to offer such a school for any families who wanted to use it. Towns, not parents, were punished for not complying with this early compulsory education statute. The implementation and enforcement of these initial compulsory education laws were scattered, with many towns refusing to comply and instead paying a fine.[9]

Over the following decades of the seventeenth and eighteenth centuries, similar compulsory education laws spread throughout the mid-Atlantic and southern colonies. As the population grew, more schools were erected and parents could choose whether to send their children there, when to send them, and for how long. The family remained the primary institution of early America, and parents retained full control over the upbringing and education of children.

While parents were responsible for their children's education, they were not the only ones teaching them. They often hired tutors and relied on apprenticeships. As schools emerged in the early settlements, local parents were frequently the ones responsible for hiring, housing, and firing teachers. Colony schools complemented the ways children learned at home, and early "dame schools" freed parents of young children to do chores and tend to the household. But school was never seen as a replacement for the education provided by parents at home and managed by parents using the wider resources of their community.[10] As historian Carl Kaestle declares: "Society educates in many ways; the state educates through schools."[11]

The conversation around compulsory education continued through the Revolutionary era, as the Founding Fathers grappled with the understanding that ensuring liberty in a thriving new democracy required an educated citizenry. Thomas Jefferson, for instance, recognized the essential connection between education and freedom, writing in 1816, "If a nation expects to be ignorant and free in a state of civilization, it expects what never was and never will be."[12] Still, the institution of the family prevailed over the interests of the state. Jefferson advocated for a highly decentralized system of education, locally controlled by parents in small districts, or "wards" as he called them, with little government involvement. He also believed that parental rights and individual liberty outweighed mandatory compliance. In 1817, Jefferson wrote, "It is better to tolerate the rare instance of a parent refusing to let his child be educated, than to shock the common feelings and ideas by forcible asportation and education of the infant against the will of the father."[13] Make education accessible, highly treasured, and free for the poor, Jefferson proposed, but don't mandate it under a legal threat of force.

In the mid-nineteenth century this all changed. The population grew larger and more diverse, and state institutions concentrated government power in a more centralized way, weakening the once dominant role of the family. Horace Mann, a Massachusetts legislator and state senate majority leader, played an instrumental role in this growing institutionalization of society in the 1800s. Mann, the proclaimed "father of American public education," also has the distinction of creating the nation's first mental institution in 1833, shortly before turning his full attention to centralized schooling.[14]

Mann became enamored with the Prussian model of compulsory schooling. It was orderly and efficient, and it facilitated the inculcation of a uniform set of moral values. The Prussians, who lived in a broad area that now includes modern-day Germany, were among the first in the world to create a taxpayer-funded, compulsory system of schooling focused on order and compliance. The Prussian model emphasized a nationalized curriculum, standardized teacher training, and punishments for parents who refused to send their children to school.[15]

Recently elected as the first secretary of the newly created Massachusetts Board of Education, Mann had the authority to create a new educational landscape. He was dissatisfied with the decentralized and dispersed system of education that Massachusetts currently had, with an array of locally controlled public schools, private schools, church schools, charity schools, homeschooling, tutoring and apprenticeship programs, and so on. There was no state control of schooling at the time, no way of centrally directing what all children learned and compelling them to learn it. There was also no regimented teacher training program or standardized certification process to ensure that teachers all taught the same things in the same way. This was troubling to Mann and his colleagues. The systematic, compulsory Prussian model of education seemed like an ideal solution. As Mann famously said: "Men are cast-iron, but children are wax."[16]

Many of us believe the myth that the catalyst for universal compulsory schooling was that illiteracy was rampant in the early 1800s. In truth, literacy rates were quite high throughout the United States prior to compulsory schooling. Slaves were often the least literate, as it was typically illegal to teach a slave to read—although many slaves took extraordinary measures to teach themselves to read, as Heather Andrea Williams reveals in her book, *Self-Taught: African American Education in Slavery and Freedom.*[17] Women and immigrants also had lower literacy rates. Historians Boles and Gintis report that approximately three-quarters of the total population, including slaves, was literate, and Massachusetts had especially high literacy rates.[18] According to Folger and Nam, the overall US illiteracy rate in 1840 was 22 percent, including women, immigrants, and slaves.[19] This high literacy rate is particularly striking when we consider that this was an era when books were quite costly and often inaccessible, and public libraries were only just beginning to emerge. The nation's first public library opened in Peterborough, New Hampshire, in 1833, followed by the Boston Public Library in 1852.

The reality is that nineteenth-century politicians and citizens were fearful of and overwhelmed by rapid societal change as thousands of immigrants streamed into American cities in the mid-1800s. The total US population exploded between 1820 and 1860, with the most immigration occurring in the 1840s and 1850s, at the peak of the Irish potato famine. Over four million immigrants arrived during those two decades.[20] Particularly troubling to lawmakers at the time was the fact that many of these new immigrants were Irish Catholics who threatened the dominant Anglo-Saxon Protestant cultural and religious customs. In 1847 alone, thirty-seven thousand Irish immigrants came to Boston, a city of just over one hundred thousand people.[21] Boston's population more than doubled between 1820 and 1840, prompting members of the Massachusetts state legislature to mourn in 1848: "Those now pouring in upon us, in masses of thousands upon thousands, are wholly of another kind in morals and intellect."[22]

In advocating for compulsory schooling statutes, Horace Mann and his nineteenth-century education reform colleagues were deeply fearful of parental authority—particularly of immigrant parents. In his book *Horace Mann's Troubling Legacy*, University of Vermont professor Bob

Pepperman Taylor elaborates further on the nineteenth-century distrust of parents and its influence on compulsory schooling. He explains that "the group receiving the greatest scolding from Mann is parents themselves. He questions the competence of a great many parents, but even worse is what he takes to be the perverse moral education provided to children by their corrupt parents."[23] Forced schooling was then intended as an antidote to those "corrupt parents," but not, presumably, for morally superior parents like Mann, who continued to homeschool his own three children with no intention of sending them to the common schools he mandated for others. As Mann's biographer, Jonathan Messerli, writes:

> From a hundred platforms, Mann had lectured that the need for better schools was predicated upon the assumption that parents could no longer be entrusted to perform their traditional roles in moral training and that a more systematic approach within the public school was necessary. Now as a father, he fell back on the educational responsibilities of the family, hoping to make the fireside achieve for his own son what he wanted the schools to accomplish for others.[24]

In 1852, thanks to Mann's vision and advocacy, Massachusetts passed the nation's first compulsory schooling law. For the first time ever in the United States, children were forced to attend school. This law required all children between the ages of eight and fourteen to go to school for at least twelve weeks per year, of which six weeks needed to be consecutive. In the following decades, all US states adopted similar versions of the same law, with Mississippi the final holdout, not passing its compulsory schooling law until 1918.[25] Unlike the previous compulsory *education* laws that were loosely monitored and enforced, these new compulsory *schooling* laws had teeth. James Carter, who was instrumental in creating Massachusetts's first education board, wrote in his *Essays on Popular Education*: "The ignorant must be allured to learn, by every motive which can be offered to them. And if they will not thus be allured, they must be taken by the strong arm of government and brought out, willing or unwilling, and made to learn, at least, enough to make them peaceable and good citizens."[26] If parents did not comply with the compulsory attendance law, they could be fined or face jail time, or even lose their parental rights.

These nineteenth-century compulsory schooling laws gradually became more far-reaching and restrictive, mandating more time spent in school beginning at earlier ages and extending into later adolescence. Compulsory education now meant compulsory schooling. With passage of the 1852 law, education in America shifted from a broadly defined social good with an assortment of formal and informal modes of learning, to a clearly defined, institutionalized method of schooling. From then on, education would be inseparable from schooling. Mann's biographer Messerli writes:

> In other words, Mann proposed to expand the scope of train-
> ing and schooling, with its potential for control, orderliness,
> and predictability, so that it would encompass almost all the
> ends achieved by the far broader process of formal and infor-
> mal socialization. That in enlarging the European concept of
> *schooling*, he might narrow the real parameters of *education* by
> enclosing it within the four walls of the public school classroom.[27]

Enclosed within the four walls of the public school classroom is where most American education has remained now for over 165 years. As state-controlled schooling gained strength and influence, families gradu-ally lost their power. Some of this was due to changing economic norms. The Industrial Revolution took many parents out of their homes and into factories, and schools became an obvious, and now required, place to keep children while their parents worked. But much of the decline in family empowerment was due to the increasing grip of mass schooling.

Many families rebelled. Catholics, for example, were outraged by compulsory schooling laws mandating that their children attend schools that were allegedly secular but were clearly focused on the Puritan beliefs and texts of their Anglo-Saxon Protestant founders and teachers. In response, many Catholic parishes created their own private, parochial schools. Throughout the late nineteenth and early twentieth centuries, citizens and lawmakers used various legislative tactics to restrict the development and growth of private and parochial schools. This effort came to a peak in 1922 when Oregon passed an expanded compulsory schooling law requiring all children to attend a public school, prohibiting attendance at parochial and other private schools. In 1925, in the landmark case of *Pierce v. Society of Sisters*, the US Supreme Court struck down the Oregon law as unconstitutional. In delivering the opinion of the court, Justice McReynolds wrote:

> The Act of 1922 unreasonably interferes with the liberty of parents and guardians to direct the upbringing and education of children under their control . . . The fundamental theory of liberty upon which all governments in this Union repose excludes any general power of the State to standardize its children by forcing them to accept instruction from public teachers only. The child is not the mere creature of the State; those who nurture him and direct his destiny have the right, coupled with the high duty, to recognize and prepare him for additional obligations.[28]

This tug-of-war between parental rights and government power continued throughout the twentieth century. Compulsory schooling laws tightened, high school expanded and attendance became mandatory, and kindergartens became integrated into primary schools. Parents often pushed back, sending their children to private schools or starting their own. In the 1970s, homeschooling began its modern revival, first among countercultural hippie liberals and closely followed by a much larger group of religious conservatives. Through the pioneering efforts of twentieth-century homeschooling and unschooling advocates, such as Holt and others, compulsory schooling laws loosened or became more clearly defined to grant families renewed control over their children's education. Today, there are more signs of change as a growing number of parents and educators look to free the next generation of children from the confines of the classroom.

Homeschooling

While parents and education activists were celebrating the full legalization of US homeschooling in the mid-1990s, I was knee-deep in college education textbooks. I read the rosy stories about American public schooling as the great equalizer, designed to provide opportunity and social mobility to every child regardless of birth or background. But at the same time, I also discovered that other stories I had been taught about American history, from Christopher Columbus to Thomas Jefferson, had a darker side not often revealed. I began to see that the origins of American forced schooling had a similar shadow. Educational historian Charles Glenn writes in his book *The Myth of the Common School,* "The objective of this state-controlled system of popular education had little to do with economic or egalitarian goals; it was to shape future citizens to a common pattern."[29] I was growing increasingly curious about education ideas and practices that broke free from the century-old model of legislated sameness.

Nearing graduation, I was starting to understand more about the game of school that I had played for so long, and to challenge the noble story I had been told about its inception. I grew fascinated by alternative education and progressive schools, as well as the education choices parents made or could not make. In a senior seminar, I had a chance to explore these topics more fully for an independent research project. A classmate of mine had a family member who homeschooled her daughter and who was willing to talk to me.

I arrived at this homeschooling family's cozy home on a brisk fall day in 1998 and was warmly welcomed by a mom and her eight-year-old daughter, who was playing her violin as I sat down at the kitchen table. When the girl finished, I chatted with her a bit about her music and homeschooling. I was awestruck at how articulate, interesting, and comfortable with adults this young child was. She was quite unlike the other second graders I had just spent weeks observing in a nearby public elementary school for a teaching practicum. This little girl was enthusiastic and confident, curious and content.

But was she socialized? That was my first question for the homeschooling mom after her daughter left us alone to chat. Like most people, I thought socialization was the key reason for sending children to school, although I admittedly didn't have a good grasp of what it meant. The dictionary definition of "socialize" means *to place under government or group ownership or control,* or *to cause to accept or behave in accordance with social norms or expectations.* By contrast, being "social" means *interacting with other people and living in communities.* Asking if this girl was social was what I really wanted to know. My engrained idea of school socialization and arbitrary age segregation distorted my view of what being *social* really meant. The mom enlightened me. She explained that because her daughter was not in school, she did not spend her days interacting only with same-age peers and a static handful of teachers. She was free to interact with children of all ages, and did so through her local homeschooling network and through various extracurricular activities and other community offerings. Furthermore, her daughter interacted with many grown-ups throughout the community who served as her teachers and mentors, and she frequently engaged with others at the library, at the market, at the post office, at the park, and so on.

This was authentic "socialization," I thought: learning social norms, behaviors, and expectations by being out in the community interacting daily with a diverse assortment of people doing real work and engaging in other creative pursuits. That to me seemed far more genuine than the forced socialization I experienced as a student and that I had observed most profoundly in my recent student-teaching rotation. School socialization is based on an expectation of obedience, compliance, and conformity. It was about rule following. Learning was secondary. Exuberance was a liability.

At the local district elementary school where I did my student-teaching practicum that same semester, the scene was quite different from that warm and welcoming home. The children, arbitrarily divided by age, were all organized into their rows, worksheets piled at their desks. Bells and buzzers and rigid routines orchestrated their movements. They needed permission to pee. While no one was threatened to be thrown out the window, they were frequently reminded to raise their hand and not speak out of turn. They were also reprimanded when they spoke to the person sitting next to or behind them, with a reminder that "socializing is for after school." I could see right away who was good at playing the game of school and who was resisting.

I wondered if the kids who were resisting—the troublemakers, the daydreamers, the failures—were really the wise ones. Did they realize, much sooner than I did, that schooling is a game, that the odds of winning are low, that the rules aren't fair, and that in order to play they had to surrender to external expectations and lose parts of themselves?

In her book *Troublemakers*, author Carla Shalaby writes about these "canaries in the mine," as she calls the children who refuse to play the game. She explains:

> These troublemakers—rejected and criminalized—are the children from whom we can learn the most about freedom. They make noise when others are silent. They stand up against every school effort to force conformity. They insist on their own way instead of the school's way. These young people demand freedom even as they are simultaneously the most stringently controlled, surveilled, confined, and policed in our schools.[30]

The troublemakers I saw refused to play the game and taught me more about teaching and learning than any education textbook ever could.

Observing conventionally schooled children also taught me something else: teachers are caught up in this game just as much as their students. They have their own rules to follow, their own mandates to administer. They have curriculum directives, assessment protocols, and the daily work of crowd control with a highly variable group of young people with different needs, backgrounds, and abilities who are compelled by law to be there.

Teachers must conform to arbitrary expectations in the same way their students do. The only difference is that teachers can quit. On the editorial pages of the *Wall Street Journal*, New York State Teacher of the Year, John Taylor Gatto, did just that. After teaching in New York City for nearly thirty years, Gatto proclaimed in his opinion article, "I Quit, I Think," that he could no longer "hurt kids to make a living."[31] He went on to write and speak about the damages of conventional schooling on children and society. In his most popular book, *Dumbing Us Down: The Hidden Curriculum of Compulsory Schooling*, Gatto reveals how teachers are as powerless as their students. He writes:

> *Successful* children do the thinking I assign them with a minimum of resistance and a decent show of enthusiasm. Of the millions of things of value to study, I decide what few we have time

for. Actually, though, this is decided by my faceless employers. The choices are theirs—why should I argue? Curiosity has no important place in my work, only conformity.[32]

Students and teachers alike are caught up in the conformity-driven culture of mass schooling, leaving little opportunity for true creativity and individuality.

The contrast between the traditionally schooled children I observed and the alternatively schooled one led me to graduate school, where I studied education policy. I was interested in alternative education, but I had a nagging sense that while alternative schools were a step in the right direction, alternatives *to* school were where we really needed to go. Most of the education efforts I had seen up until that point still operated within a schooling model of education, not a learning one. The grip of schooling remained tight. Even the homeschooling family I met had a packaged curriculum and replicated school at home. Could education and schooling be separated? It wasn't until I became a mom that I would really understand what learning without schooling looks like.

Learning Without Schooling

A decade after college, when my daughter Molly was two and my son Jack was an infant, I hadn't yet decided what their education would look like. We simply lived our lives together, spending time exploring city parks and museums, enjoying mornings at the library story time and sing-alongs, visiting with friends and relatives, reading and coloring, cuddling and napping and snacking, and playing. Lots of playing. It was too soon, I thought, to decide what Molly's "real" education would look like. For now, being immersed in our community, following the daily rhythms dictated by a life with little ones, seemed enough. Yet it was true that many of Molly's young friends had already enrolled in preschool, beginning their formal schooling while just barely out of diapers. In fact, most two-year-olds in my city were in some type of school.

As the fall went on, I would repeatedly get asked the same questions from various strangers in various places throughout the city:

"How old is your daughter?"
"Two and a half."
"Oh, so where does she go to school?"
"She doesn't. She's two."

Sometimes these questioners would then say, "So are you home-schooling?" The more I was asked these questions, the more I began to think critically about the role of formal schooling in our culture, particularly the increasing focus on enrolling children in schools at ever-earlier ages. I wondered about the potential ramifications of such a trend, the possible impact of shortening childhood and accelerating institutionalized education. I had read the work of Dr. Raymond Moore and his wife, Dorothy, two central figures who, along with Holt, ushered in the modern homeschooling movement. In their popular book *Better Late Than Early* they urged parents to delay formal schooling for their young children and nurture them at home. They write, "In principle, a young child, given reasonable freedom and personal guidance, develops better outside the classroom than within it. This is particularly true of the first 8 years or so."[33]

Later academic research would reinforce the Moores' claim. Most significantly, a 2008 longitudinal study by Kern and Friedman at the University of California, Riverside concluded that "early school entry was associated with less educational attainment, worse midlife adjustment, and most importantly, increased mortality risk."[34] Friedman asserts:

> Most children under age six need lots of time to play, and to develop social skills, and to learn to control their impulses. An over-emphasis on formal classroom instruction—that is, studies instead of buddies, or staying in instead of playing out—can have serious effects that might not be apparent until years later.[35]

As I read this research on the potential harm of early schooling for many children, I thought also about how engrained the idea of schooling has become in our culture. School was the default. It was where learning took place. The societal message was clear: children couldn't be properly educated without being schooled.

Yet I recalled my time visiting with the homeschooling family ten years earlier. I remembered the startling differences I observed between the authentic learning at home and throughout one's community, and the contrived and authoritarian learning in school. Those images stuck with me. Prompted by the strangers' questions that fall, and wondering what my own children's education would look like, I decided to revisit homeschooling and alternatives to school.

The first book I read about homeschooling as a mom and not a student was a gem. *Better Than School* by homeschooling mother Nancy Wallace was first published in 1983. Sitting on the shelves of my local public library, it resonated with me. Like me at the time, Nancy had two children, a boy and a girl. Also like me, she watched as her children's early learning unfolded organically, without coercion. But when she sent her son, Ishmael, to school in the first grade, everything changed. She writes:

> Our school troubles with Ishmael started during his very first week in first grade. He was told that he couldn't go to the bathroom without first raising his hand and getting permission, and apparently he sat there for a long, long time with his hand raised before he finally wet his pants: not a very auspicious beginning. Then he was upset because all they seemed to do was to color in mimeographed papers, but when he went up to the teacher and explained that he already knew how to color and wanted to learn something else, she told him to go back to his seat and work on coloring more neatly. I watched Ishmael struggling to resign himself to school, to the boredom and seemingly arbitrary rules.[36]

Nancy Wallace waded into homeschooling at a much different time than I did. Raising her children in the 1970s and '80s, she recounts the process of gaining permission to homeschool before the practice was fully legal and the challenges of embracing schooling alternatives before they were commonplace. While homeschooling families still face hurdles, it is much easier now thanks to the hard work of earlier education activists who fought to re-empower parents and loosen the clamp of schooling on education.

As I began to explore the modern homeschooling movement and connect with local homeschooling families, I learned that in contrast to the systematic environment of public schools, homeschooling was a legal designation that allowed families greater freedom and flexibility. That might help explain why the number of homeschooled children doubled from 850,000 in 1999, when I wrote my college research paper, to nearly two million young people a decade later.[37] More recent estimates indicate that there are over two million homeschoolers in the United States, placing their numbers on par with charter school enrollment figures.[38] The homeschooling community has also become much more diverse since its earlier days, with the number of black homeschooling families doubling between 2007 and 2011 to nearly 10 percent of homeschoolers, and Hispanic homeschoolers representing 15 percent of its population, up from 5 percent in 2003.[39] According to the US Department of Education, "concern about the environment of other schools, such as safety, drugs, and negative peer pressure" was the top motivator for contemporary homeschooling families.[40] While Christian families remain the majority of the US homeschool population, Muslim families now represent a fast-growing demographic.[41] Secular homeschoolers are also on the rise.[42]

Among the homeschooling parents I met, I learned that they tailored learning and teaching to the specific needs of their children and focused their days around family and community. They also spent a lot of time exploring outside in nature, visiting public spaces, taking classes tied to interests and needs, volunteering with local organizations, and interacting with a wide assortment of community members, shopkeepers, neighbors, family members, and friends. In his study of homeschooling and socialization, psychology professor Richard Medlin found that most homeschoolers were tightly connected with their larger community and had solid social skills and strong relationships with both peers and adults. Medlin also suggested that homeschooled children may have more community involvement and participation in extracurricular activities than schooled children due to their more flexible schedules and interaction with a wide assortment of community members.[43]

I was hooked. Why would I want my kids playing an increasingly regimented game of school when they could be living and learning authentically in and from the people, places, and things around us? It seemed to me that enclosing my children within the four walls of the classroom would cause their learning to contract, not expand. As Nancy Wallace wrote, "The thought of having them spend so much time in school when there were so many more interesting things going on right in the community seemed absurd."[44]

We spent the following years doing those interesting things. We visited parks and playgrounds, went often to the library, museum, and bookstores, spent vast amounts of time outdoors near woods and water, gathered together with friends and neighbors, enjoyed uninterrupted time with grandparents and aunts and uncles, and generally lived our lives without any attention to school or school-like activities. We reveled in the freedom that homeschooling provided and the opportunity it allowed for abundant childhood play. Still, as Molly neared kindergarten age and I now had my hands full with a toddler and an infant, I started to consider what curriculum I would purchase for her. After all, ample playtime and freedom were great for her early childhood, but now that she was five her learning would need to have some school-like structure to it. Or so I thought.

As I researched various curriculum choices and plotted my role as kindergarten teacher, I became familiar with the various performance expectations of five-year-olds. Lots of books and resources shared "what my kindergartener should know." The subject matter was comprehensive, the learning objectives were clear, the assessment was straightforward. There were games to make learning fun and prizes to keep my child motivated. Each curriculum package had its own style and approach but the result was the same: a distinct and coordinated process of teaching my child reading, writing, and arithmetic.

With my curriculum choices finalized and my kindergarten plan ready, out of nowhere Molly taught herself to read. She was also learning many other things from the world around her, like the habits of our neighbor's hermit crabs, the proper way to plant seeds in her great-aunt's garden, the origins of the solar system at the museum's planetarium, and so on. Sure, I could create a curriculum around these ambient learning resources, but why would I want to? I began to wonder if curriculum and assessment, subject matter and learning objectives, lessons and outcomes were really the best way to facilitate education. We had already opted out of conventional schooling, so why did I feel the need to replicate school at home? Was there another way to learn without being schooled—even homeschooled?

I began to read everything I could about natural learning and nontraditional homeschooling. I became immersed in Holt's writings about "unschooling," as well as the books of other self-directed education pioneers. One such trailblazer is Wendy Priesnitz, who has been an active and vocal international advocate for learning without schooling (or life learning, as she calls it) since the 1970s. In her book *School Free* she asks, "Why do we assume that five-year-olds are no longer able to learn in the way they did when they were four and instead need a structured curriculum taught by specially trained and certified adults?" She goes on to suggest that learning is natural and doesn't need to be reined in with curriculum: "When children are small, much learning (like how to walk and talk) goes on while we aren't really paying attention . . . except to the result. The early learning of a large number of complicated concepts occurs somewhat spontaneously as a result of desires and curiosity."[45] This piqued my interest and reflected what I was already witnessing with my own young children. Why would I want to halt their natural, spontaneous learning with a top-down, school-like curriculum?

Curriculum, regardless of how engaging and child led it attempts to be, assumes that there is specific content that someone should learn at a specific time, in a specific way, using specific materials and resources, for a specific outcome, with a specific form of assessment. These specifics may vary widely depending on educational philosophy and approach. For instance, the Montessori curriculum is quite different from the Waldorf education curriculum, which is quite different from a Common Core–based public schooling curriculum, and so on. Each educational framework has its own curriculum focus and its own agenda, and many times the success of that curriculum depends on the quality of teachers to effectively interpret and execute that curriculum. The difference with unschooling, I learned, is that there is no set curriculum and the learner—not the teacher—is the central figure. To make the leap to unschooling, I needed to stop thinking of myself as my children's teacher and instead become their follower.

Unschooling Tips

• **Build community**. Whenever I get asked how to get started with homeschooling or unschooling, the first thing I suggest is for parents to connect with their local homeschooling community. It's incredibly valuable to meet real-life homeschooling families and explore their different philosophies and approaches. No matter where you are located, you are likely to find a group of like-minded families who appreciate learning without schooling. Many places have statewide, grassroots homeschooling organizations that help connect homeschoolers to each other and explain local polices and regulations. You may also be able to find homeschooling networks targeted to your specific city or county. Online groups often exist to connect homeschoolers in your area, as well as social media pages for homeschoolers near you. Google homeschooling and your location and see what pops up. You can also check with your local librarians and museum educators to see if they know of homeschooling resources nearby.

• **Find unschoolers.** Homeschoolers generally rely on some established curriculum, teaching framework, and assessment protocol, whereas unschoolers focus on interest-based, self-directed education. To find other families who share your views on natural learning, connect with local unschooling families through online communities and social media, as well as more national and global unschooling networks and conferences. Here you will find other families choosing a more child-directed path to learning, albeit with many different approaches underneath the unschooling umbrella.

• **Consider your family values**. What is most important to you as a family, and how can unschooling reflect those values? Maybe you want to make sure your children have abundant playtime and spend long hours outside exploring nature. If so, that will be a major focus of your unschooled approach. Maybe you want to spend much of your time volunteering in your community, or traveling to different cities and countries, and that will be a foundational family commitment on which your unschooling rests. Maybe unschooling is part of a broader goal to spend more time together as a family or to adopt a slower, simpler lifestyle. Focusing on these values will enable you to craft an unschooling lifestyle that is meaningful for everyone.

• **Talk with your kids!** Hopefully, your children are active participants in helping to identify your family values and decide if unschooling makes sense. What do your kids want? What has their education experience been? If they have been to school and now you are turning to unschooling, you and your children may need to go through a significant "deschooling" process to shed preconceived notions of learning and education. It may take time for those natural learning tendencies to reemerge. Deschooling could take months to years, depending on how much time your child has been in school and how much of an impact schooling has had on their natural learning tendencies. In fact, deschooling may never really be over for any of us living within a schooled society. Good communication, patience, and an open mind toward new ways of living and learning can help create a smoother transition from a schooled mind-set to an unschooled one.

• **Get ready to question everything**. In her popular book *Free Range Learning*, Laura Grace Weldon warns that "homeschooling changes everything."[46] Once you begin to challenge assumptions about education and learning you may find that you start questioning other cultural norms. Why do I continue to go to this job that I hate? Why do we have this big mortgage? Why must the kids take piano lessons? Why are organized sports consuming so much of our family time? Why must we all learn calculus? Why has college become the holy grail? You may be in for an avalanche of questions as you start to challenge the status quo.

2

What Is Unschooling?

"Unschooling is essentially a curiosity-led approach to learning devoid of testing and predefined curricula. It leaves the exploration and implementation of knowledge to children, instead of relying on the passing of information from adults and books, based on what is believed (by adults) to be necessary learning."

—Akilah S. Richards[1]

"I HAVE BEEN IN THE classroom my entire life, since the womb," says Katie Lane-Karnas, an unschooling mom to two daughters, Mae and Juniper. Both of her parents were professional educators in traditional classrooms and school administration. Katie's earliest school memories are as a toddler joining her mom at the remedial summer school classes she taught. Getting a degree in education and becoming a public school teacher were almost predestined for Katie. It was an obvious and well-trodden path.

After teaching in several states from the late 1990s to the mid 2000s, she grew increasingly distressed by what she was seeing in schools. "It was unsettling to me how easily a child, at any age, could be dismissed, quieted, belittled, judged in small ways," she recalls. "A second grader with his hand in the air, answering a question, could be shown with body language and response that his idea, or attempt at participating, is somehow not right enough. A third grader who barely speaks English can know that his literacy in his own language is just not relevant to graduating to fourth grade. A middle schooler whose main interest is dance, or farming, or hunting, or babysitting, has no way to bring these skills to support her education. So many high schoolers who play in the band are missing major pieces of understanding how to read music—yet know it's too dumb to ask questions to get a full grasp of music."

Frustrated by the coercive system of mass schooling, Katie eventually quit her teaching job; but she still expected to send her own children to her local public schools. Despite her reservations as a teacher, she believed in schooling and wanted it to work for her children. Nevertheless, she decided to see what kindergarten would be like for her five-year-old daughter, Mae, and asked to observe the classroom before enrolling her. Katie remembers:

> My child suddenly seemed quite a bit too loud, too fast, too opinionated, alternately dressed in a wedding party gown or stark naked, to go to school. I tried to envision Mae alongside the little girls with their hands obligingly in the air while a few exuberant boys were chastised and then called on over and over, the quiet girls never calling out, during a half-hour seated circle time. I felt sad thinking of how willingly she would color in the picture of the Olympic rings in the lesson plan exactly the way the teacher said was the *only* correct way to do it, of her avoiding experimenting with the glue because clearly only the naughty boys dared try that.

What Katie observed in that classroom mirrored what she saw previously in her own school classrooms as a teacher. She knew she couldn't subject her children to schooling and watch their creativity and curiosity diminish.

After exploring different schools and education options, Katie and her husband decided to homeschool their daughters. They immediately gravitated toward the unschooling philosophy of natural, child-directed learning. It was like a weight was lifted. Katie didn't realize the many subtle ways the schooled mind-set had influenced her parenting until she let it go. "Suddenly, without school expectations looming," she recalls,

my relationship with my daughter improved dramatically. I realized how many things about her I was trying to "gently" change
to make her more acceptable in school, which she was resisting.
I realized how much I wanted to protect her by making her less
like herself. Letting go of school was letting go of changing her.
Without school as the framework within which I saw my five-
year-old, I began to see more of her strengths and trust her as we
had in her early childhood development. I soon began to notice
how much "schoolish" thought was diminishing my respect of my
child's freedom of mind. The more we released school from our
family plan, the more we could relax and embrace our child again.

Katie continued to release her schooled mind-set, looking more
honestly at her own school experiences as a student and a teacher and
witnessing the many, often hidden ways that schooled thought surrounds
us. A schooled culture is reflected in our calendars, in our fiction, in
our conversations with neighbors, and in the town spirit of Friday night
football games. It's in back-to-school snapshots and prom photos, summer reading programs and school plays, student-of-the-month awards
and bumper stickers, graduation speeches and a host of other trivial
rituals that distract us from the fierce reality of schooling. In just over
a century and a half, schooling has taken over so much of our collective
psyche that we cannot imagine a civilized society without the institution
of school. Breaking free of the schooled mind-set is no easy feat.

In moving from schooling to unschooling, Katie reconnected with the
ways she facilitated her children's interests and nurtured their development when they were babies and toddlers. She watched as they naturally
learned to discover their world, to experiment and take risks, to walk and
talk and comprehend. She now draws on those experiences to support
her girls' learning as they grow. She listens to them, trusts them, and
surrounds them with abundant resources and opportunities. Like most
unschoolers, Katie does not use a packaged curriculum. Instead, she rec-
ognizes her children's interests and then connects those interests to the
people, places, and things around her, including books and materials, digital resources, activities, classes, community members, and public spaces.
Mae is now eight and loves drawing, art, makeup, and math as well as

many other ephemeral and emerging interests. Juniper is six, and her main passions are chickens and geology, and anything related to beauty, fairies, and dress-up. Learning happens all the time, fueled by these interests, facilitated by attentive grown-ups, and supported by the shared wisdom of the larger community. For Katie, moving from schooling to unschooling, from teacher to follower, has been particularly cathartic. She says, "As a teacher, I was trained to respectfully control all the people around me, to encourage them to express their needs and selves only within a well-defined scope of what's appropriate in that environment. I was so good at it! And it felt awful to be in a relationship that way."

Unschooling, Defined

Unschooling is more than an educational approach. It is not about teaching and learning, about progressive educational ideals over conventional ones. Unschooling is about challenging dominant structures of control and searching for freedom and autonomy. It is about understanding the ways in which our schooled lens influences how we see learning and knowing, and also determines what we don't see. It is about reexamining what it means to be educated. In some ways, the idea of unschooling is quite simple: give children more freedom and control over their lives and their futures by letting them learn instead of making them schooled. The complexity comes in the execution. What does freedom in learning look like in a widely schooled society? What is the balance of freedom and responsibility? Who decides? These questions lie at the root of the philosophy of unschooling and of self-directed education in general. There are no easy answers.

Every unschooling family will look and act differently. Every unschooling cooperative or learning center will create a distinct culture. Every self-directed school or camp or community program will have its own essence. Some may think that their approach is better, kinder, purer. None is perfect. Diversity is a strength of the unschooling approach. Unschooling is both a philosophy and a lifestyle—an ideal and a practice—and therein lies its blessing and its burden. The ideal is to give children freedom to learn without coercion, following their own interests, using the full resources of their community. The practice is to do this within a complex web of interpersonal relationships, social dynamics, family values, cultural realities, and community responsibilities. Practice is the key word.

With this messiness in mind, we can arrive at an imperfect definition of unschooling. Most simply, unschooling is the opposite of schooling. It is learning without schooling—including school-at-home. Unschooling rejects the schooling prototype of education and instead values a learning one that looks nothing like school. The unschooling approach to education is noncoercive, meaning that children are not required or expected to learn things the way they are in compulsory schools or school-like settings. Like grown-ups, unschooled children have the freedom to say no. Unschooling dismisses the common accoutrements of school, including adult-imposed curriculum, grade levels, subject silos, age segregation, lesson plans, rewards and punishments, and arbitrary tests and rankings. Unschooling separates schooling from education.

When studying homeschooling families and their different approaches in the early 1990s, University of Michigan researchers discovered a clear distinction between the school-at-home homeschoolers and those whom we would now call unschoolers. They defined the difference as a split between *schooling* and *education*: "With systematic curricula, teacher-directed lessons, and external rewards and punishments, schooling provides a structure that requires extrinsic motivation of the student. Conversely, education implies the development of the learner and includes the notion that the learner is responsible for deciding what is learned."[2] Unschooling reflects this definition of education, focused on learner autonomy and detached from the system of schooling—including school-at-home. With unschooling, learning is an intrinsic, personal, continuous process of education.

Unschooling means trusting humans' propensity to learn about their world—to become educated—by following their innate curiosities when surrounded by plentiful resources and opportunities. Schooling is about control whereas unschooling is about freedom. This means even the term unschooling may tilt too much toward schooling. As Wendy Priesnitz says, "If we truly are living as if school doesn't exist, we can stop describing ourselves in school terms! We can de-couple learning—and the life we're living with our families—from the institution of school."[3] The term "self-directed education" is quickly becoming a more popular term for this type of learning, both because it explains what unschooling is versus what it's not, and also because it is more embracing of the wide variety of unschooling approaches now available—from family-centered unschooling, to "free schools" and Sudbury-style democratic schools, to unschooling camps and after-school and community programs, to self-directed learning centers and teen immersion experiences. I use the terms "unschooling" and "self-directed education" interchangeably throughout this book, as they share underlying ideals, practices, and philosophical roots.

Schooling has become so engrained in our culture and conversations that disentangling it from learning takes time and thought. Not only do we need to unschool our own thinking but also we need to help others do the same—and to show compassion when they might not yet understand. Unschooling disrupts everything we have been taught about learning and knowing. It is bound to cause confusion. One day when Jack was eight we went to our family doctor for a check-up. We love our physician, and she has always been very supportive of our education choices—even if she didn't quite understand this unschooling thing. Homeschooling seemed straightforward, but unschooling? What does *that* look like? She and Jack talked about his passion for skateboarding, the long hours he spends each week at the skate park. He explained the latest trick he was working on and defined some of the skateboarding vernacular for her. She listened attentively and then, sweetly though stumblingly, asked Jack, "So what are you learning in, um, school? I mean, I know it's not school but, well, you know what I mean."

Jack replied, "Well, right now I am really interested in chemical bonds and I want to have as much time as possible to spend with my dad figuring out these chemical bonds, the protons and electrons and the periodic table."

"Hey," our doctor laughed, surprised by Jack's response. "I thought you said you don't do school! This sure sounds like school!"

"Yes," I answered, "unschooling is not un-learning or un-education; it's just that the learning isn't tied to a set curriculum but rather—" The doctor finished my sentence, "—it's tied to their interests."

Exactly. With unschooling, learning is tied to young people's interests. Sometimes that learning will involve what we think of as "academic" topics, and sometimes that learning will consist of topics that don't resemble school subjects at all, like skateboarding. But it is all learning. I think our doctor was relieved that Jack could talk about chemical bonds as well as skateboarding; but the larger point is that when we don't separate learning into certain silos—when we don't say learning only happens at these certain places, at these certain times, with these certain people and materials—all learning becomes interesting. Children are naturally curious. They want to know how things work, what things mean, why things are. Any parent can testify to the barrage of questions young children ask, sometimes incessantly. Schooling disengages a child's natural curiosity about the world by ignoring his interests and questions, placing knowledge into buckets, and then forcing him to learn what is in those buckets. Schooling and learning are strikingly different.

I don't actually know where Jack's interest in the periodic table of elements came from, or why he latched on to chemical bonds so enthusiastically. He probably saw or heard or read something throughout his day about the periodic table and wanted to learn more. My husband, Brian, and I searched with Jack for information about the periodic table on the Internet, watched some streaming Khan Academy videos together as well as other online, instructional videos about chemical bonds, went to the library for additional books and resources, visited our local science museum's exhibit on the periodic table, and so on. This was not tied to any lesson plan or learning objectives. Jack was just very interested in this topic, so we noticed his interest, gathered appropriate resources, learned alongside him, and supported him as he learned more on his own. When his interest in knowing more about chemical bonds waned, he stopped. That is unschooling.

With information now so accessible, and learning resources so abundant, the static process of schooling becomes obsolete. It used to be that school was where the books and knowledge were; now the books and knowledge are all around us, with a vibrant network of widely available and talented instructors and facilitators to help us learn whatever we want, whenever we want, with whomever we want. Unschooling can lead to deeper, more meaningful, more authentic learning because it is driven by the learner, using the varied tools around him. In a new, networked world with information at our fingertips, a set curriculum may actually hold us back.

Curriculum

An important differentiator between schooling (including traditional homeschooling) and unschooling is that unschooling avoids a prescribed curriculum. Unlike other educational approaches, including those that attempt to make curriculum more nonlinear or emergent or child-focused, unschooling dismisses the very notion of adult-imposed curriculum. It discards the idea that learning needs to be preplanned and assessed with certain measures of achievement. Cleveland State University education professor Karl Wheatley defines unschooling families as those "who primarily or entirely let children learn about whatever they are interested in, and use little or no formal adult-chosen curricula."[4] Like schooling, curriculum is an artifact of an earlier time. The history of curriculum is closely tied to the history of schooling and gained prominence with the rise of mass schooling around the globe. The word curriculum comes from Latin origins meaning "racing chariot" (*curricle*) and "to run" (*currere*). In the first textbook on the topic, *The Curriculum* in 1918, Franklin Bobbitt defines the ideal curriculum as "that *series of things which children and youth must do and experience* by way of developing abilities to do the things well that make up the affairs of adult life; and to be in all respects what adults should be."[5] It is, in short, a race to an end.

In his book *Towards a Theory of Schooling*, David Hamilton traces the origins of schooling from loosely organized courses during medieval times to the rise of mass schooling to bring about order and conformity. It was in the seventeenth century that the term curriculum first gained its modern meaning and was thought of as an academic tool that ensured both a whole and sequential course of study. Hamilton argues that at that post-Reformation historical moment curriculum became something that was not only "followed" but also "completed." Knowledge was to be acquired in a set order with a specific outcome, providing "a greater sense of control to both teaching and learning."[6] Specific content was to be mastered in a specific way with a specific result.

Curriculum rests on control. It is about deciding what subject matter others should study and master, and when. It may be a gentle curriculum with songs and games and colorful stickers, but it is still a method of controlling another's learning—sometimes through prodding, bribery, and punishment. Unschooling is about challenging that control. Without a predetermined curriculum, learning becomes less regimented and more organic, springing from developing interests and passions. There is no need to prod, bribe, or punish a child because learning comes from within. Instead of someone else deciding what a learner should know or do, it is the learner who decides what to know and do. Instead of someone else assessing a learner's knowledge, it is the learner who decides when her learning is complete. Unschooling is far less authoritarian than schooling. Learning happens naturally, and much more meaningfully, when it is driven by the learner's personal motivations.

The idea that children can learn without being schooled is contrary to how most of us were trained to view education. We take for granted that adult-chosen curriculum is required and instruction is necessary for real learning to take place. Wheatley calls this belief the "instruction assumption." Wheatley argues that the assumption that one must be taught in order to learn is so engrained in our culture that we often cannot imagine another way, and may, in fact, be deeply skeptical of learner-directed education. Not only does the instruction assumption dismiss unschooling ideas and findings, Wheatley argues, it also sees more instruction (longer school days, lengthier academic years, more teaching and testing) as the rational cure for educational problems.[7] Instead of more freedom for children, as unschooling advocates suggest, the instruction assumption leads to tighter control and more intervention.

The instruction assumption upholds all of the features and functions of conventional schooling, ignoring more natural ways of learning. Wheatley argues that "accepting the instruction assumption typically goes hand and hand with dividing education into academic subjects, dividing subjects into a series of learning objectives, and planning standardized curricular sequences by which students will be directly taught

those objectives."[8] A complete and sequential curriculum, with predetermined subject matter, objectives, and desired outcomes, upholds the
instruction myth. Interest-based learning theories like unschooling that
arise from a child's genuine curiosity about her world challenge the
instruction myth and contradict what most of us have been taught about
how humans learn.

Ever since my younger daughter, Abby, was a toddler, she has been
fascinated by bugs. Many young kids enjoy bugs, and I thought her
interest would be fleeting, but four years later she still loves bugs. She
has shifted from her early days of collecting and observing them to now
learning more about insect identification and how to pin and preserve
her specimens. My older daughter, Molly, hates bugs—which makes for
some interesting negotiations in car rides home from family hikes with
full bug jars! Molly has different interests, such as sewing, baking, and
math, that also began to sprout when she was quite young and that have
also remained and strengthened over the years.

If I had imposed a curriculum unit on insects or sewing, regardless of my individual child's interest, I would be asserting my control
over a topic while stripping my child of her power to determine and
expand her own interests. If I taught her a specific curriculum, rather
than letting her explore various resources, I would be seizing control of
her learning. Instead, Abby's interests in bugs led to us going together
to gather many books at the library on bugs, watching YouTube videos
about bugs, joining a local entomological society, going on lots of "bug
walks," connecting with mentors who know more about bug identification than we do, visiting the natural history museum and seeing their
pinned bug collection, gathering bug-preserving materials, and so on.
Molly's interests in crafting and handiwork led to a similar path, with
many books and videos and mentors. She also decided to take some local
community classes on knitting and sewing to get started, and now she is
able to use advanced books and YouTube videos to enhance her skills.

Some may argue: *Even with a curriculum the girls would still be able
to explore their interests in bugs and crafting, respectively. Curriculum
shouldn't shut down other interests.* Perhaps curriculum shouldn't shut
down our self-educative tendencies, but it often does. For instance, a

reading curriculum positions reading as something separate from living. Rather than reading happening naturally through a child's interests in a particular topic, it becomes a subject to be covered in a certain way, following someone else's agenda. Learning to read and write because you want to know more about your bugs and how to properly label them on your preservation tray can be much more powerful than learning to read because your mom or teacher tells you so. The more far-reaching a curriculum becomes, consuming more time and more content areas, the more it may dull our self-educative tendencies and zest for learning. We learn to be led.

A curriculum can sometimes help to expose young people to topics they may not otherwise have known about, therefore facilitating an interest where there wasn't one. It's true that curriculum can expose learners to new and different topics, but so can the library—and the museum, and the park, and their friends, and the shopkeeper, and the Internet. Curriculum is a shortcut. It is a one-dimensional representation of various topics disconnected from the real world in which we live. Connecting young people to the larger world and the various resources of their community can lead to much more layered, spontaneous, authentic learning than is possible in a canned curriculum. For example, Abby gained her appreciation for bugs by being outside often, taking nature walks, spending long hours in the woods. There was no need for a curriculum; nature was her teacher. Molly's interest in crafting and sewing sprang from regular conversations with the artisans at our local knitting shop, and spending time with her great-aunt who sews and crafts. These are immersive experiences, using real people, places, and things in the community.

Without a curriculum determining what content to learn, knowledge of certain subject areas will be incomplete. With unschooling, there is no expectation of "completeness" or mastery of arbitrary content. If Abby decides to be done with bugs (or if she decided after only a day to stop), then that's it for bugs. There is no expectation of a whole, sequential, or completed curriculum. With unschooling, there is no set curriculum— there is only living and learning. In so many ways, the unschooling approach to learning is similar to the way most museums approach learning. Information, exhibits, and lectures are offered, usually centered on the museum's focus (art, science, nature), and museum guides are available to answer questions or lead a demonstration. Nothing is forced. If you want to explore a particular exhibit for a long period of time and ignore the other ones, you can. If you want to spend time in the contemporary art wing and ignore the impressionist painters, go for it. If you want to listen to a lecture on animal behavior or do a hands-on geology activity, it's there for you. If you don't want to, that's OK too. You can come and go as you choose. The museum won't cajole you or evaluate what you know. With unschooling, as with museum learning, resources, materials, and opportunities are made widely available for exploration and discovery—without coercion.

Without a set curriculum there will be gaps in one's knowledge. Curriculum, as Hamilton revealed, is both whole and sequential. It is a neatly presented set of content and expectations detailing the whole of what someone else decides should be covered and the sequence in which that should be covered. It is linear and complete. This is what makes curriculum so appealing: it takes the guesswork out of learning. But its linearity is also its drawback, because it doesn't allow for meandering questions on various topics that prompt further exploration. If I bought or created a curriculum that determined when and how we would cover the periodic table of elements, Jack probably wouldn't have been nearly as interested—because it wouldn't have arisen from his own questions and curiosity. He may have learned the periodic table through a curriculum and scored adequately on a test about its various components, but something important would be lost. Most of us learned the periodic table through a preestablished schooling curriculum with various learning objectives and assessments. How much do you remember?

With unschooling, learning is circuitous, not sequential. Content is explored, not completed. Will there be gaps in unschoolers' knowledge? Most certainly—just as there are gaps in schooled children's knowledge. We all have gaps in our knowledge. It is now widely accepted that there is so much information and data available to us that it would be impossible for any of us to know everything—or even a fraction of everything. Former Google CEO Eric Schmidt explains that "every two days we create as much information as we did from the dawn of civilization up until 2003."[9] This is jaw-dropping. Curriculum, core competencies, testing—none of that can possibly keep up with the knowledge needs of the Imagination Age.

The term Imagination Age was first coined by Charlie Magee in a 1993 symposium on open source technologies. In his essay "The Age of Imagination: Coming Soon to a Civilization Near You," Magee writes: "The task we should undertake now is to learn to develop our imaginations, for it is the most imaginative people of any period of human evolution who are the leaders. The problem is that we'll need many more imaginative people, as a percentage of the population, than we've ever needed before."[10] In more recent years, the term has been popularized by writer and global strategist Rita J. King, who identifies the Imagination Age as the post-industrial era that precedes the coming "intelligence age," when robots outsmart people.[11] Human creativity will be the most crucial characteristic to differentiate people from machines. A forced schooling model weakens creativity and smothers individuality as it compels young people to learn specific content of questionable relevance for the future. In the Imagination Age, it will be the innovators, entrepreneurs, and original thinkers whose creative intelligence will distinguish itself from an artificial antipode.

Curriculum allows content to be taught and tested to gauge complete learning. When content is taught and tested, it often reveals how successful a child is at playing the game of school: at effectively memorizing and regurgitating information. It may reveal what a child has been taught but not necessarily what he learned. This can help explain why most of us probably don't remember much about the periodic table and chemical bonds. It also explains the schooled phenomenon of summer learning loss, or "summer slide," in which children purportedly lose knowledge over the summer break. Content that children are tested on in the spring is forgotten by fall. Efforts to reduce summer slide abound, with schools and organizations dedicated to reinforcing schooled content all summer long so that nothing will be lost in September. These well-meaning initiatives overlook a basic point: maybe the children never really learned at all. Maybe they simply repeated information taught for the test and quickly forgot it because it wasn't meaningful or useful to them. They may have shown their test-taking prowess but not necessarily their learning ability. Indeed, one large study found that most participants forgot half of their high school math content within five years of learning it, and nearly all of that content within twenty-five years.[12] Real learning cannot be so easily forgotten. What is a covalent bond again?

Sometimes kids like to learn from a curriculum. Yes! This is entirely true. Some unschoolers want a structured curriculum, like workbooks or textbooks. Many unschoolers choose to take very formal classes, led by very traditional teachers using a very rigid curriculum. Molly takes an intense Korean language class, with rigorous weekly assignments and assessments. It is very structured and highly curriculum-based, but she chose to do it. I didn't tell her that she should learn a foreign language or suggest Korean; her growing passion for martial arts led to a natural curiosity of Korean language, history, and culture. She explored various options for learning Korean, and selected a formal curriculum taught by an expert instructor with workbooks and linear lessons. Curriculum isn't the problem; an *adult-imposed* curriculum can be.

As Molly's Korean language learning shows, unschooling doesn't mean that young people never learn "school-ish" subjects or never take formal classes. A great many of them do! It simply means they choose to do it, or not. When curriculum and instruction are chosen, tied to specific interests or personal goals, they become noncoercive. A learner decides for herself to gain knowledge in that particular way, from that particular instructor or source. She can also decide not to do it as well.

Jack's recent passion is photography. He spends hours taking online classes on Lynda.com, available for free through our public library, to sharpen his skills. His favorite instructor is someone I find very boring and monotone, but Jack prefers him over the other available instructors, listening intently for hours to this instructor's lectures and completing the assignments he suggests. These are very structured, lecture-based classes, but they are chosen by Jack to serve his particular purposes. He learns about and experiments with angles and shutter speed, distance and depth, editing and uploading. I am often astounded by his commitment to these courses and the effort he makes to practice his skills and improve his craft.

These online courses complement other ways he learns photography. In addition to lectures and practice, Jack has also developed a mentoring relationship with an adult friend of ours who is a hobby photographer. He devours books about photography, watches documentaries, and reads about famous photographers. His favorite photographer is the renowned twentieth-century landscape photographer Ansel Adams, whose father removed him from school at age twelve when the school found Ansel to be inattentive and hyperactive. The school said Ansel needed more discipline. His father disagreed, saying he needed more freedom. In his autobiography, Adams writes:

> I often wonder at the strength and courage my father had in taking me out of the traditional school situation and providing me with these extraordinary learning experiences. I am certain he established the positive direction of my life that otherwise, given my native hyperactivity, could have been confused and catastrophic. I trace who I am and the direction of my development to those years of growing up in our house on the dunes, propelled especially by an internal spark tenderly kept alive and glowing by my father.[13]

Curriculum can be a great resource, as long as it is chosen freely by the child and just as easily ignored. It can be available but not required. For instance, my kids love doing workbooks. Just as we have books and pencils and play dough in our home, we also have workbooks. They are always available, and sometimes the kids will grab one, flip to a page that interests them, and work through a whole section, asking questions when necessary and stopping when they have had enough. My kids have never been to school so they don't have any mental model to view workbooks or worksheets as drudgery. To them, workbooks—like all of the other resources around them—are simply tools with which to interact when and how they choose.

In his excellent book *From Socrates to Summerhill and Beyond*, retired education philosophy professor Ronald Swartz discusses the key problems with a prescribed curriculum and a top-down, teacher-led approach to education. He finds that curriculum-driven educational models breed authoritarianism, even when educators believe they are not being authoritarian at all. Swartz argues for educational frameworks that reject authoritarianism in favor of those based on freedom and personal responsibility, like A. S. Neill's famed Summerhill School discussed in greater detail in the following chapter. Swartz writes that rejecting traditional authoritarian structures of education is necessary "partly because authoritarianism in all its forms can be viewed as one of the great threats to human freedom and the development of human potential."[14] An imposed curriculum, as a method of educational control, necessarily limits freedom and potential to within the parameters of that set curriculum.

As a schooled society, we take for granted the instruction assumption and the curriculum myth. The entire foundation of conventional schooling rests on the belief that young people must spend most of their childhood passively absorbing specific content deemed by others to be important. It assumes that young people are incapable of choosing what to learn, when, and how, and that teachers are the only ones who can effectively impart knowledge. With curriculum comes gatekeepers. Without an adult-imposed curriculum—an agenda for determining what a child should know and when—learning happens as a direct result of living. Children absorb the environment surrounding them, become fascinated by various ideas and topics at various times, and dig deeper into those areas with the help of adults when necessary. And when they are done with a certain topic or interest, they are done. With unschooling, authoritarianism is ousted.

Beyond School-at-Home

For Deanna Skow, moving from schooling to homeschooling was easy, but making the leap from homeschooling to unschooling proved more challenging. A public elementary school teacher before motherhood, Deanna witnessed firsthand the ways that schooling can crush creativity and exuberance. She recalls holding a stopwatch (as subtly as she could) to time the children's ability to read and answer questions in preparation for standardized tests. She saw the disconnect between the way she was teaching reading and the way she was expected to test it. Deanna felt that she could no longer be a part of the coercive system of schooling—and also couldn't subject her own children to its methods. She and her husband, a university professor, decided not to send their children to school and to homeschool them instead.

Deanna started a blog, *Adventures in Teaching My Own*, to catalogue the kind of homeschooling she expected to do. It would be much more child-centered and interest-based than conventional schooling, she envisioned; but she was still committed to re-creating in her home many of the features of her second-grade classroom, including daily schedules and lesson plans and learning objectives. At first her older son was OK with the structure and idea of school-at-home, but then his enthusiasm waned. It became harder and harder for Deanna to get him to focus on his schoolwork and embrace a new lesson. She began to question whether homeschooling was a good idea after all. Why was he resisting her efforts to teach him?

Deanna continued her homeschooling research and kept stumbling upon the idea of unschooling. "My initial reaction to unschooling was not a positive one," recalls Deanna. "It felt too extreme, too risky, too drastic. Yet, over and over I was meeting homeschoolers who identified as unschoolers, and I thought to myself: they don't seem all that extreme." She researched more about this approach and talked to more unschooling families. She began to see that she was hung up on the semantics of unschooling more than the overall philosophy:

> I feel as though the word unschooling has a negative implication. It projects more of what it does *not* do rather than what it *does* do. Its synonyms—natural learning or child-led learning—do a better job of putting forth its true meaning. The more I opened my mind to this idea the more I realized that unschooling is simply allowing your children to guide their education based on their interests. Natural learning takes place in your everyday world. You learn what you need and want to know, based on how you live your life.

As so often happens with homeschooling families, we realize that schooling isn't the preferred path. It's not just *school* we reject; it's the very idea of *schooling*, of determining what someone else should know and getting them to know it. We choose not to send our children to school for a reason, so why do we feel the need to replicate that narrow educational approach at home? Many of us begin to question the schooling approach to learning and gradually find our way to unschooling. While Deanna's blog retains its original title, her kids are now the ones teaching her. "When I loosened up on the curriculum reins and allowed my children's intrinsic motivation to dictate what we learned about," says Deanna, "I discovered that their enthusiasm is endless and motivation is strong. Their education path thrives in a more eclectic, unplanned, organic, and spontaneous learning environment. We take the time to really listen to every question our children have and run with their ideas. Unschooling, natural learning, child-led learning, life learners—call it what you will, but I find more each day that it is our chosen path to educating our children."

Unschooling is not for the indolent. It takes effort to preserve the time and space for true learning. It takes tolerance of ambiguity and a more unpredictable path of learning than the neat and linear schooled model. It takes keen observation to identify children's budding interests, and it takes resourcefulness in connecting them to tangible and digital tools to explore those interests. It takes a personal commitment to modeling the behaviors we hope our children will develop, rather than demanding they develop them. Unschooling takes a commitment to broadening their world, expanding their perspectives, and exposing them to new tools and ideas. It takes a willingness to take our children to interesting places and to meet interesting people when they are young, and it takes courage to let them go off on their own to those interesting places with interesting people as they grow. Mostly, unschooling requires trusting our children's natural, self-educative abilities, listening to their ideas and interests, and helping them to explore those ideas and interests throughout their community. It also takes trusting ourselves. As Holt writes: "Trust Children. Nothing could be simpler, or more difficult. Difficult because to trust children we must first learn to trust ourselves, and most of us were taught as children that we could not be trusted."[15]

Trusting Children

Trusting children, and ourselves, may be one of the biggest hurdles to fully embracing unschooling. After all, most of us have been schooled—and those schooled beliefs run deep. The reality is that most of us grew up in an authoritarian classroom. We were told what to learn, what to do, and how to act. We were told that our interests and enthusiasms didn't matter. We were told that our natural creativity was not nearly as important as coloring in the lines. We were told that freedom was for others. As Herb Kohl writes in his book *The Open Classroom*, "For most American children there is essentially one public school system in the United States and it is authoritarian and oppressive."[16]

It's hard to break this cycle of authoritarian education in favor of natural learning. It's hard to trust that our children will learn by following their interests and exploring their world when we were taught to bury our interests and remain caged in a classroom for much of our childhood. But just as many of us were spanked as children and now far fewer parents spank their kids,[17] authoritarian tendencies can weaken in favor of more open, respectful ways of living and being. We can learn to trust children.

"The biggest difference between school or school-at-home and unschooling is being willing to trust the child," says Adam Bloom, who grew up unschooled in the Pacific Northwest.

Children are very curious. Human beings want to learn if they're not taught that learning is frustrating or boring. If you let them learn on their own terms, with some guidance because they're still kids, they'll learn. Trusting them to learn what and how they want instills in them a lifelong enjoyment of learning. This is a long-term benefit, not just a benefit in the immediate, pre-college sense.

Adam never went to school and spent much of his childhood reading and playing. While both of his parents earned master's degrees, neither felt they learned much in all of their years of schooling, including college. Given their experiences, both parents felt that schooling wasn't the best path for being educated. Adam's father had read some Holt and was influenced by A. S. Neill's book *Summerhill*. He was drawn to the ideas of unschooling and self-directed education and became a stay-at-home dad who could help facilitate his children's learning.

Adam was an avid reader, so his father often gathered books on various topics and gave them to Adam. When Adam was ten, the books he most enjoyed were about computer programming. This became a passion that would ultimately stay with Adam throughout adolescence and adulthood. "A big part of my early education was playing games," says Adam. When he was eight, his parents gave him a box set of a fantasy strategy war game (Warhammer Fantasy Battles), and he spent much of his time playing these games. "One example of comparing my unschooling to someone who went to regular school is that I effectively learned my timetables by building army lists through the game. I would have twenty guys in one unit and thirty guys in another, and they were each worth a certain number of points, so I learned how to multiply quickly. I could always multiply faster than my friends." He continued to enjoy math, reading math books as he got older and teaching himself algebra.

Adam says that he never had an interest in a more structured school environment. As a teenager, he took occasional Japanese and Spanish classes at a local homeschool resource center that offered a variety of different classes, and he enrolled in a writing course at a community college; but mostly he learned through books, by following his interests, and by being surrounded by the resources of his family and community. He decided to go to college not so much for the classroom experience, he says, but for a change of scenery. He got an SAT prep book, studied it and took some practice exams, and then scored well enough on the SATs to get accepted to several colleges of his choice. "We looked at colleges that at least mentioned something about being open to home-schooled students." Often, these colleges required an extra step or two for homeschoolers, such as an additional application essay. "For my application transcript, my dad and I sat down and tried to list out all of the books I had read. Books were my curriculum."

In college, Adam took a variety of classes but ultimately gravitated toward technology, graduating with a bachelor's degree in computer science with minors in Japanese and political science. Now in his thirties, Adam credits his unschooled upbringing for giving him a love of learning new things and a sense of agency over his life's path. He is a full-time software developer, where managing ambiguity and self-teaching are key qualifications. "The most interesting times I have had at my jobs are when I am put on a task or project and I know nothing about the tools or language we'll be using. With programming, you have to be constantly learning new things. If you want to settle in and coast, you're going to get stuck."

As Adam reflects on his unschooling experience, he says: "I think it was pretty fantastic. I am not always the person I might want to be, but I think it would be significantly worse if I didn't have the unschooling experience." Adam can appreciate the hesitation parents might feel in pulling their child from school or moving from homeschooling to unschooling. His advice to parents considering unschooling comes back to trust: "Trust that your kids want to learn, they just may not want to learn the way people around them think they should learn. If you give them the opportunity to figure out how and what to learn, they will do it."

Trusting children to learn, when appropriately supported by grown-ups, is not a revolutionary idea. In fact, progressive educators have long advocated for providing young people more freedom and autonomy in their learning, for surrounding them with gentle teachers, and for making the curriculum more interactive and more relevant to childhood experiences. Unschooling has its roots in this progressive educational ideology and shares many of its essential beliefs about children and learning. The difference between progressive education and unschooling, as we will see in the next chapter, is both subtle and profound.

Unschooling Tips

- **Understand regulations**. Homeschooling is legal in all fifty US states (international legality varies by country), and unschooling is one method of homeschooling. Regulations for homeschooling differ among states and within states, with some places requiring notification and approval and others not. Some homeschooling regulations mandate periodic assessments, including testing. Unschoolers often comply with regulations that typically follow a schooled set of subject matter criteria by listing the people, places, and things that their children learn from in any given "subject." For example, for a history requirement, unschoolers might list the biographies their children read, the documentaries they watched, the historical sites they visited, the library lectures they attended, and so on. Research your local homeschooling requirements and try to connect with other like-minded families in your area to determine how best to comply.

Also, if standardized testing is required for homeschoolers in your state, you can take action to challenge this mandate. Join together with like-minded families to lobby state legislators or alter local district policies that authorize testing for homeschoolers. Standardized testing may force learning into certain subject silos and grade levels that are inadequate in assessing overall learning. Just as many private school students are exempt from standardized testing requirements and are free to adopt their own educational approach, homeschooling families should be granted these same freedoms. Parent portfolios and samples of children's work throughout the year can be much more revealing of a child's learning than a score on a standardized test.

• **Create structure**. A common question from new unschoolers is: How do I create some structure to our days, or is it just a free-for-all? Unschooling families create structure in several different ways, often guided by how much structure the parent or child wants or needs. First, it can be helpful to let go of the idea of daily, weekly, and seasonal *routines* and instead focus on *rhythms*. Much more fluid than routines, rhythms are guided by your child's interests at that time, the classes and activities they may be doing, family circumstances (such as work schedules, relatives who are visiting, holidays, illness, a new baby), seasonal changes that may determine how much time you are outside, and so on.

Within these rhythms you can create as much structure as you want. Meal times can provide nice benchmarks to guide your day. Maybe every day after breakfast you and your children take a walk, maybe every night after dinner you play a board game together. Maybe on Mondays you meet up with homeschoolers at a weekly park day. Maybe every Tuesday Grammy visits. Maybe every Wednesday you go to a museum. Maybe every Thursday is ballet class. Maybe on Fridays you go to the library. Maybe on fall weekends you go apple picking. You probably already have more structure to your days and weeks than you think.

If you are coming to unschooling from a schooling environment, the daily and weekly schedule may seem quite different from what you are used to. Writing out your daily and weekly activities, errands, and responsibilities may help you to reveal some existing checkpoints. You can then build your rhythms from there, knowing that they will change frequently—perhaps much more frequently than in a schooled schedule—as your children's interests and family's needs change and evolve. Creating structure in your days and weeks can be helpful, but it is not the same thing as structuring your children's learning. You can give them the freedom to learn within the rhythms of your life.

• **Facilitate learning**. Most unschooling parents consider their role as facilitators of their children's learning. But what does that mean? If I am not instructing them or deciding what they should know, then what do I do? You have an important role in cultivating a rich learning environment for your child. Stock your home with basic supplies, like paper, pens and pencils, crayons, markers, scissors, glue and tape, clay, paints and other art supplies. Scatter books and magazines around on all different topics for curious fingers to flip through. Provide access to technology and the Internet to answer children's endless array of questions. Connect them to the wide assortment of resources available in your community. Gather with local unschooling families and research local self-directed learning centers or co-ops.

You may even have workbooks in your home—or a curriculum if your child asks for it. To unschooled kids, these are materials and tools just like everything else around them, to use when and how they choose. As your children get older, give them full access to the kitchen if they want to bake, to the toolbox if they want to build, to the garden if they want to cultivate. Accompany them to community spaces, like the library, the museum, the bookstore, the market, the flower shop. Then, when they are ready, encourage them to go to these places on their own or with their friends, becoming more immersed in the people, places, and things around them.

What if my kids are bored or don't know what to do? Can I offer suggestions or is that interfering too much with their learning? Part of facilitating learning is being helpful and responsive. If you and your partner are contemplating what to do for your date night, or you and your friend are deciding how to spend your Saturday afternoon together, you are not cajoling. You are brainstorming. The same is true with your children. You can offer your thoughts and suggestions, and maybe begin a project together. Being helpful is quite different from being coercive. Just be willing to take no for an answer.

3

The Roots of Unschooling

*"I believe that education, therefore, is a process of living
and not a preparation for future living."*

—John Dewey[1]

NANCY WAS CONCERNED FOR HER SON. At eight years old, in school for
the first time in his life, Tom was not doing well. After three months,
his teacher, Mr. Engle, called him "addled," or unable to think clearly.
Tom had spent his childhood up to that point freely playing and exploring near his home, and he found the adjustment to school difficult. He
especially disliked the emphasis on sitting, memorizing, and repeating, and
he found the teacher's ways harsh and rigid. Tom was miserable. Nancy
went to speak to Mr. Engle about her son, but she was turned off by his
sharp ways. Frustrated by the teacher's tactics and his low opinion of her
son, Nancy removed Tom from school and homeschooled him. Thomas
Edison was done being schooled.

At home, free to be a curious boy once again, Edison developed a
passion for books and knowledge. Nancy mostly allowed Tom to learn
naturally, following his own interests. Edison biographer Matthew
Josephson writes that "she avoided forcing or prodding and made an
effort to engage his interest by reading him works of good literature and
history that she had learned to love."[2] A former teacher, Nancy Edison
facilitated her son's learning by noticing the things that interested him

and gathering books and resources to help him explore those topics more fully. Tom became a voracious reader, reading at age nine the great works of Dickens and Shakespeare and many others. Also at nine, Tom became interested in science, so his mother brought him a book on the physical sciences—R. G. Parker's *School of Natural Philosophy*—and he performed every experiment within it. This led to a passion for chemistry, so his mother gathered more books for him. Edison spent all of his extra money to buy chemicals from a local pharmacist and to purchase science equipment, and he conducted his first experiments in a makeshift lab in his home's basement while still just a tween. Josephson writes that in allowing Edison so much freedom and autonomy, his mother "brought him to the stage of learning things for himself, learning that which most amused and interested him, and she encouraged him to go on in that path." Edison himself wrote about his mother: "She understood me; she let me follow my bent."[3]

With over a thousand US patents, Thomas Edison went on to become one of the greatest inventors of all time, creating the phonograph, the motion picture camera, and, most famously, the first commercial lightbulb. Books were the foundation of Edison's education. At fifteen, he became one of the first cardholders at the Detroit Free Library, and later in his massive laboratory in New Jersey he placed his desk in the center of the lab's library, surrounded by thousands of books. One of Edison's chemists, Martin Andre Rosanoff, concluded: "Had Edison been formally schooled, he might not have had the audacity to create such *impossible* things."[4]

Nancy Edison was wise. She saw the energy and creativity in her young son, and she also spotted quickly the ways in which schooling smothers both. In 1855, when she removed Tom from school, compulsory schooling was just beginning to gain its stronghold throughout the nation, and homeschooling hadn't yet disappeared to the extent that it eventually would in the late nineteenth and early twentieth centuries. Nancy removed her son from school and allowed him to learn at home in a self-directed way, through books and hands-on experimentation, all while following his own passions. She connected him to resources to help him learn and then allowed him the freedom to direct his own education. With a strong foundation in and appreciation for literacy and numeracy, Edison was able to leverage both to pursue his interests in science and expand his knowledge of complex principles. Not tied to a curriculum, and given great freedom and support, Edison was able to creatively explore various subjects and invent the "impossible things" that brightened our world.

In many ways, the confrontation of Nancy Edison and Mr. Engle concerning young Tom's education reflected a larger philosophical trend in the nineteenth century. There were the conventional educators focused on rote learning and memorization, order and conformity, discipline and passivity. Then there were what came to be known as the progressive educators, who sought to reform mass schooling to be more child-centered and experiential. The progressive educators, with their roots in earlier philosophers such as John Locke and Jean-Jacques Rousseau, believed in the essential goodness of children and wanted to help them to reach their full potential through a more nurturing, child-centered, natural educational approach that challenged dominant education methods of the time.

Progressive Education and Unschooling

Unschooling may seem like a new-age idea, but really it is a contemporary offshoot of something much older and more revolutionary: a view of human development that starts with the child and individual growth versus one that places nearly all responsibility on a directive expert. Early modern philosophers, such as Rousseau in the eighteenth century and Locke in the seventeenth, planted the seeds of child-focused pedagogy. An English philosopher, Locke was considered one of the eminent Enlightenment thinkers, arguing that humans are not born with pre-existing beliefs; rather, experiences create our knowledge. He did believe, however, that we all have innate talents and gifts and that caring adults should help a child reveal these inclinations. Locke was also an early advocate of gentle parenting, less coercive education, and childhood play. He understood well that children, when forced to learn, will not willingly enjoy it. Locke advocated for abundant free playtime for children and for acknowledging children's various interests and developmental stages when educating them. In his 1693 book *Some Thoughts Concerning Education* he wrote:

> For a child will learn three times as much when he is in tune, as he will with double the time and pains when he goes awkwardly or is dragg'd unwillingly to it. If this were minded as it should, children might be permitted to weary themselves with play, and yet have time enough to learn what is suited to the capacity of each age. But no such thing is consider'd in the ordinary way of education, nor can it well be. That rough discipline of the rod is built upon other principles, has no attraction in it, regards not what humour children are in, nor looks after favourable seasons of inclination. And indeed it would be ridiculous, when compulsion and blows have rais'd an aversion in the child to his task, to expect he should freely of his own accord leave his play, and with pleasure court the occasions of learning.[5]

Locke's milder approach to child development later influenced the Swiss-born French philosopher Rousseau, who in 1762 wrote his famous treatise *Emile, or On Education*. In this work, Rousseau revealed his theory, through the fictional character Emile, that children are born innately good and that their experiences are what either corrupt or nurture them. In *Emile*'s early pages, Rousseau writes: "Everything is good as it leaves the hands of the author of things and everything degenerates in the hands of man."[6] *Emile* aimed to show how adults could cultivate a child's inner goodness and support his successful moral development through experience and hands-on learning, in sharp contrast to the prevailing education methods of the time such as student subordination and rote learning.

These earlier philosophical ideas of children as innately good who benefit from more tender, child-focused education and experiential learning influenced the burgeoning progressive education movement. In the nineteenth century, as conventional schooling was gaining its foothold, a flurry of Romantic philosophers and progressive educators spread the idea of a more nurturing, child-focused education. The Swiss philosopher Johann Heinrich Pestalozzi was an early advocate of child-centered education, encouraging mothers to implement at home what Locke and Rousseau espoused. The German educator Friedrich Fröbel, a student of Pestalozzi, is credited with creating the concept of "kindergarten" as a play space for young children to complement the education provided by mothers at home.[7] In the latter half of the nineteenth and early twentieth centuries the Italian physician and educator Maria Montessori perfected the Montessori method of education that continues to be practiced in Montessori schools around the world. Rudolph Steiner created his model of Waldorf education in Germany. And in Spain, Francisco Ferrer sparked the modern school movement that swept through the United States in the early twentieth century and would later become the template for many of the progressive American "free schools" of the 1960s and '70s (discussed more in chapter 8).

It was the psychologist and philosopher John Dewey, though, who became widely known as the torchbearer of progressive education, often overshadowing other progressive educators like Montessori, Steiner, and Ferrer. A contemporary of Dewey who is far more obscure but much more highly influential for the unschooling movement is the American educator Homer Lane. Like many educators at the turn of the twentieth century, Lane was influenced by Dewey's writings and became increasingly leery of conventional schooling as a result, but the men differed on one critical issue.[8] For Dewey, and his twentieth-century acolytes, the teacher and the curriculum remained essential components of the proper education of children. In contrast, Lane's vision rejected the idea that teaching and curriculum are essential for learning. Instead, Lane believed that giving young people greater freedom and control over their own learning and actions is what leads to human flourishing.

John Dewey and Homer Lane represent a progressive education movement that would fork along two separate paths during the twentieth century.[9] Dewey would influence reforms to expand and refine schooling, while Lane's legacy would focus on disrupting the very structure of forced schooling in favor of freedom. Dewey was undisturbed by the compulsory nature of schooling and didn't seem bothered by coercing young people to learn according to a certain curriculum as long as the teaching was more nurturing and the curriculum was more child-focused. As Hook writes, "Only those unfamiliar with Dewey's work can believe that he rejects the active role of the teacher in planning the classroom experience by properly organized subject matters."[10] In *Compulsory Miseducation*, Paul Goodman echoes this claim: "Dewey's principle is, simply, that good teaching is that which leads the student to want to learn something more."[11] According to this view, the teacher is a critical player in education. Lane and his followers challenged this idea.

Twentieth-Century Unschooling

At the turn of the twentieth century, Lane was a woodworking teacher at a Sloyd School, a turn-of-the-century group of schools devoted to handicraft. There, he became convinced of the fundamental principle of noncoercive education: do not force a child to learn. He later moved to Detroit to lead a program for troubled boys. He created a novel approach to working with these children—many of whom were in and out of the criminal justice system—that focused on freedom, respect, and autonomy. Specifically, Lane gave the boys an active role in self-governance, giving them more control and influence over their surroundings.[12] In 1913, Lane was invited to England to run the Little Commonwealth reform school for problem youth in Dorset. At Little Commonwealth, Lane's philosophy of education really emerged, emphasizing love, freedom from coercion, and democratic self-governance that was quite successful in helping these young people to thrive.[13] Lane wrote, "The only true authority is love, and the only true discipline is founded upon hope. The authority that is based upon force will transform love into hatred and hope into fear."[14]

While at Little Commonwealth, Lane was visited by Scottish educator, Alexander Sutherland Neill, the eventual founder of the renowned noncoercive school Summerhill. A. S. Neill immediately gravitated to Lane's education philosophy, and Lane quickly became Neill's most influential mentor. Little Commonwealth closed in 1918, but its vision remained with Neill when he opened Summerhill in England in 1921. Neill said that Lane was the one who most inspired him, and the one from whom he adopted the powerful ideas of self-governance and non-compulsory studies for Summerhill. Neill writes, "Forget the idea that education means learning school subjects, conditioning children, moulding character. The only true education is in letting a child grow in his own way, in his own time, without outside fears and anxieties. Homer Lane showed the way."[15]

Neill, like Lane, believed that young people learn best without coercion, enabling them to follow their own interests without being directed by adults on what, how, and when to learn. Neill described his educational philosophy as "freedom, not license," meaning children (as well as adults) should be granted freedom with responsibility, not permissiveness. To mediate this freedom, students at Summerhill, which still exists today, are key players in determining the rules and policies of governance, with each member of the community given the same voting status. Children and adults each get one vote, weighted exactly the same. At Summerhill, young people are placed in command of their own learning, free from coercive classes, curriculum requirements, and testing. Traditional classes are offered by teachers, but they are not mandatory. Some children may not attend traditional classes for months or even years, particularly if they arrive at Summerhill with baggage from an unpleasant schooled experience.[16] Young people use the people, resources, and spaces around them to pursue their own interests, develop their own mastery, and gain essential skills and knowledge.

Being forced to learn, even if that learning is presented more openly and kindly, deprives young people of their agency and can set them up for a lifetime of authoritarian influence. For Lane and Neill, the basic tenets of schooling—such as forced curriculum and teaching—should be replaced with interest-based, self-directed learning; noncoercive, optional instruction; and democratic ideals of freedom and responsibility. Dewey focused on reforming mass schooling, while Lane laid the groundwork for education without conventional schooling, or unschooling.

The ongoing interest in learner-centered over teacher-directed education found an enthusiastic audience amid the social tumult of the 1960s. There was a surge of writing and experimentation as many educators tried to create new schools, or tweak traditional schools, to become less coercive and more child-friendly. Some of those educators looked to Summerhill as an ideal model. In 1960, Neill's book *Summerhill School: A New View of Childhood* was first published, selling over two million copies in its first decade in print. In *Summerhill*, Neill reflected on his score of years as the school's leader and shared a vision for what education could be. He writes:

> The function of the child is to live his own life—not the life that his anxious parents think he should live, nor a life according to the purpose of the educator who thinks he knows what is best. All this interference and guidance on the part of adults only produces a generation of robots.[17]

Neill's message resonated. Educators worked to give children more freedom and autonomy, but the divide between Deweyan educators and Lane-inspired ones became increasingly apparent. To the Dewey educators, less restrictive classrooms, better curriculum, and improved teaching methods would enhance schooling. To the Lane educators, the learner was the leader, free from compulsion. The world was her classroom.

Following *Summerhill*'s publication, author and social critic Paul Goodman wrote his book *Compulsory Miseducation* in 1964, excoriating conventional schooling. Even then, before the onslaught of federal No Child Left Behind legislation, Common Core curriculum frameworks, high-stakes testing at ever-earlier ages, and the widespread lengthening of school days and years, Goodman warned about the problem of focusing on schooling as synonymous with education, acknowledging that in just over a century forced schooling had weakened many of the previous informal educational models, like family-based learning and community apprenticeships. Influenced by Lane and Neill, Goodman was a proponent of non-compulsory education and more authentic, community-based learning. In his 1970 book *New Reformation* he writes:

> The present expanded school systems are coercive in their nature. The young have to attend for various well-known reasons, none of which is necessary for their well-being or the well-being of society . . . In all societies, both primitive and highly civilized, until quite recently, most education of most children has occurred incidentally, not in schools set aside for the purpose.[18]

Goodman's critique of compulsory schooling and coercive curriculum was shared by another cultural reformer of the 1970s, Ivan Illich. Illich was a Catholic priest and philosopher who linked institutionalized education with a general institutionalization of society, in which people are not fully able to be free and flourishing because they have been stripped of their self-direction. Conditioned by coercive schooling, young people lose their autonomy and natural learning inclinations and are instead trained to be taught. This process, according to Illich, then translates into a lifetime of institutionalized thinking that eradicates personal power. In his 1970 book *Deschooling Society* Illich begins:

> Many students, especially those who are poor, intuitively know what the schools do for them. They school them to confuse process and substance. Once these become blurred, a new logic is assumed: the more treatment there is, the better are the results; or, escalation leads to success. The pupil is thereby "schooled" to confuse teaching with learning, grade advancement with education, a diploma with competence, and fluency with the ability to say something new. His imagination is "schooled" to accept service in place of value.

"Not only education," Illich continues, "but social reality itself has become schooled.[19]

Inspired by Illich's writing and vision for a deschooled society, John Holt began to correspond with Illich and to visit him at his research center in Mexico. Holt's 1964 and 1967 books, *How Children Fail* and *How Children Learn*, respectively, became bestsellers. But Holt gradually began to feel that these books, which exposed in compelling detail the problems of institutionalized learning, didn't go far enough. Illich's message helped to crystallize Holt's thinking. Unlike other progressive educators at the time, Holt no longer felt that schooling could be reformed and he instead began to embrace alternatives. Throughout the 1970s, Holt advocated for learning separate from schooling, encouraging parents to remove their children from school to homeschool them. In his 1981 book about homeschooling, *Teach Your Own*, Holt writes, "What is most important and valuable about the home as a base for children's growth in the world is not that it is a better school than the schools but *that it isn't a school at all.*[20] Holt coined the term "unschooling" to encourage further distance from a schooled way of thinking, even at home.

At the same time that Illich and Holt were imagining a deschooled society, Daniel Greenberg was building a US school based on this vision. In the mid-1960s, Greenberg left his job as a physics professor at Columbia University to move to Massachusetts. He and his wife couldn't find a school that they liked for their son and decided, along with a team of founders, to create their own school that, like Summerhill, would be based on the democratic principles of self-governance and personal responsibility and a philosophy of self-directed learning. In 1968, the Sudbury Valley School opened its doors in Framingham, Massachusetts. It remains one of the few progressive schools born in the 1960s to survive and continues to be an inspiration for parents and educators interested in unschooling and self-directed education. There are no required classes and young people pursue their own interests, spending time on the things most meaningful to them.

Unschooling Today

While many progressive and self-directed schools floundered in the latter half of the last century (I explore some reasons why in chapter 8), the family-centered homeschooling movement gained momentum. John Holt's call, along with others, for parents to remove their children from coercive schooling resonated, and homeschooling numbers swelled. Patrick Farenga worked closely with John Holt until Holt's death in 1985, unschooled his own children, and now runs Holt Associates in Boston. He says that Holt never expected more than 2 percent of the overall US K–12 population to choose homeschooling.[21] Yet today, homeschooling numbers hover around two million children, or about 3.5 percent of the overall schooled population.

All indications are that unschooling is growing in popularity. The most recent data from the US Department of Education reveal that 20 percent of homeschooling families in 2016 "mostly" or "always" use an informal approach to learning with little to no reliance on formal curriculum, up from 13 percent in 2012.[22] Many parents who choose homeschooling wholeheartedly reject the uniformity and standardization of conventional schooling and are unwilling to bring that same model into their homes. They are opting out of the whole idea of schooling in favor of learning.

One refreshing change with today's unschooling movement is that it is being driven not by philosophers but by parents. Unlike Illich and Holt, who never had children, today's unschooling advocates increasingly choose this educational path from observing and listening to their own children. In many cases, unschooling parents saw their child's learning unfolding naturally and didn't want to halt it with formal schooling, or they sent their child to school and realized it was a mistake. For Chanda McCreary, choosing a nurturing, child-focused education environment for her daughter was a top priority. She initially gravitated toward progressive education before discovering unschooling.

A former public school teacher, with bachelor's and master's degrees in education, Chanda witnessed the ways in which mass schooling dulls curiosities and child-driven passions. Once she became a mom, she knew that the dominant schooling model was at odds with her parenting values. "We practiced attachment parenting and didn't feel that public school was an extension of that," says Chanda. "In addition, we are a two-mom family and we hoped to send our daughter to a school that made a point of celebrating diversity in many ways, including family structure." Chanda hadn't yet learned about unschooling and self-directed education when her daughter hit kindergarten age, so she enrolled her child in a certified Montessori school that was highly regarded as a model for similar schools, and a site for teacher training in Montessori practices. Chanda herself became so interested in the Montessori education approach that she began substitute teaching at her daughter's school, ultimately earning her Montessori teaching certification and becoming a full-time Montessori teacher.

At first, the child-centered Montessori curriculum, colorful classroom environment, and gentle teaching approach seemed like a good fit for her daughter; but gradually Chanda noticed that the curriculum expectations and teaching practices began to compromise her child's natural learning. While Chanda says the classroom was self-directed to some extent, it was limited. "The shelves in the classroom are set up with materials in each area, from easiest to most difficult," she says. "Students can make choices about what area to work in, but they must use the materials in order on the shelf. So if they have not completed one activity on the shelf in that area, they cannot move to the next activity. And, the materials are only to be used in one way, the way the teacher had taught the lesson, step-by-step exactly as they were meant to be used." Extensive progress reports evaluate a child's curriculum mastery.

Chanda's daughter began to feel stifled by these practices and expectations. She became increasingly frustrated at not having the time and space to work on projects that most interested her, and she grew bored at having to complete assignments that she found unfulfilling. Chanda also noticed how her daughter was developing a fixed mind-set around various subjects, like math and art, internalizing a belief that she was "good" in certain subjects and "bad" in others. At the end of fourth grade, Chanda and her spouse pulled their daughter from school and began the deschooling process. They began with homeschooling, but they ultimately found that unschooling and self-directed education would allow their daughter the time, space, and environment to pursue projects that she loved.

Today at thirteen, their daughter continues to forge her own educational path, pursuing personal goals, taking classes that are meaningful to her, and learning through everyday living. In hindsight, Chanda says that she is glad they chose Montessori schooling over other educational options, but she wishes that unschooling and self-directed education had been in her lexicon. "You would think that it would have been since I was in schools of education for both my undergraduate and graduate experiences!" Chanda continues:

> Even now, knowing about self-directed education and practicing it at home and in the community, is only a beginning. I hope that by being an example of a family that leads our life this way, and speaking out about it, in the future there will be many different choices for families who want to embrace self-directed education. There is much evidence that mass schooling is not working for

the masses. We should look at what does work, and put money and energy toward those choices for all families.

Now that the first generation of modern unschoolers has reached adulthood, we have initial evidence that self-directed education works. In 2013, academic researchers Peter Gray and Gina Riley reported on their survey of over two hundred unschooling families about their experiences with unschooling, including benefits and drawbacks. They found that most unschooling parents were overwhelmingly satisfied with unschooling and its outcomes, but the researchers wanted to know what the unschoolers themselves thought about their educational experience.[23]

In a 2014 survey of grown unschoolers, Gray and Riley found that the unschoolers were also widely satisfied with their experience and had gone on to lead fulfilling, independent, self-directed lives in a host of different career paths. Of particular interest is that more than half of the surveyed unschoolers went on to become entrepreneurs in various fields. The vast majority of the unschoolers surveyed went on to college and performed well academically, despite little to no formal academic training prior to college. According to the survey, the unschoolers who attended college at the highest rates were the "always unschooled" ones, as compared to more short-term or intermittent unschoolers. Most of the unschoolers who attended college found the admissions process to be straightforward and easy, even though the majority of them did not have a high school diploma or GED, and most did not take SAT or ACT exams. Colleges are increasingly accepting of, and even actively recruiting, alternatively educated students. Many unschoolers in the study took community college classes prior to enrolling in four-year university degree programs to prepare for the admissions process.[24]

Most unschoolers reported adjusting well to college life and formal academics but noted that their biggest complaints were "the lack of motivation and intellectual curiosity among their college classmates, the constricted social life of college, and, in a few cases, constraints imposed by the curriculum or grading system."[25] Research conducted on Sudbury Valley School graduates over the past fifty years shows similar results of self-directed education and is described in chapter 8. These preliminary findings on the outcomes and satisfaction of grown unschoolers are small but promising, and should be encouraging to today's parents considering this educational approach for their children.

Freedom, Not License

Although unschoolers often share common convictions about learning and parenting, we are a rather hodgepodge bunch. There is a wide spectrum of unschooling approaches, ranging from relaxed or eclectic homeschooling approaches that are mostly self-directed but incorporate a tiny amount of curriculum (math, for instance), to "radical unschooling" approaches that extend academic unschooling ideas to all areas of living, granting children full autonomy in determining things like bedtimes, food choices, personal hygiene decisions, and screen time. While today's unschooling families may move fluidly along this spectrum as their children hit different ages and stages, most families likely hover somewhere in the middle, embracing what I call an "open unschooling" approach.

In his 1969 book, *The Open Classroom*, Kohl describes three environments for learning: authoritarian, open, and permissive.[26] Authoritarian environments are the most common and the strictest, demanding acquiescence to authority figures. Permissive environments are overly indulgent and unruly. Open environments can promote the deepest learning because they don't control children, but they also don't let children control the adults. In unschooling circles, you often hear the phrase "unschooling is not un-parenting." This would be an example of fostering an open learning environment versus an authoritarian or permissive one.

In an open unschooling environment, there is shared respect, freedom from coercion, and trust in each other's motives. But there is also a social contract. That arrangement will vary for each unschooling family or organization, and may continually change and evolve. In A. S. Neill's terms, this is "freedom, not license." Providing the freedom is straightforward; ensuring that freedom doesn't turn into license, or permissiveness, is much harder to impart and will vary to ensure that one person's freedom does not negatively impact another's freedom. In Neill's 1966 book, *Freedom—Not License!*, he explains this idea more fully: "Freedom, over-extended, turns into license. I define license as interfering with another's freedom. For example, in my school a child is free to go to lessons or stay away from lessons because that is his own affair, but he is not free to play a trumpet when others want to study or sleep."[27]

Unschooling families develop their own sets of ideals and their own degrees of freedom, not license, based on family values and priorities. For example, unschooling parents may not force their children to do writing exercises, but they may ask them to write thank you notes for the birthday gifts they receive. They may not demand that a child do a certain craft, but they may ask that he clean up the paper trimmings on his bedroom floor before his friends come over. They may not choose what books their children read, but they may decide to read *The Hobbit* aloud at bedtime to whoever wants to listen. They may not limit their children's screen time, but they may choose not to have a television in their home.

Freedom, not license looks different for each unschooling family. The key is mutual respect and shared responsibility. Children are granted tremendous freedom in how they spend their time and on what activities they do or do not engage in, but they also have a responsibility to their family members, to their household, and to their larger community. Similarly, unschooling parents appreciate their educational freedom but also recognize their responsibility to be good parents who care for their children's health and well-being and are attentive to their children's needs and interests. There is also the issue of common sense. Parents have a responsibility to protect their children from harm, something young children in particular are notorious for seeking. I can't tell you the number of times my toddlers, upon seeing their neighborhood friends across the street, tried to jump in front of oncoming city traffic. I held their hands tightly, knowing that self-regulation only goes so far with little ones. Sometimes parents know best. We can encourage self-direction and self-regulation, within reason. Neill reminds us of this in *Summerhill*: "Of course, self-regulation, like any theoretical idea, is dangerous if not combined with common sense. Only a fool in charge of young children would allow unbarred bedroom windows or an unprotected fire in the nursery."[28]

Family Values

Family values will necessarily influence unschooling, as they do in any home life, and may define childhood experiences and exposures. For Saira Siddiqui, her conservative Muslim views may seem incompatible with her role as an unschooling mother of three children in Texas. Yet she finds that she is able to create a life centered around faith while also providing freedom and autonomy for her children. As Saira says, "I have a very conservative view of faith, so there are a lot of things that I think and believe that do seem contradictory with unschooling. For example, we have a lot of discipline in our faith. A Muslim at the age of puberty is required to pray five times a day. That is something that I personally uphold in my life and that I want my children to uphold." But Saira is clear that she wants faith to be something her children think critically about, question, and discuss so that their faith will come from an internal belief system, and not be something imposed by force by external author- ity figures. Since her children, who are now nine-year-old twins and a six-year-old, were very young, Saira has presented faith as an important and defining part of their family life but also as something that should come from within and be continuously examined. As Saira says, "I don't think that questioning is antithetical to being a person of high faith. I don't want to grow robotic people of faith."

Saira's approach to unschooling springs from her gentle parenting tendencies, in which she follows her children's lead, responds to their needs, and creates a nurturing home life that encourages individual flourishing. She has a graduate degree in education and was a teacher prior to motherhood. Saira thought she would send her children to public school, but as she explored local schools when her children hit school-age, they all seemed too sterile and top-down. At home, she watched how her children's learning unfolded organically—how they naturally gravitated toward books and conversation and exploration. She felt that schooling would be less able to facilitate her children's natural learning and personal growth.

Instead of public school, Saira decided to homeschool her kids, begin- ning with a more conventional school-at-home approach that incorpo- rated adult-selected activities and projects and eventually finding her way to unschooling. She began unschooling at about the same time she started writing her popular blog, *Confessions of a Muslim Mom*, which now has many thousands of followers. Her ideas about child-directed learning and natural parenting resonated with both religious and secular parents. Today, Saira's children learn by following their interests, without a set curriculum. The family travels frequently, exploring new cultures and languages, and becoming immersed in new experiences that shape her children's learning.

Faith remains a central feature of the family's living and learning. Saira acknowledges that unschooling is not un-parenting, and that parents can and will extend their personal and philosophical beliefs onto their children. "It's the nature of living in a household and in a community that certain values will be passed down. That is how culture functions," says Saira. She feels that the best way to reconcile unschooling views with strong religious beliefs, or other lifestyle convictions (like veganism, for example), is to approach these ideologies from a place of openness and assurance, rather than fear and coercion. As Saira says:

> Sometimes when you come from a place of very strong beliefs, there is a fear that your children will not subscribe to those beliefs and that fear determines how you interact with your children. I don't think that belief driven by fear is the best way to inculcate those beliefs in others. I think one of the antidotes to fear is to be in a place of complete confidence, assurance, and faith yourself and then that fear dissipates.

Unschoolers will define freedom and responsibility in different ways, and family values will create the contours of a child's life, but a common theme is likely to emerge for these families: with unschooling, learning and living become seamless and synonymous. There is no separation of one from the other. There is no separation of children from the "real world." It is all real. As Grace Llewellyn and Amy Silver write in their book, *Guerrilla Learning*, "Unschooling is really just a fancy term for 'life,' or 'growing up uninstitutionalized.'"[29] Children are eager to explore and discover their world and to engage in meaningful work and actions tied to their interests and fueled by their limitless curiosity. Our job as unschooling parents is to listen to their questions and ideas, support and encourage them, and help connect them to the wider world around them. Facilitating our children's natural learning, free from coercion, is a primary goal. Separating ourselves from the influence of schooled thinking can be a more daunting objective.

Unschooling Tips

• **Acknowledge the unschooling spectrum**. There is a wide range of unschooling approaches underneath the unschooling umbrella. Unschooling is a catchall term for interest-based, self-directed learning that uses the full resources of one's community. It is centered on freedom and respect for children's individual development and distinct passions. "Freedom, not license" will look different for every family because values and expectations vary.

• **Start with interests.** Parents interested in unschooling may wonder how to take the first step from a schooling model to a learning one. Start with your children's interests! Maybe they already have extracurricular activities that fill their week as an add-on to academics. Make these the focal point of the week. There is nothing "extra" about them. The activities your children enjoy, and the interests that continually emerge from their daily life within their community, become your children's education.

• **Appreciate noncoercive learning**. A primary characteristic of unschooling is its emphasis on noncoercive education, or the ability to say no. Perhaps you place some math problems on the table for your child to do, or you set up a craft for him, or you offer to read him a book about the Revolutionary War. He should have the freedom to say no. (Although usually if you start reading that book out loud or doing that craft yourself, he'll want to join in too!)

The trickier piece of noncoercion is what happens when one person's no infringes on another's yes. This gets back to the point of "freedom, not license." If your family wants to go for a hike in the woods and one child doesn't, it may require some discussion and communication around family give-and-take, why you all value time in nature, and so on. Or maybe the child who really doesn't want to go on that hike can find another option, like going to a friend's or family member's house. An older child may be able to simply stay home. Offering freedom without allowing one's freedom to negatively impact another's is an ongoing challenge, and each challenge will have a different solution.

• **Accept the dichotomy of unschooling.** Unschooling parents are both very involved and very uninvolved. They are very involved in recognizing their children's distinct interests and individual approaches to learning and actively facilitate these interests and learning by helping to connect them to broader resources. But they are also very uninvolved in terms of giving their children a lot of freedom, not hovering over them as they learn and grow, and encouraging them to explore and make sense of the world on their own terms. Unschooling parents are very attentive to their children's ideas and well-being, and they are also able to let go and give their children the freedom to learn.

4

Childhood Isn't
What It Used to Be

*"How has childhood become so unnatural? Why does
the dominant culture treat young humans in ways which
would be illegal if applied to young dogs? Born to burrow
and nest in nature, children are now exiled from it. They
are enclosed indoors, caged and shut out of the green and
vivid world, in ways unthinkable a generation ago."*

—Jay Griffiths, *A Country Called Childhood*[1]

HAVE YOU EVER EATEN A perfectly ripe cherry tomato right off the vine?
Or plucked a sunshine-warmed strawberry straight from the summer
fields? Or taken that first crunchy bite of a just-picked apple from an
autumn orchard? If you have, you know that nothing can compare to the
real thing. There is an intangible authenticity to real food.

In his book *In Defense of Food*, well-known food writer Michael Pollan contrasts real food with what he calls the "edible foodlike substances"
that now pervade our Western diet: packaged and processed imitations
of the real thing.[2] These foodstuff imposters are causing serious harm.
Recent US Centers for Disease Control and Prevention (CDC) data
reveal that 40 percent of American adults are obese and over 70 percent are overweight or obese; 20 percent of kids are also now considered obese. Obesity is often linked to our culture's skyrocketing rates of

chronic illness, like type 2 diabetes, high blood pressure, heart disease, and stroke.[3] In straying too far from the natural foods that humans have evolved to eat, these "edible foodlike substances" are making us sick.

In much the same way that artificial food is causing harm, artificial learning is doing the same. We have steadily replaced real learning with what I call "packaged, education-like systems," or schoolstuffs. You may be thinking that like "edible foodlike substances," these schoolstuffs have been around for a long time without causing significant harm. We all likely ate Twinkies and went to school and we're fine, right? The problem is that there are more artificial foodstuffs and schoolstuffs today than when we were kids. Yes, we might have had a Twinkie but we also probably had a nutritious home-cooked meal for dinner. Yes, we might have gone to school, but it was for a tolerable few hours a day with wide-open afternoons, weekends, and summer vacations to play freely. We humans can readily absorb and adapt to some degree of artificiality in both our food and our learning; we just can't do it so well when the abnormal becomes the norm.

The Rise of Schoolstuffs

In just a generation, the landscape of learning has dramatically changed. Children are now spending more time in conventional schooling, and other school-like settings such as day care, after-school care, and structured extracurricular programming, than ever before. In a 2004 report, researchers at the University of Michigan compared the time use of American children in 1981–82 to their time use in 2002–03. They discovered that over that twenty-year period, American children aged six to seventeen spent much more time in school in the early 2000s than they did in the early 1980s. While children in all age groups saw increases in time spent in school over those two decades, the rise was particularly steep for young children ages six to eight, whose schooling increased from an average of five hours a day in 1981–82 to an average of seven hours a day in 2002–03.[4] More significantly, these data did not include time spent in out-of-school programming and day care settings that are often quite school-like as well.

Not surprisingly, the University of Michigan researchers also found that children in the early 2000s were spending less time in "active sports and out-of-doors activities" than children growing up in the 1980s. Play was vanishing. In addition, children are consuming more schoolstuffs for more of the year, including during summertime. According to data by the US Bureau of Labor Statistics, 42 percent of children were enrolled in school in July 2016, compared to only 10 percent in July 1985.[5]

The evaporation of free playtime, coinciding with the increase of schoolstuffs, has been documented by other researchers as well. According to a 2001 paper by Sandra Hofferth and John Sandberg, childhood play declined by 16 percent between 1981 and 1997. The drop in free play correlated with a rise in structured activities, including school. Interestingly, Hofferth and Sandberg found that it wasn't just the influx of mothers into the workplace during this time period that led to rising time in school and declining play. Nonworking mothers also began to rely more heavily on schoolstuffs.[6] If school was good, more of it was better—or so parents thought.

Many of us remember play-filled afternoons running around with the neighborhood kids, and wide open summer vacations filled with sunshine and fresh air. Adults weren't around, but we knew how to find them and where to get help—even before cell phones. Today, this kind of free, unstructured, unsupervised play is virtually nonexistent. Many children today spend nearly every waking hour consuming some type of schoolstuff, mostly orchestrated and observed by adults. Street hockey and flag football and a good game of neighborhood catch have disappeared, replaced by organized activities for toddlers to teens.

Abandoned neighborhoods aren't the only consequence of this trend toward more schoolstuffs and away from play. Mounting evidence reveals a rise in childhood mental health issues as children's play declines. A 2011 article in the *American Journal of Play* argues for a causal link between the systematic decline in play and the corresponding rise in childhood anxiety, depression, feelings of helplessness, narcissism, and other mental illness indicators.[7] Other researchers have found similar disturbing trends regarding play deprivation. In her book, *Balanced and Barefoot*, pediatric occupational therapist Angela Hanscom describes the importance of free play and its healthy impact on emotional and physical development. She describes the trends away from free, active play and what she observes as a steady rise in sensory and motor development delays. "The cold hard truth," says Hanscom, "is that when you compare today's children to past generations, they just can't keep up. Children are getting weaker, less resilient, and less imaginative."[8]

The more time children spend in structured, adult-led activities the less time they learn through free play. This can have a significant impact on their overall physical, cognitive, and emotional development. Researchers at the University of Colorado, Boulder published a 2014 report showing that young children who spent more time in structured activities, such as music lessons, organized sports, and homework, had worse "self-directed executive functioning" skills than children who spent time in less structured activities, such as free play, pleasure reading, and going to a library or museum.[9] These executive functioning skills were defined as the ability to set and accomplish personal goals. Children whose time was most tightly controlled by adults fared worse on executive functioning measures. According to the researchers, childhood executive functioning skills are also an important indicator of long-term outcomes, including health, academic achievement, and financial success. As children spend more time in coordinated activities, their ability to self-direct weakens.

Despite this alarming rise in schoolstuffs and decline in play, many parents don't seem particularly bothered by these trends. According to a 2017 Gallup report, parents of children ages ten and younger acknowledge that free play "fosters creativity and problem-solving," but they do not think these qualities are especially important. In fact, the study found child-led unstructured play ranked near the bottom of the priority list for parents, while academic skills were highly ranked. The report concludes that many parents don't appreciate the importance of unstructured childhood play on children's development and tend to be anxious about their children's free time.[10] Parents now believe that schoolstuffs are more important than good old-fashioned play. The heightened focus on early childhood success and academic achievement may result in children who grow up to be less creative, less collaborative, and less emotionally resilient than they were just a generation ago.

Declining childhood creativity is a serious problem. The rise of school-stuffs and the decline of play, coupled with parents who don't seem to prioritize the conditions necessary to cultivate creativity, are leading to a generation of young people who are less creative than earlier cohorts. In a startling discovery, Kyung Hee Kim, a professor at the College of William and Mary, found that creativity scores had been rising for each generation up until 1990. At that point, creativity scores began a steady decline. Kim analyzed hundreds of thousands of scores on the well-regarded Torrance Tests of Creative Thinking, considered by many to be the gold standard of creativity measurement tools. While she uncovered an overall signifi-cant creativity decline since 1990, kindergartners to sixth graders had the steepest drop.[11] Kim finds that Americans are much less creative today than they were twenty-five years ago, and there are no signs of improve-ment. In her book, *The Creativity Challenge,* Kim writes, "Despite all the innovation that has brought America to where it is today, the culture has changed in ways that have stifled creativity instead of encouraging it. America must reclaim what it does best: fostering creativity."[12]

For Dan Sanchez, an editor and writer, preserving childhood cre-ativity is a major reason why he and his wife decided not to send their daughter, Evie, to school. Through the process of watching his daughter and reading more about natural, noncoercive learning, Dan realized how much of his own childhood creativity and passion were extinguished by schooling. "My earliest memories of myself are of an energetic, passion-ate little boy," he recalls. "I obsessively immersed myself in my interests, which ranged from collecting the scientific names of animals to memo-rizing every detail about Transformers characters. But then school wore that down. The exploration of topics became an imposed obligation, which made me apathetic. Instead of pursuing my own interests, the goal became winning good grades."

Now, Dan sees his five-year-old daughter's similar passions and interests and the way she becomes deeply focused on her imaginary play. He doesn't want to replace that natural creativity and curiosity with a diet of schoolstuffs filled with artificial additives.

> I see in my daughter the enthusiastic, fascination-prone nature
> that I had as a very young child. She is fascinated with certain

character-based toy lines. She is learning how to obsessively master a subject inside and out under her own initiative and volition. She is also learning that the world she has found herself in is an accessible, enjoyable, and fascinating place full of rewarding opportunities. And she is learning about herself: that she is a capable being, able to create experiences for herself that she finds meaningful.

For Dan and his wife, neither schooling nor homeschooling were appealing options. Homeschooling, while gentler and more child-centered than conventional schooling, still imports many of the schooled expectations around forced assignments, curriculum guidelines, rote learning, and a singular mode of assessment. Dan wanted to avoid having these school-stuffs in his home and instead to allow Evie's insatiable curiosity to drive her learning and doing throughout her childhood. "I came to understand the real problem with conventional schools. It's not that schools are bad at schooling. It's not that parents themselves could do schooling better at home. Schooling itself is the problem, wherever it is done."

Schooling separates children from their community, and imposes a particular framework for what they should know and when. Schooling, whether at home or elsewhere, ignores what children themselves want to learn and do, and dismisses their powerful drive for knowledge. Children are wired to learn. Our job as parents is to give them the freedom and opportunity to do so within the wider world, following their own distinct interests and timetables. As Dan concludes, the primary problem with schooling is "the very idea of cloistering children from the wider world and placing them under constant adult oversight, direction, and correction. This remains true even if the home is the cloister and if parents are the overseers, directors, and correctors." Schooling is the problem; learning—freely and naturally within the wider world—is the solution.

Quality, Not Just Quantity

It's not just that people are consuming higher quantities of edible, food-like substances that are making them sick. It's also that the ingredients of these substances are more toxic than before. Similarly, it's not just more schoolstuffs that are causing harm today; it's also the type of schoolstuffs that children now consume compared to earlier generations. Conventional schooling today is much more standardized and test-driven than it used to be. In 2001, the US Congress passed the No Child Left Behind Act (NCLB) as part of a reauthorization of the Elementary and Secondary Education Act, first enacted in 1965. It broadened the role of the federal government in public schooling and focused on frequent standardized testing to increase school and teacher accountability.

The accelerated focus on standards, accountability, and regular testing over the subsequent years culminated with the Common Core State Standards Initiative, an effort to establish a uniform set of curriculum and testing frameworks for all public school students. These curriculum standards were launched in 2009 and adopted by the majority of US states. To entice states to adopt these new standards and receive generous funding packages, the federal government offered "Race to the Top" grants. In December 2015, the Every Student Succeeds Act (ESSA) replaced NCLB. It retains federal oversight of education goals and accountability, though it pushes responsibility toward the states to develop their own standards and metrics. It also maintains an expectation of regular standardized testing within all public schools. Under the ESSA, states must adopt "challenging" curriculum frameworks, which may or may not be Common Core standards, and students are tested annually from third through eighth grades and again in high school. Aghast at these rising schoolstuffs, parents and teachers alike are seeking alternatives.

After working for Teach for America and then earning a master's degree from the Harvard Graduate School of Education, Jessica Yarmosky became a high school English teacher in a large, urban public school district. At first she was eager and optimistic, but she quickly became disturbed. "In my interview, the first thing they asked me was what I knew about the test," Jess said, describing the tenth-grade statewide standardized exam that was also a graduation requirement for students. "That should have been a red flag. Everything we did was based on the test." Jess recalls that the way she was told to teach English and writing was focused squarely on the requirements of the test. There wasn't anything in her teaching that focused on real enjoyment of certain texts or the art of how to write well.

Learning was standardized and test-driven, both for students and for teachers. "I went into the classroom with a real passion for deeper learning," she says. "But midway through that fall semester, I was so disappointed that we were not serving kids in the way that I felt they should be served because of the standardized curriculum and the testing. It felt really disgusting to me. I would have kids say to me, 'I used to like writing, I used to like reading, and now I hate it.'" Jess left that teaching job, believing that she could no longer be complicit in that pressure-filled environment for kids. She had listened to a talk by someone who was starting a self-directed school and it validated what she had been feeling. Jess began to explore unschooling and alternatives to school that were more aligned with her beliefs in how young people should be treated.

"Kids need freedom and choice," says Jess.

> We are literally barring them from making daily choices, from being in the community doing things with others. We have this thing now called "school refusal," where kids don't want to go to school. It's a new label. It is so bad we have to create an academic research community around it. The reason kids hate school is because it's school. They don't want to be there.

Like many of the educators featured in these pages, Jess is committed to expanding unschooling and self-directed education options to more kids. She is one of a growing number of teachers who reject the standardization of schooling and see unschooling as the future of education. Learning shouldn't hurt.

Even with this heightened attention to standardized curriculum and testing over the last two decades, the outcomes don't appear good. By their own metrics, schools are failing. Recent data from the Organization for Economic Cooperation and Development (OECD) show that the United States spends more on education than most developed countries yet current schooling outcomes are disappointing.[13] On international comparison tests, such as the well-regarded Program for International

Student Assessment, US students are lagging far behind their peers in other nations, with US fifteen-year-olds ranking thirty-eighth out of seventy-one countries in math and twenty-fourth in science.[14] According to the National Assessment of Educational Progress report, also known as the Nation's Report Card, student reading and math scores declined between 2013 and 2015.[15]

Not only is the standards and testing movement not working, one of its most damaging legacies is the elimination of play-based early childhood education. New kindergarten curriculum standards shift academic work previously reserved for first and second graders to kindergarteners and, increasingly, preschoolers as schooling trumps playing. Children are being fed schoolstuffs much earlier and more often than when we were kids. It's becoming more apparent that valuing these schoolstuffs over time-honored childhood play is leading to less curious, more formulaic kids. As author Erika Christakis writes in the *Atlantic*:

> Preschool classrooms have become increasingly fraught spaces, with teachers cajoling their charges to finish their "work" before they can go play. And yet, even as preschoolers are learning more pre-academic skills at earlier ages, I've heard many teachers say that they seem somehow—is it possible?—less inquisitive and less engaged than the kids of earlier generations.[16]

Children become conditioned to be taught, giving up the unschooled ways in which they are wired to learn. The earlier this conditioning occurs, the more quickly children lose their creative, self-educative aptitudes. In September 2011, two separate research laboratories conducted different experiments on young children but reported similar findings about the impact of instruction on learning. Researchers at the Massachusetts Institute of Technology wanted to see how direct instruction of young children might impact their overall learning. They assembled two groups of four-year-olds, telling one group that they had just found a great new toy with four tubes that could squeak. For the other group, the researchers showed the children their new toy and proceeded to demonstrate how it worked. The first group was learning through play and exploration, while the second group was learning through direct instruction.

The researchers discovered that while both groups made the toy squeak, the group that was taught failed to discover many of the other features of the toy. The untaught group, on the other hand, was able to uncover these other toy functions as a normal part of their play and exploration. The researchers concluded that direct instruction "promotes efficient learning but at a cost: children are less likely to perform potentially irrelevant actions but also less likely to discover novel information."[17] In other words, teaching can quickly pass on information but it can also limit creative discovery by stifling the natural drive to play and explore.

At the same time, researchers at the University of California, Berkeley also showed a new toy to separate groups of four-year-olds, with one group receiving direct instruction and the other not. This toy had various features, but it would only play music if two features were pressed in the same sequence. For the first group, the researchers provided no instruction and the children were able to quickly discover on their own the basic two-part sequence that would make the toy play music. For the second group, the researchers acted as teachers. They demonstrated how their toy worked and showed its various features, concluding with the two-part sequence that would make the toy musical. When this second group of children was then given the toy, the children simply imitated the instructor. These taught kids followed the same set of sequences they were shown and were not able to uncover the basic, two-sequence step that the untaught children had naturally found.[18]

Alison Gopnik, one of the lead researchers of the UC-Berkeley study, explains that while direct instruction has its place, natural learning can be particularly powerful for young children. She writes, "Adults often assume that most learning is the result of teaching and that exploratory, spontaneous learning is unusual. But actually, spontaneous learning is more fundamental . . . Knowing this, it's more important than ever to give children's remarkable, spontaneous learning abilities free rein."[19] Both of these studies reveal how adept young children are at learning and discovery. They also show how easy it is for adults to turn off a child's natural learning tendencies.

Unequal Impact

More schoolstuffs at earlier ages can swiftly dull children's curiosity and creativity, but that is not their only harm. There is mounting evidence that our increasingly restrictive system of forced schooling may be most damaging to poor and minority young people. Mass schooling can amplify and embed disadvantage very early on in a child's life, fueling a massive school-to-prison pipeline and perpetuating inequality. According to US Department of Education data from 2013 to 2014, 6,743 children who were enrolled in public *preschool* received one or more out-of-school suspensions—with black children much more likely to be suspended than white children.[20] What does it say about the state of American childhood when preschoolers are being expelled?

Beyond this disturbing trend is the revelation that many minority children don't appear to be faring well academically within the existing mass schooling model. According to National Center for Education Statistics data, only 14 percent of African America eighth graders scored at or above the proficient level in reading, and only 17 percent of Hispanic eighth graders did so.[21] These disappointing outcomes may explain why more parents, particularly minorities, are opting out of mass schooling altogether and are instead embracing alternatives to school. In a 2012 research paper published in the *Journal of Black Studies*, Temple University professor Ama Mazama revealed that black families were increasingly turning to school alternatives such as homeschooling as a form of racial protectionism. She found the growth in African American homeschooling to be "an exercise in agency inspired by the desire to defeat racism through physical removal from one of its major spheres of operation, school."[22] The *Atlantic* reports that black families are one of the fastest-growing demographics of homeschoolers.[23]

For Shaylanna Graham the path to homeschooling, and ultimately unschooling, was premised on the freedom to learn and the freedom to create. When her firstborn was sixteen months old she knew she had to make a choice: either put him in daycare or give up her newly founded

business so that she could be home with him and give him the attention that he demanded as a toddler. As she explored various preschool
programs for her son in his early years, she was disappointed. "Most of
them were indoor-based, academically focused, and all about kindergarten
prep," she remembers. "I don't know what it was but something inside
of me just knew something was not right about what I was witnessing in
preschools. I knew our son thrived in an environment where he had a lot
of free time to play and create from his own imagination." This caused her
to become a stay-at-home mother and seek alternative educational options.

She soon gave birth to her second child and knew that her feelings
were correct when she witnessed, continuously, how both her son and
daughter grew and learned naturally, without much interference. "I was
watching them learn so much without my help," says Shaylanna.

> The high demands that the traditional school system puts on
> young children these days just didn't seem right to me. So, their
> dad and I decided that we would homeschool. It felt right for us
> to allow them to gravitate toward their own interests and grow
> and learn organically, exactly as they had already been doing
> at home. We also knew that we wanted to create somewhat of
> a mobile lifestyle for our family and wanted our children to be
> free to travel and learn about the world through exploring and
> experiencing the world in real life.

Race also played a role in Shaylanna's decision to choose homeschooling. As an African American, she felt that mass schooling can be
particularly harmful for children of color. "There is a clear disadvantage
for children of color and it can be damaging emotionally and psycho-
logically for many children of color," says Shaylanna.

> We wanted to shelter our children from having that experience
> in school. We also wanted to make sure that they learned the
> true history and origin of our ancestors and the great impact
> that our African ancestors had in the history of the world. It
> clearly did not begin with slavery, as we are taught in traditional
> schools. We want our children to see themselves as equals to

everyone else and to know that they are just as great as anyone else, despite a difference in the hue of their skin tone. Schools systematically treat our brown children as if they are less-than and less deserving than the rest and it is our intention that our brown children have a much more positive life-experience.

While getting acclimated to her new role as an at-home parent, Shaylanna began to miss running her own business. "I have a degree in business management, I love business!" she says. She sought a way to merge the two roles. Shaylanna created what she believed was the ideal learning environment for her own children and founded a holistic, play-based, self-directed preschool in her home. She offered her preschool services to other families who shared similar beliefs on the importance of self-directed learning and free play in early childhood.

While Shaylanna embraced self-directed learning for the preschool years, she initially thought her children would need a more structured, curriculum-based learning environment as they grew. When her son hit kindergarten age, Shaylanna started to research homeschool curriculum offerings. She felt that as a responsible homeschooling parent, selecting a highly ranked elementary school curriculum would be the obvious path. But as she read various curriculum reviews and identified the pluses and minuses of each, she was watching her children grow and learn all by themselves, from their environment and with her support. "From watching my own children and also the children in my preschool, I came to the conclusion that children really can learn without a lot of adult intervention." She began to wonder about non-curriculum-focused homeschooling options and discovered the term unschooling from a YouTube video about homeschooling. Shaylanna recalls, "I bought John Holt's books and I said, 'Wow, this is it! We're unschooling!' And now I see them learning and doing exactly what he said they would."

With a name for her natural approach to learning, Shaylanna feels increasingly confident about this education choice. Now that her son is six she says:

I allow him to freely do what he wants, following his interests. If he has questions, he asks and I help him. I try to make his everyday living a part of his learning. We do a lot of cooking, baking, measuring, trips to the grocery store where he sorts the money. Are we sitting and doing workbooks? No. He's learning on his own. When he was five he wrote a letter to his dad and not one day did I teach him how to write. My daughter began writing her whole name when she was three, and again it was not something I taught her. We have an alphabet chart on the wall and they are using that to learn to write on their own. If they need help spelling a word, I spell it for them, they look on the alphabet chart for the letters, and then they reproduce it on paper without my help.

Surrounding her children with resources and being attentive to their needs and interests is how Shaylanna facilitates her children's natural learning.

Shaylanna plans to continue on this unschooling path indefinitely. She and her husband hope to expose the children to as much of the world as possible and allow them to forge their own educational path with assistance when they need it. She tells her children:

You are powerful. You are creative beings. You can create whatever you want. If I place them in the school system, they are going to get the opposite message; there is no focus on the person inside. I want them to have a strong foundation of knowing who they are at their core, and how much power they have to create their own reality and how much influence they can have in their environment and in this world in which we live.

Pathologizing Childhood

The environment of today's schooling often emphasizes control, order, and conformity at the expense of freedom, play, and originality. For some children, the increasing time and intensity of schoolstuffs at earlier ages pushes them to the very limits of their adaptability. More young children are exhibiting school-related behavioral and attention disorders now than ever before, and they are more likely to be treated with potent psychotropic medications for what are often normal childhood actions that can become pathologized within an early forced schooling context. The US Centers for Disease Control and Prevention (CDC) reports that approximately 11 percent of children ages four to seventeen have been diagnosed with ADHD, and that number increased 42 percent from 2003–04 to 2011–12, with a majority of those diagnosed placed on medication. Perhaps more troubling, one-third of these diagnoses occur in children under age six.[24]

In young children especially, these "disorders" may just be a cry for help. As psychologist Enrico Gnaulati writes in his book *Back to Normal: Why Ordinary Childhood Behavior Is Mistaken for ADHD, Bipolar Disorder, and Autism Spectrum Disorder:*

> Kindergarteners these days are being dealt a double whammy. Their overall stress is elevated due to their being confronted with academic tasks and social expectations that are beyond their developmental capacities. Then they are deprived of the means to cope with that stress—animated, kinetic, imaginative play . . . When they wander off, tantrum, hit, dillydally, squirm, squeal, or cuss, they are at risk of being caught up in the kindergarten psychiatric dragnet, when their behavior is often merely a negative reaction to stress.[25]

Not able to cope with the demands of standardized, test-based schooling at early ages, young children may be improperly flagged and diagnosed for ADHD when they are simply exhibiting normal childhood behavior that becomes problematic within a developmentally abnormal learning environment.

A team of University of California, Berkeley professors discovered that some of the increased ADHD diagnoses were highly correlated with the growing emphasis on standardized testing pushed forward by federal education policies such as No Child Left Behind (NCLB). In their 2015 report, the researchers revealed that between 2003 and 2011 there was an uptick in children, particularly low-income children, diagnosed with ADHD in states where high-stakes testing first became prevalent. Low-income children were particularly targeted due to NCLB's expectation that disadvantaged children show yearly progress on standardized tests. In states with laws that prohibited schools from recommending psychotropic medications for children, the number of children medicated for ADHD fell slightly during the 2003–11 timeline, in contrast to the states without such laws that saw a 23 percent rise in ADHD medication rates.[26] The surge in ADHD diagnoses since the early 2000s may be due, at least in part, to efforts to help children conform to the demands of mandatory testing, or as a strategy for helping school districts to improve their test scores by recommending medication to get young children to sit still and concentrate.

Curious about mounting data showing possible correlations between school attendance and ADHD diagnoses, psychologist Dr. Peter Gray conducted his own informal, online survey of children who left conventional schooling for homeschooling or other forms of alternative education. He found that for children previously labeled ADHD, often with related anxiety issues, children's behavioral and emotional problems were dramatically reduced, or disappeared altogether, and their overall learning improved when they left conventional schooling. Results were particularly positive when children engaged in self-directed education, or unschooling, where they had more freedom and control over their own learning.[27] Dr. Gray concludes that ADHD is essentially a "failure to adapt to the conditions of standard schooling."[28]

For Tarryn Anderson's son Miles, adapting to the conditions of standard schooling was difficult. It all started in kindergarten. "His teacher was the sweetest thing," recalls Tarryn, but there were soon mentions of Miles's 'attention' issues." Then there was the classroom behavior chart, and Miles was frequently getting marked down for poor behavior. He was five. "I would get upset because of the behavior chart," says Tarryn, "and would find myself shaming him for his poor behavior in school." Still, Tarryn didn't know what else she could do. She and her husband both worked full-time and private schools were too expensive. Their choices were limited.

In first grade at Miles's public elementary school, the teachers continued to complain about his attention issues and hyperactive behavior. They urged Tarryn to take Miles to a doctor for assessment. In second grade, she finally relented. The doctor diagnosed Miles with ADHD and prescribed medication. It did not sit well with Tarryn. She felt, instinctively, that her son didn't need this label or these medications. She believed that the symptoms he exhibited—inability to sit still in school, inability to pay attention to the teacher, talking out of turn, inability to focus on worksheets—were typical of young boys. But medication has replaced the schoolmarm's knuckle-rapping ruler. Tarryn ultimately gave in and allowed her son to be placed on ADHD medication.

Once medicated, Miles's attention and behavior issues improved. The teachers no longer complained about his lack of attention, his behavioral problems ended, and he was able to focus on his schoolwork. This was a win then, right? One could argue that Miles was properly diagnosed with a mental health issue and appropriately medicated. It is true that Miles's ADHD diagnosis and treatment enabled him to comply more fully with the expectations of conventional schooling. The more consequential question, though, is at what cost? What did Miles give up in his effort to go along?

Those questions were answered for Tarryn when Miles began third grade. Tarryn was the creative director of a fashion magazine, a job that kept her days busy and full. The magazine folded as Miles started the new school year, leaving Tarryn with unexpected free time. She decided to volunteer at Miles's school, and for the first time she got a close-up look at what was really going on. "When I saw him at lunchtime, I thought, 'This is not my child.' He was totally zoned out. I realized that in the afternoon when he got home from school the meds wore off and he was my typical kid, but at school I saw that he was completely different. I could feel his pain. It didn't sit well with me."

Tarryn started researching her options. Homeschooling was the furthest thing from her mind, she says. And yet, here she was in the midst of a career change and wondering what was next. "I had this moment where I said to myself, 'What are you doing with your life?' I decided that we were going to give homeschooling a try." She pulled Miles from school and stopped his ADHD medication.

Like many parents who leave a conventional schooling environment for homeschooling, Tarryn began with a traditional curriculum, attempting to replicate school-at-home. It can be tricky to imagine education without schooling. After all, most of us went to school. It is a dominant cultural institution reflected in so much of our everyday living. For many of us, education and schooling are indelibly linked. Even if we reject conventional schooling, we may still be drawn to replicate its structure elsewhere. How else could we learn if it wasn't for school?

This was the common trap Tarryn found herself in during those initial few weeks of homeschooling. She bought a pricey, traditional homeschooling curriculum that reflected standard schooling subject areas, with standard worksheets and assessments. "I was drawn to a more child-led approach to learning, but I was scared to do it," Tarryn says. She trudged along with the standard curriculum, coercing Miles to go through the motions of school-at-home. He continually resisted; she continually pushed. Neither was enjoying the experience. Maybe homeschooling was a mistake, they thought.

The typical pattern of moving from conventional school to school-at-home homeschooling is also frequently followed by a typical turning point moment. Something happens that creates a catalyst for pause and reevaluation and, often, introspection. Does learning have to be this way? Does education have to be painful? Do we really need to do school? For Tarryn, this turning point arrived three months into their fledgling homeschooling journey. They had friends arriving shortly from out of town. Tarryn was feeling the pressure to have Miles finish his schoolwork before they arrived. She was pushing him to buckle down and complete his assignments for the day. "Then," Tarryn says, "he had a full-blown anxiety attack."

All the pressure to re-create school, with its daily assignments and coercive tactics, had escalated and ultimately unleashed. There must be another way, thought Tarryn. She began researching child-led learning and found information about unschooling and self-directed education that do not replicate school-at-home. "We dropped everything: the $4,000 curriculum, the room we had set up in our home, complete with a chalkboard. We dropped it all and began deschooling for a while. Then we gradually moved toward more project-based, eclectic homeschooling, where we would do certain projects together or use bits of curriculum here and there." Ultimately, Tarryn and Miles fully embraced unschooling, moving away entirely from a schooled model of education to a natural learning one. Now, she is the cofounder of a self-directed learning collaborative for unschoolers in Texas called Thought Quotient.

Children like Miles are everywhere. With disturbing frequency, young children are being labeled with disorders for what are often common adaptive responses to a stressful situation—school. While some of these diagnoses are likely caused by factors other than the rise in schoolstuffs, the growing numbers are alarming. The rise in schoolstuffs and the corresponding decline in play may simply be pushing children beyond their limits.

Tracy Ventola is a certified teacher who taught elementary school Spanish before becoming a stay-at-home mom. Her mother was a classroom teacher. Her father taught special education in public schools for over thirty years. Unschooling was the last thing Tracy thought she would embrace. Like so many parents who make the leap from schooling to unschooling, Tracy gradually realized that the problems her older daughter was experiencing in school (first in a traditional preschool and then in a more progressive private school) were a result of schooling and not of her daughter. "When she started preschool, my already shy girl got even quieter," says Tracy. "She pulled further into herself, to the point that she stopped talking. Her reaction to school earned her a diagnosis of selective mutism. School had the opposite effect on my friend's son. Her incredibly bright, super-verbal, high-energy kid got louder; he went further outside of himself and therefore has been diagnosed with ADHD. There is nothing wrong with either of these children. They are simply coping differently with the stress of school."[29]

After much reading and soul-searching and second-guessing, Tracy and her husband finally decided to pull their daughter from elementary school after kindergarten. The results were astonishing. She became happy, talkative, and engaged. The parents immediately gravitated toward unschooling, not wanting to replicate the schooled mind-set and routines that had been so stressful for their daughter. They created a slow, peaceful rhythm to their days. There was abundant playtime, lingering hours at the library, long walks to parks and playgrounds. As she deschooled, Tracy's daughter also grew more confident and more extroverted. She spent hours at homeschool park days playing with friends, as well as fueling her growing interest in, and talent for, drawing and making art. She taught herself to read just before she turned nine and quickly became a voracious reader, devouring *Harry Potter* and other classic book series.

Today, Tracy's daughter is a content and vibrant twelve-year-old unschooler who still loves reading and drawing, but her growing passion is theatre—particularly comedy. The little girl who was so stressed by schooling that she stopped talking now regularly performs live in front of large public audiences. For Tracy, trusting her parenting instincts enabled her to question the prevailing trend of labeling children for alleged disorders that are often just extreme adaptive responses to the artificiality of school. In many cases, these "disorders" may simply be allergies to schoolstuffs.

As schooling shifts to earlier ages, for longer hours, some children simply cannot adapt. They are often the ones labeled as troublemakers, diagnosed with various impediments, or told they are failing. They are the messengers. We should listen to them. These children tell us, loudly and clearly, that our industrial framework of test-driven mass schooling doesn't create learners. It creates mimics. Those who do well in the system are those who have adapted effectively to the schooling norm. They have been trained but not educated. The answer is not more schooling. The answer is less schooling and more learning. The answer is to transform an archaic system of factory schooling and instead embrace the ideals of authentic, self-directed education for all young people.

It's Not the Kids, It's the School

A big challenge for the educators and parents embracing schooling alternatives is fighting the enduring myth that children must be forced to learn. You hear it everywhere: Kids these days are lazy, entitled, disruptive. They lack curiosity and a strong work ethic. Young children don't know how to sit still and listen. Older children complain about their homework and just want to play video games. Teens spend so much of their time on their phones and social media that it's like pulling teeth to get them to write a coherent sentence for a school paper. Kids these days are graduating with fewer skills, less independence, no grit, and hardly any commitment to excellence. Without coercion, like clear rewards and strict punishments, these kids would never amount to anything. But we mostly see how children act *in school*, how learning happens *in school*. School is as far from natural for a child as a zoo is for a zebra. In school, children learn quickly that their ideas, interests, and individual freedom are insignificant. They learn quickly how to play the game of school, which means losing their natural learning tendencies in the name of education. Cajoled with gold stars and praise, and threatened with lost privileges and humiliation, schooled children adapt to their rigid world. Learning, which was so organic and enjoyable in infancy and toddlerhood, becomes a job.

Even those kids who say they like learning in school when they are young often grow into tweens and teens who gradually lose their love of school—and of learning. According to a 2016 Gallup student poll of nearly one million children from approximately three thousand different schools, enthusiasm for school dropped dramatically between fifth grade and twelfth grade.[30] The 2009 High School Survey of Student Engagement revealed that 66 percent of high school students say they are bored in class every single day.[31] The more time they spend in school, the more young people begin to exhibit the behaviors of "kids these days," eagerly finding ways to escape the coercion and regain some semblance of control over their programmed lives. In school, other people direct their thoughts, actions, and outcomes. For even the most enthusiastic students, that coercion can take its toll. In one large-scale 2003 study, psychologists tracked several hundred elementary and secondary school students over the course of a week. The students wore watches that signaled them several times a day to record, at that moment, what they were doing and how they were feeling. The results disclosed that children were unhappiest while they were at school, and happiest when out of school. Their happiness was the highest, for instance, on Saturdays and the lowest on Mondays.[32]

That's life, someone might respond to the idea that Mondays bring gloom and work shouldn't be fun. But it doesn't have to be this way. We can challenge the default of conventional schooling and explore alternatives that support humans' natural, self-educative instincts. Unschoolers show that learning can and should be joyful. In his book *Originals:*

How Non-Conformists Move the World, Wharton Business School professor Adam Grant writes about the need to question defaults, to challenge
what is and always has been. He says:

> Justifying the default system serves a soothing function. It's an
> emotional painkiller: If the world is supposed to be this way,
> we don't need to be dissatisfied with it. But acquiescence also
> robs us of the moral outrage to stand against injustice and the
> creative will to consider alternative ways that the world could
> work. The hallmark of originality is rejecting the default and
> exploring whether a better option exists.[33]

Frustrated by rising schoolstuffs, outraged by a decline in childhood
play and creativity and a corresponding bump in childhood disorders,
and nudged by a tickling sense that learning and living should be joyful, more parents and educators are challenging the default of conventional schooling. They are exploring education alternatives that look
nothing like school but that lead to real, authentic learning. In many
instances, challenging the schooling default contradicts everything these
parents and educators have been taught about how humans learn and
how knowledge is shared. Once we question what we have been taught,
we may begin to wonder what more there is to learn.

Unschooling Tips

• **Challenge defaults**. Parents can get swept up in a wave of
diagnoses regarding their child's development. Sometimes these diagnoses are important and helpful, but sometimes they may be a direct
result of a child's schooling—not of the child herself. When removed
from a coercive schooling environment, problematic behaviors can be
lessened or may disappear completely. Parents should challenge defaults,
question labels, and seek alternatives.

• **Prioritize play**. The rise of schoolstuffs and the decline of play
may be major factors in dwindling childhood creativity and increasing

mental health disorders. Prioritize unstructured, child-directed play. Create the time and space for this type of play, and fiercely protect it. Avoid the cultural pressure to place kids in many adult-led activities and classes—as fun as they may sound—and opt instead for wide-open hours of free play.

- **Reduce schoolstuffs**. The steady increase of schoolstuffs can subtly invade our homes. It can be hard to value play over academics, free time over classes—particularly when schoolstuffs are so prevalent and accepted. Just as you may avoid consuming too many Twinkies, you may need to be equally vigilant about reducing schoolstuffs.

- **Enable self-direction**. Parents sometimes ask me how they can encourage self-directed learning when their child isn't self-directed. My response is that nearly all children are self-directed if they are given the full freedom to learn what, how, when, and with whom they want. These children must know that they are fully responsible for their own education—not that a parent or other adult decides what they should know or do. It also means that parents and other adults don't make judgments on what is or is not "educational." Kids will likely be bored sometimes. They may have stretches where they appear adrift or restless or lazy. That's OK. These periods are often transitional and will likely lead to new interests or inquiries if young people know that they are the ones owning their own education, setting their own present and future goals. Your job is to provide the time, opportunity, and resources for learning. If children come to unschooling from a school or school-at-home environment, where they have been conditioned to assume that learning comes from adults, allowing for ample deschooling time is essential. In fact, it may never really end.

5

Natural Literacy and Numeracy

*"If we ever, God forbid, manage to make each child suc-
ceed with his peer group, we will produce a race of bland
and faceless nonentities, and all poetry and mystery will
vanish from the face of the earth."*

—Madeleine L'Engle, *A Circle of Quiet*[1]

JAKE HATED SCHOOL. AS A first grader, he was boisterous and inquisitive, active and inventive. The increased emphasis on seat work and a
Common Core curriculum fueled by high-stakes testing were tough on
him. He often resisted the typical constraints of schooling, and his teachers' murmurs of ADHD grew louder. Jake also wasn't reading. At age six,
this was a problem for curriculum frameworks that increasingly pushed
academic work previously reserved for older children to younger ones.
Daphna Bassok and her colleagues at the University of Virginia discovered
that in 1998, 31 percent of teachers believed that children should learn
to read while in kindergarten. In 2010, that number was 80 percent.[2] His
teachers were concerned. Jake should be reading. They wanted to label
him with a learning disability and give him an individualized education
plan (IEP) so that he would more quickly catch up to the pack.

Jake's parents, Beth and Mike Harris, were torn. They believed
that their son was fine, that his energy was typical for a six-year-old,
that he would eventually read, and that it was the rigid structure of mass

schooling that was causing these issues. But they also felt pressure from the school staff to intervene and "fix" him. They waited a bit longer, debating their options and wondering about alternatives. As the stay-at-home parent at the time, Mike was pushing to homeschool; Beth was a bit more reticent. Then one day she took her son to the bookstore and told him he could choose any book he wanted, anything at all. She desperately wanted him to value reading and make the effort to learn. Instead, Jake grabbed a book off the shelf, threw it across the room, and shouted, "I hate reading!"

That did it. Beth and Mike removed their son from school halfway through his first grade school year and haven't looked back. They are grateful that Jake now loves reading and books, but it required a transition period from a schooled mind-set to an unschooled one. At first, the family went through a deschooling process. They allowed a few months of downtime where they didn't push Jake to do any school-like activities; but when fall came, they felt that back-to-school buzz and started introducing some phonics lessons. "It brought back those feelings of hating books, huge fits," remembers Beth. So they quickly gave it up. "We switched to just going to the library, reading to him, and taking out lots of books. Looking back, and with the knowledge I have now, we should not have tried to teach him because it was only when we stopped teaching and focused on enjoying books that he learned on his own." They stopped pushing him to read. They didn't force, or cajole, or evaluate. They brought him home, let him play, gave him freedom, respected his autonomy and individuality, and allowed him to be himself. Eventually, Jake learned to read. He did it on his own timetable, focused on his own interests, with books that mattered to him.

As part of their state's homeschooling reporting requirements, Jake's parents had different assessment options from which to choose in order to comply with regulations. One year they decided to do the Iowa Test of Basic Skills for both fourth grader Jake and their second-grade daughter, Abby. After Jake's schooling experience, Mike and Beth decided not to send Abby to school and not to do any direct reading instruction with her. She was completely unschooled from the start. The parents recognized the limitations of standardized tests but chose to use them as a comparative marker for both of their children and to comply with state regulations.

After the test results came back, Beth told me:

> The boy who was in tears in first grade, with all that the school was pushing on him—and us—for him to learn to read, scored at a sixth-grade reading level. Abby, with whom we did no reading instruction, showed she is reading at a fourth-grade level. She would be in second grade. I know tests don't really matter, but it was such a hard decision at the time to make. I guess pulling him out and trusting in him and letting it naturally happen was the right choice.

Now in fifth grade at home, Jake loves to read and spends hours devouring books. Mike and Beth's biggest problem today is wondering if they should cut off his nighttime reading so he will go to bed before midnight! For now, the flexibility of their unschooled lifestyle means that Jake can sleep in as late as he wants, making up for his late-night reading marathons.

Jake's schooling experience is tragically common, and becoming more so. I hear frequently from parents who say that their kindergartener is in danger of being held back because she is not reading, or their first grader has been diagnosed with learning disabilities because he is not reading at "grade level." Unfortunately, most parents don't challenge these recommendations and take the leap that Mike and Beth took. Instead, they keep their child in school, believing the educators who tell them that their child has behavioral problems, learning difficulties, or other issues that separate him from the norm. They become convinced that their child is flawed and early intervention is necessary, rather than recognizing that schoolstuffs may be the real culprit. Retired public school teacher and author John Taylor Gatto writes about the disturbing tendency to label children in school: "In 26 years of teaching kids rich and poor I almost never met a 'learning disabled' child; hardly ever met a 'gifted and talented' one either. Like all school categories, these are sacred myths, created by the human imagination. They derive from questionable values we never examine because they preserve the temple of schooling."[3] Schools say they value difference, diversity, and individuality; the reality is that they don't. They can't. Childhood energy and enthusiasm are incompatible with schoolstuffs. Reading later than the established curriculum norms dictate is unacceptable and grounds for intervention. All must be the same.

With unschooling, diversity and difference are treasured. We don't need to hurry our child's literacy or numeracy; rather, we can support her in learning these important concepts naturally when immersed in environments that value both. It is our ultimate obligation as parents to ensure that our child is literate and numerate, but it's the child who leads the way. We connect our child to resources rich in literacy and numeracy, and then allow her to explore the ones most appealing to her, in her own way. We don't need to push *Dick and Jane* or urge a child to complete a problem set. Instead, we pay attention to her interests, surround her with tools, and allow her to learn to read and compute in an organic, unforced way tied to her individual enthusiasms and on her own unique timetable.

Natural Literacy

In 1969, psychology professor Jane Torrey recorded a case study of how a child learned to read without being taught. The report, "Learning to Read Without a Teacher," was published in the journal *Elementary English* and was subsequently widely cited as an example of natural reading. In this study, Dr. Torrey followed a poor, five-year-old African American boy named John from a segregated southern school who, teachers discovered, had learned to read prior to entering kindergarten. Testing showed that John was of average language ability. John's father was a truck driver, his mother was a hospital maid. They had five children and had a combined income level that qualified them for subsidized housing. How then could a boy whose parents had only a minimal amount of schooling in the segregated South learn to read on his own before going to school?

John's case was so startling to his teachers that they asked Dr. Torrey to research further. She spent several hours a day for several weeks in John's home, observing his environment and approach to reading and writing. From conversations with John's mother and grandmother,

Dr. Torrey discovered that John learned to read spontaneously, mostly from watching and singing frequent television commercials that emphasized simple words or phrases. He also learned from reading the familiar labels on food cans in his kitchen and from being exposed to the books in his home that the family owned or borrowed from the library. Eventually, reading clicked for John, earlier than for most children. Torrey concludes her case study with some thoughts on reading instruction:

> Reading is learned, not taught. Even in school the teacher can only provide guidance, motivating circumstances, and answers to questions. No teacher has time to tell each child everything he has to learn, much less to drill him enough times on each element. The key for learning to read may be the child's asking the right questions of his environment. If the child does that, he will be able to get the answers from a variety of sources, not necessarily including a consciously teaching older person.[4]

To be sure, this was just one case study of one boy, but Torrey became one of the first academic researchers to suggest that becoming literate is an act of *learning* rather than *teaching*.[5] A decade after her observations with John, Torrey concluded: "The findings on the histories of early readers might be summarized by saying that they were not taught to read, they just learned in an environment that contained enough stimulation and material."[6]

Today, with the growth in the numbers of children who learn outside of conventional schooling environments, it is possible to apply Torrey's findings to older children as well. Anecdotal reports of unschooled children reveal an average age of reading proficiency of between eight and nine years old, but more rigorous academic studies have shown similar results. In their research, Alan Thomas and Harriet Pattison found that young people who learned to read outside of formal school settings most often learned to read spontaneously, frequently resisting attempts at formal instruction. These children were surrounded by resources and opportunities to read and did so on a widely variable timetable. According to the authors: "Our research has found much to question in both the views that children should learn to read by a certain age and that in order to do so they need to be taken through a structured and staged learning programme. On the contrary, we have found that many children learn to read aged eight or older (sometimes much older) without experiencing any adverse effect."[7]

For Phoebe Wells's three now-grown unschooled children, natural reading occurred at different ages in dramatically different ways. The common thread, though, was that they were surrounded by literacy and they were allowed to read on their own developmental timing, without being pushed. One of Phoebe's children learned to read at age four, one at age eight, and one not until he was thirteen. The "wicked late" reader, says Phoebe, didn't read anything at all until he was about ten. He was then really into soccer and his soccer schedule was the first thing he read. Her son would go through various cycles where he really wanted to try to read, and he would sometimes feel frustrated that he couldn't, so Phoebe supported him in his reading efforts without forcing him. It wasn't until he was thirteen that he became a fluent reader, going from "*Cat in the Hat* to Shakespeare in a matter of a month," she recalls.

Phoebe wasn't particularly worried about her son's later reading. In Holt's *Growing Without Schooling* newsletters, she had read stories of later readers who quickly became fluent. She could also see the many other ways in which her son was flourishing: reading music, performing complex mental math, memorizing lines for theatrical performances, and so on. "So many people believe that reading ability is a proxy for intelligence, and that was never a worry for me," says Phoebe. "If he were just learning to read for the sake of reading and didn't care about the material, it would have been even longer and harder," she adds.

Recognizing her son's many other strengths and talents helped Phoebe to accept his late reading. "I went on the premise that learning to read is not that hard to do or why would so many little kids be able to do it," she says. She surrounded her son with a literacy-rich environment, went often to the library, read to him frequently, and played games that focused on literacy skills, but she didn't push him to read. She also didn't want to test him for a reading delay. "It's hard to shed a label," says Phoebe. "It's hard not to be held back. I felt the potential risks of testing outweighed any benefits."

Phoebe's son, now thirty, left home at age seventeen and became a professional ballet dancer, performing with some of the most prestigious ballet companies in the nation. In between performances, he began taking some online courses. As Phoebe says: "Having never been to school and not doing anything academic mathematically or with writing, he did some very basic classes and progressed really smoothly." He realized he liked math and science, so he enrolled in community college classes. Once he retired from the ballet company, he was accepted into a pre-med program at a large university, is now studying for the MCAT exam, and has his sights set on medical school. "Had he been stuck with an IEP and a reading disability label, would he ever be pre-med? I doubt it," says Phoebe. "I don't know how many kids ever escape that label to become something intentionally academic."

The timetable on which Phoebe's children learned to read seems almost impossible within our current schooled context. Reading is now being taught in kindergarten, and third grade looms large as a literacy endpoint. At the completion of third grade (or roughly ages eight or nine), children are expected to be reading proficiently. The reason third grade is such a critical year for literacy is that it signals a curriculum shift from *learning to read* to *reading to learn*.[8] The school curriculum changes in fourth grade to assume a certain level of reading proficiency, and it requires children to understand that content in order to then learn specific subject matter in a specific way.

The trouble with the third grade theory is that, once again, it focuses on how children learn *in school*. Yes, in school it is true that the curriculum changes by fourth grade, leaving nonreaders at a disadvantage. But this indicates a *schooling* problem, not necessarily a *reading* problem, and certainly not a *child* one. For unschooled children, like Phoebe's, late reading outside of the schooled context is simply later reading. It occurs on the far end of what we might visualize as a normal bell curve distribution for learning to read. One of her children was on the far left margin of the curve, one was on the right, and the eight-year-old reader was more in the middle of the curve, a spot where most children would likely fall if allowed to learn to read naturally, without school.

Further research on homeschooled children and reading acquisition confirms the strong probability of this natural reading bell curve. In her book *Rethinking Learning to Read* Harriet Pattison analyzed survey results for four hundred home-educated children. She discovered a wide range of ages at which children first learned to read. Many of the children in her sample began reading after age seven, or what she calls the "designated school norm." Pattison also found that the later readers would quickly achieve proficiency, often reading complex books very quickly after first learning to read. Pattison concludes: "It really cannot be stressed enough how different these experiences are to those of children in school. Re-thinking learning to read must take this important evidence into account; if we do not then we are doing an immense disservice to all the children whose lives are blighted both in school and beyond by reading difficulties."[9]

We tend to accept normal human variation for some developmental milestones but not for others. For instance, we generally do not feel the need to hurry up our children's first rolls or first crawls or first steps. Yet, as children age, we often increasingly feel the need to intervene in their learning: to start teaching them instead of allowing them to learn, in their own way, in their own time, when surrounded by caring adults and plentiful resources. We are expecting children to learn to read at earlier ages, interfering with their own distinct reading timelines. The vast majority of children, when surrounded by literacy, will naturally learn to read.[10] Some will be early readers, some will be late readers; but most children will learn to read all on their own when surrounded by books, by reading, and by people who value and encourage books and reading.

Forcing reading instruction before a child is developmentally ready to learn to read can cause more harm than good. Aware of this danger, some researchers are pushing back against standardized school curriculum frameworks that accelerate reading instruction for kindergarteners. In their report *Reading in Kindergarten: Little to Gain and Much to Lose* education professor Nancy Carlsson-Paige and her colleagues warn about the hazards of early reading instruction. They write, "When children have educational experiences that are not geared to their developmental level or in tune with their learning needs and cultures, it can cause them great harm, including feelings of inadequacy, anxiety and confusion."[11] While Carlsson-Paige and her colleagues advocate for developmentally age-appropriate reading instruction over natural literacy, they acknowledge that the costs of early forced reading can significantly outweigh potential benefits.

Accepting a normal distribution curve for reading, with average reading proficiency around age eight, may help to explain how some progressive educators approach literacy development in independent schools. In Waldorf education, for example, reading and other academic topics are not taught in kindergarten, and "there are no rigid, time-specific goals for reading or any other subject towards which a class will be driven." In first grade, Waldorf students learn letters and letter sounds through story, song, movement, creative artwork, and play, with more formal reading instruction not beginning until second grade.[12] This delayed instructional approach ensures that more children are at the peak of a natural reading curve and are therefore more likely to be developmentally ready to read.

In a large 2012 academic study, researchers examined reading achievement data of two groups of children in New Zealand. One group attended conventional state schools that began formal reading instruction at age five, while the other group attended Waldorf/Steiner schools, where formal reading instruction didn't begin until age seven. Researchers controlled for an assortment of variables, including children's existing vocabulary skills, socioeconomic status, the literacy environment of the children's home, and so forth. The research team, led by Dr. Sebastian Suggate, found that the early reading group showed higher initial reading skills than the later reading group, but this reading differential was gone by age eleven. In fact, the researchers found, the later reading group actually had higher reading comprehension skills at the end of their primary school education than the earlier reading group.[13] Early forced reading may backfire.

Challenging the standard schooling timelines of literacy development
and showing the different ways and ages that children naturally learn to
read can help parents to more honestly examine their schooled expectations of reading proficiency. But parents are powerful. If a parent thinks
that a real learning disability could be a factor in her child's delayed
literacy—or any other developmental area—then she should trust her
parenting instincts and seek appropriate counsel. That said, I often hear
from parents who say that their child was not reading by the end of
second grade and was labeled with a reading disability. That may be
true—or it may be that the child just wasn't yet ready to read, but the
third grade school reading expectation created an artificial closure. In
Free at Last, Daniel Greenberg writes about the noncoercive Sudbury
Valley School, reporting that in its first two decades of operation, they
never had a case of dyslexia. He says: "The fact is, we have never seen
it at the school. It just might be because we have never made anyone
learn how to read." Despite not forcing kids to read, Sudbury students
all learned how to read—albeit on wildly disparate timetables.[14] Standardized schooling cannot adequately accommodate the vast differences
in normal childhood development and the variety of ways that humans
absorb and negotiate their world.

Education professor Karl Wheatley argues that unschoolers can
begin to influence larger educational policy by challenging the schooled
assumptions of learning to read. He writes: "Unschoolers are not so
interested in what educators mean by 'reading achievement,' because
that mostly means scores on tests that largely assess low-level reading
subskills. Thus, when others talk about 'reading achievement,' we can
say that low-level skills are the wrong focus, and that we really need to
focus on 'reading comprehension and love of reading.'"[15] These outcomes—strong reading comprehension and a love of reading—are frequently cited by unschoolers as evidence that cultivating natural literacy
is far more effective than the dominant schooled approach to reading
instruction.

Learning to read in a schooled context often involves an arduous,
artificial process of breaking down books into sentences and big ideas
into a meaningless jumble. In school, children are told what to read,

when to read, and for how long to read—with that dire warning, "Don't read ahead!" There are now digital bookmarks available that beep when a child's assigned nightly reading time is up. If ever we wanted young people to dislike reading, we would force them to read things they don't care about, place reading into a subject silo separated from daily living, assign mundane homework so that reading becomes more chore than pleasure, time them, test them frequently on decoding skills, and give them a label. Those of us who still enjoy reading after all of that do so in spite of school, not because of it. Is it any wonder that more than one-quarter of American adults reported not reading any books in 2016?[16] And 29 percent of American adults read at only a "basic" level or worse.[17] The schooled approach to reading instruction leaves much to be desired.

My son Jack learned to read proficiently at age seven. We never pushed reading nor did reading exercises with him. We didn't encourage him to sound out words or practice phonics. Instead, we read to him a lot, took him frequently to the library, surrounded him with a literacy-rich environment, and modeled a love of reading. Unlike my daughter Abby, who taught herself to read at age seven using classic *Dick and Jane* texts, Jack wanted nothing to do with early readers. They were silly to him. He learned to read when it mattered to him, centered around his interests. First, he began reading the lyrics of the rock 'n' roll songs he enjoyed listening to. We printed out the written words of his favorite songs and he looked at them intently as he listened to his music. Next, he began to read the Amazon.com reviews of certain items he wanted to buy to find out whether or not they were worth his money. Finally, he wanted to read articles about the latest iOS updates and other technical content from tech industry magazines. I remember the day when he read a full *New York Times* article aloud about the latest iPhone release—and understood every word. Now at nine, he loves biographies, juvenile fiction, and skateboarding magazine articles, but technical articles about software and hardware remain some of his favorite things to read. These are topics that matter to him, not content that others decide is important. We spotted his interests and helped to connect him to reading materials related to those interests, but we didn't force or prod. Jack now loves to read and, like Jake's parents, debating whether or not we should cut off his reading before midnight is our biggest concern regarding his literacy.

Jack learned to read closer to the midpoint of a natural reading bell curve, but other unschooled children learn to read much later. As a grown unschooler, Peter Kowalke recalls that being a late reader and writer were not problems within an unschooled environment. He remembers being a very verbal child, but he had no real reason to read. His mom read to him and he drew a lot, using pictures in place of words. It wasn't until he was ten that reading became a priority for him. "I loved G.I. Joe," says Peter. "I had all the toys, watched all the shows, then I discovered that there were comic books of G.I. Joe." His mom got the comic books and read them to him, but comics, Peter found, work better if you read them yourself. With their simple words and engaging pictures, and content that was captivating for Peter, he swiftly learned to read. For the next few years, Peter read mostly comic books, but by the time he was thirteen his reading catapulted. Like many other late readers, Peter quickly became proficient, jumping swiftly from comic books to classic texts. The fourth book he read was Plato's *Republic*.

In his article on how children learn to read and write naturally, William Teale theorized that "the practice of literacy is not merely abstract skill in producing, decoding, and comprehending writing; rather, when children become literate they use reading and writing in the performance of the practices which constitute their culture."[18] Children will naturally learn to read and write—to become literate—when it is meaningful and purposeful to them, if they are surrounded by a literacy-rich environment and supportive grown-ups. For Peter, learning to write only became a need when it involved a girl. At thirteen, he and his family attended a homeschool conference in Michigan. There, he met a girl he liked and he wanted to stay in touch with her. "The first letter I wrote was one long paragraph," Peter recalls. He wanted to impress this girl, who became his first girlfriend and continues to be a good friend today. He asked his mom, a former English teacher, for initial help in sentence structure, paragraph formation, editing, and other writing basics. By his sixth letter, he had learned all of the basics of grammar and writing.

Hooked on writing in his teen years, Peter started a national magazine for homeschoolers and unschoolers. This boy, who didn't read until after he was ten and didn't write until he was thirteen, majored in journalism in college (with a minor in math) and became a professional journalist and editor in New York City.

The stories from the Harrises, Jane Torrey, Phoebe, Jack, and Peter highlight a wide variability in the timing and methods of kids learning to read. Some children will be early readers, some will be late readers, and most will fall in a broad mid-range of reading proficiency that likely hovers around eight years old. Our conventional system of schooling that pushes younger and younger kids to read, expects proficiency by an arbitrary endpoint of third grade. The high-stakes standardized exams to enforce this unnatural reading timeline can cause significant harm to children who may not be developmentally ready to read at a given age. This should be concerning to parents of conventionally schooled and unschooled kids, and both groups should advocate to eliminate this standardized education. For unschoolers in particular, some of whom may live in states that require standardized testing for homeschoolers, curriculum approval and regular testing can limit their educational freedom, forcing them to push their children to read earlier than they should. Working hard to change these regulations will give parents more autonomy and children more respect for their individual learning differences. Families who are tied to schoolstuffs, even indirectly through state and local policies, face a much more difficult time separating from a schooled framework of education.

Natural Numeracy

One recent night, Molly and Jack were playing math games with their dad. I could hear the laughter from the kitchen as they mastered increasingly complex calculations and took turns trying to stump my husband. It occurred to me that laughter and fun and collaboration and play were never concepts that I associated with math while growing up. I never liked math until college. I learned to play the game at school—to memorize and regurgitate—but I never liked it. I never *learned* it. I got As, but they were superficial—markers of good short-term memory and a keenness for the game of school. As Andrew Hacker writes in his excellent book *The Math Myth: And Other STEM Delusions*: "Mathematics, perhaps more than other subjects, favors pupils who give precisely the answers their teachers want. Perhaps for this reason, there's less inclination to indulge students who don't keep up. So Cs and Ds and Fs are more usual in mathematics than in other subjects."[19]

My children, who have never been to school, have no mental construct to consider math to be labor, something to just get through. They don't associate it with worksheets or quizzes, gold stars or hollow letters. They love math, truly and deeply. They see it, live it, know it due to their everyday living and learning. Fear of math—of how to teach it, how to learn it, how to use it, how to like it—is a grown-up problem, not a kid one. Many grown-ups don't like math or are not confident in their math abilities. We recall the painstaking ways we were taught math as kids: the dull worksheets, the boring lectures, the confusing blackboard calculations, the timed tests, the word problems. It's laced with bad memories. We project these memories onto our children, sometimes unwittingly. Determined to make math more fun for kids, many of us go to great lengths to disguise our contempt and lack of confidence. Kids see right through this and get the message that math is work. "Math anxiety" is now a new label commonly assigned to children. Like ubiquitous reading delay labels and interventions, math labeling may arise from the growth of schoolstuffs and lead to children internalizing a belief that they are "bad at math," when again it is a schooling problem and not a learning one.

Really, math is play and should be fun. Molly gravitated to math from an early age. Noticing her interest in math, we found a local math class for homeschoolers taught by an MIT-trained mathematician who has run math enrichment classes from her home for over thirty years. A gifted teacher, Beth O'Sullivan—who has been visited by the folks at Khan Academy for her innovative way of presenting math—talks often about math as play. The children simply play games together. When I asked Molly after one of her initial classes what math she learned, she said, "We don't really learn math. We just play." The reality is that she learns a tremendous amount in the class about true mathematical concepts: patterns, logic, sequences, strategy, reasoning, higher-order thinking.

"Play is, at its most fulfilling for a child, the engagement of a child's imagination with the world around him or her," says Beth.

> Through this engagement a child will discover mathematics. Shapes, symmetry, balance are all a part of a child's discovery of the world around her. We don't send our young children to language school to learn their language; they pick it up through engagement with adults and other children, from being read to, and through play. The same is true with mathematics when children are exposed to the language of mathematics. The more a child enjoys learning the language of mathematics, the more she will seek it out and the more she will learn.

Molly's younger siblings also learn math through play but have found that classes—even playful ones like Beth's—aren't for them. For now at least, they prefer to engage with math in other ways, like through math stories and board games, card games, online math programs, and math play with their dad. Unschooling provides the freedom and flexibility to allow children to explore literacy and numeracy in natural, noncoercive ways tied to a child's specific interests and learning styles. Some children will gravitate toward classes and instruction, others may prefer online learning and interactive technology, and still others may prefer books, games, or hands-on manipulatives. The key is to provide plentiful options and allow children to learn in ways that are most meaningful to them without cajoling them to do so. As Beth says, "Mathematics is wondrous and mysterious by nature. If one understands this, its impish and playful nature is also revealed."

For most of us, this natural, playful way of discovering math didn't exist. We learned math through rote memorization and high-pressure regurgitation. In her book *Mindshift: Break Through Obstacles to Learning and Discover Your Hidden Potential* author Barbara Oakley shares how she "had a passionate contempt for math and science and did poorly in both from an early age."[20] She reveals that she consistently failed those subjects from elementary school through high school and was convinced that she was simply bad at math. In adulthood, though, she became more interested in math and science, began studying both, and eventually earned a PhD in engineering from Detroit's Oakland University, where she is now a faculty member. Math isn't the problem. It's the way math is conventionally taught that leads to so much frustration and avoidance, and that ignores play and self-direction.

Frustrated by the way mathematics was conventionally taught, with poor outcomes particularly for disadvantaged children, L. P. Benezet launched a remarkable experiment in elementary school classrooms beginning in 1929. Benezet was the superintendent of schools in Manchester, New Hampshire, and he decided to make some radical changes to the math curriculum. Specifically, he chose several classrooms where he eliminated all formal arithmetic instruction below the sixth grade. Reflecting on his experiment in 1935, Benezet writes, "I had noticed that the effect of the early introduction of arithmetic had been to dull and almost chloroform the child's reasoning faculties." Instead of learning arithmetic and struggling through long division, elementary school children in Benezet's experimental classrooms gained a natural appreciation of numbers and mathematical concepts (like time and measurement) through their daily learning and natural literacy development. In sixth grade, the children (who were mostly immigrants) began their formal arithmetic instruction and quickly caught up—within that one year—to the children who had received conventional mathematical training up until that point.[21]

Perhaps most striking is that the children with delayed math instruction continued to outperform their regularly instructed peers in overall mathematical problem-solving ability.[22] Benezet's experiments challenge deep-seated assumptions about mathematical training. The idea that math is hard and therefore needs to be rigorously and methodically taught, through repetition and memorization, during the elementary school years is shown to be untrue. When they are surrounded by an environment rich in literacy and numeracy in their earlier years, children can quickly and easily learn mathematical concepts later on. This finding echoes many of the anecdotal experiences shared by grown unschoolers who say that despite not having much conventional mathematical instruction, they were generally able to take formal math classes later on, do well, and learn quite quickly. In *Free at Last*, Daniel Greenberg recounts the experiences of unschooled young people at Sudbury Valley School, finding repeatedly over the years that it takes about twenty hours to learn the entire K–6 mathematics curriculum when a child is interested in learning it.[23] Twenty hours. Just think of what children could be learning and doing in their elementary schooling years if they weren't forced to spend so much time in classroom math instruction that can be learned so quickly when they are ready for it.

In advocating for alternatives to conventional math instruction, esteemed mathematician Dr. Hassler Whitney highlights Benezet's work as an important example of moving away from the status quo. He argues that most of us calculate and use math outside of school in very different ways than how we were taught in school, but these more natural, practical approaches to numeracy are frequently dismissed. Whitney writes: "It is as though we have completely lost faith in our children. In spite of their preeminent learning when very young, we expect them (especially the 'disadvantaged') to begin to flounder in math in early school years. So we put more pressure on both teachers and children, creating more struggles with rules, discouraging them still more." Whitney, like Benezet, suggests a more natural approach to numeracy, rejecting the conventional rote learning approach. "Benezet cut out formal math teaching before grade 6; it could well be cut out throughout high school, as I see it," says Whitney. "Perhaps the most important point is that if the teacher lets the natural human powers come to the fore, with all the interconnections between widely dispersed elements, the students can do great things."[24] Encouraging children's natural curiosity about the mathematical concepts all around them can help them to not only learn math but to love it as well.

One day when Jack was eight we were sitting together on the living room couch chitchatting. He looked at the clock hanging on our wall with its Roman numerals and asked about them: "Why does that clock have those numbers and not regular numbers?" That's a good question, I thought. I realized that I had very little understanding of Roman numerals. Sure, I had been taught about them in elementary school, and

I knew that it had something to do with ancient Rome. I knew there were additional Roman numerals not shown on the clock, but I couldn't remember what they were or what value they represented. I didn't know if Roman numerals served any modern purpose other than to indicate this year's Super Bowl.

I told all of this to Jack and asked if he wanted to investigate with me. He did, so we Googled Roman numerals, found out more about their ancient origins, learned that they serve very little purpose now other than decorative, and discovered the other Roman numerals that don't appear on our clock. Jack was still curious, as was I, so I asked if he wanted to go into an online math subscription we have to learn more about these digits and play around with them. After searching various online math tools for children, we found a math website that our kids really like that charges a yearly subscription fee but allows full choice on what math areas to explore, without any expectation of completeness or sequentiality. The kids know this math software is available to them to use at any time should they choose. For the Roman numerals, it was the perfect tool for Jack to explore this particular math concept in an age-appropriate way, with my help when he wanted it, and then to stop when he chose to.

Just as unschoolers surround their children with books and literacy, model a love of reading, and take them frequently to the library to facilitate their natural reading, we surround them with a numeracy-rich environment as well. This could mean providing open access to online math tools and games and offering math workbooks and activities, with the understanding that these are available but not required. Similarly, just as reading frequently to our children can foster a love of literacy, engaging in math regularly with our children can foster a love of numeracy. This could involve doing math problems together if the child wants to, reading aloud the many children's books available that introduce mathematical concepts through story, playing board games and card games together, and so on.

"I loved school," says Heather Svanidze, an unschooling mom of four young children in California. "But looking back, I realize that very early on I relinquished all responsibility for directing my own learning.

I may have gotten excited about classes, but I never went home at the end of a school year (or even a school day!) and checked out library books on the subjects I had gotten excited about while reading the course catalog. Why should I learn on my own when I could just wait until the teacher told me what to read and think? Because I was so good at 'doing school,' I think I lost the ability to motivate myself and direct my own learning."

For Heather's own children, who have never been to school, there is no time wasted on playing the game of school. Instead, they just play.

> My kids have all learned the basics of arithmetic by just living in the world, where there are fingers and toes to count, cookies to divide with siblings, shapes everywhere. We have some "math toys" around, such as pattern blocks and mirrors, Cuisenaire rods, and base ten sets. We have workbooks around that they can use when they want to. They usually get on a workbook kick every couple of months or so. They rarely learn any new concepts from these; they just get a chance to see the math in written form. We also read a lot of picture books dealing with math, such as Stuart Murphy's *Math Start* books, *Cat in Numberland*, and *On Beyond a Million*, and math activity books like *Family Math* and *Moebius Noodles*. And board games! So many board games use math. Gosh, what *isn't* math? Our kids are never forced to do any math, so they just see it like any other activity, like a game.

Facilitating natural numeracy may seem more daunting than facilitating natural literacy because we often don't think of the many ways that numeracy is part of our everyday lives. Literacy seems so straightforward and commonplace, but numeracy may seem more hidden. When we start to consider that mathematical concepts are embedded in so much of what we do, we can begin to integrate our children into these actions. Baking, for example, requires many mathematical concepts, from measuring to fractions to time, and is often something kids enjoy doing alongside others. Grocery shopping is a great opportunity for children to see list making, price setting, currency, and change.

As so many of our transactions become automated, it may take a bit more thought to involve children in some of this real-life numeracy. For instance, rather than going to the bank and keeping track of funds in our checkbooks, we may instead check our balances online. We can simply remember to involve our children, who are so often curious about the adult world and the real, practical skills of their culture. We could print out bank statements or budgets and leave them around the house for children to spot and play with and investigate—in the same way they would play with board books before they are literate. And we can include our children in our adult world of budgeting and financing and income tax preparing to the extent that they are interested.

While technology and automation may hide numeracy and mathematical transactions from children a bit more than when we were kids, they can also be important tools in allowing young people to discover many mathematical and technical concepts through play. Canadian researcher Dr. Carlo Ricci has documented the ways that young children can develop quantitative concepts by playing with everyday digital tools, such as iPods and iPhones and other widely available technologies. Ricci reports on the ways children can learn extensive numerical concepts by exploring—based on their own interests and curiosity—the common features of these devices including the alarm, timer and stopwatch, weather, and so on. Ricci concludes that we should "appreciate the fact that technology can enhance the learning of literacy and numeracy in very natural and powerful ways." These natural and powerful ways of learning with and from technology require that children be given the freedom to access technology for their own play. Ricci writes that "we need to allow learners to freely play with the technology so that they can engage with and stumble on skills naturally and as they see fit. This is not to say that an external person cannot offer support, but that the learner needs to have a voice and she needs to be empowered to make substantive decisions and choices."[25]

For kids who have been schooled, undoing the damage of math instruction can be particularly difficult. Technology may be a playful, key tool to help overcome some of the trauma of conventional math instruction. Many kids in school internalize a belief that they are bad at math or that math is unpleasant and boring and hard. Allowing for a lengthy deschooling process, without reminders of what math instruction is like in schools (i.e., workbooks, worksheets) can be helpful. So, too, can questioning the schooled math curriculum. Is it really necessary for all kids to learn algebra, geometry, trigonometry, and calculus on a schooled path? Challenging curriculum norms is a key feature of the unschooling mind-set. *The Math Myth*'s Hacker says that advanced math, like what is taught in conventional high schools, is unnecessary for most people. He says that there is a pervasive societal belief "that every one of us is going to have to know algebra, geometry, trigonometry in the twenty-first century, because that's the way a high-tech age is going. It's a total myth," he says. "At most, 5 percent of people really use math, advanced math, in their work." Hacker argues that instead of focusing so much time on teaching advanced math to students who will likely never need it, more time should be spent on practical, albeit more advanced, mathematical literacy, such as understanding the federal budget, knowing how to read a corporate report, comprehending political campaign financing, and so on.[26] These are real-life examples of numeracy that we all could probably do a better job at understanding. Involving our children in this ongoing process of mathematical literacy can be an important part of the unschooling lifestyle.

Stories from grown unschoolers also shed light on how math is learned outside of schooling. "Unschooling in my house was, as the term suggests, very free and based on my and my siblings' own individual interests and explorations," recalls Ani Pond. "My parents spent a lot of time talking with us, playing with us, and reading to us. My mom was an elementary school teacher, but disagreed with the methodologies of formal education, and wanted my siblings and me to learn in a way that honors the more natural way that kids learn, through play." Ani, along with her brother and sister, learned math concepts through playing math games, measuring ingredients for baking, estimating time and destination and speed during car rides, and through daily commerce. Her parents supported reading and created a literacy-rich home environment, but Ani says that she and her siblings really taught themselves to read—she at age six, her brother at ten, and her sister at age eight.

"Generally," says Ani, "my parents facilitated the learning of 'the basics' as we became interested in them, or they became necessary for us to know in order to facilitate a self-designated goal."

By the time she was a teenager, Ani was accustomed to learning through everyday living and to seeing herself as the leader of her own education. She traveled extensively with her family during her teen years and also took some community college classes. She spent several months on her own in Spain, working as an au pair and learning Spanish. "I felt very free and independent as an unschooled teen, and had the time to pleasure read as many books as I could access, write novels and short stories, travel, and pursue passions such as theater, music, dancing, and gymnastics. I also engaged in assorted self-created internships throughout my teenage years." Now twenty-one, she is enrolled in a four-year university in Chicago, having transferred many of her earlier community college classes for degree credit.

Ani's advice to unschooling parents is to be present and involved with their children, but to think of their role as a facilitator, not a teacher. "The best support for children is providing opportunity, encouragement, and facilitation, while allowing freedom and autonomy and trusting the children," she says.

> When children are taught how to learn and how to teach themselves, rather than how to memorize and regurgitate information in isolation from real life, like is usual in schools, they can learn anything on their own when it becomes necessary—including, should they choose, to memorize and regurgitate. I feel that my unschooled education most importantly taught me to think critically, and to have confidence in my own ability to navigate new environments and situations.

With natural literacy and numeracy as the foundation for unschooling, other content areas can be explored and developed based on a child's distinct interests and passions. These interests and passions emerge through freedom and opportunity, surrounded by community resources and caring adults. As Ani and other grown unschoolers show, unschooling doesn't preclude formal academics or learning through memorization and regurgitation. Research on grown unschoolers shows that, despite little exposure to conventional schooled subjects and curriculum, many do just fine in formal classes and higher education, quickly learning to play the game of school if it becomes a priority for them—and when it is chosen rather than forced. With abundant resources now available to facilitate natural learning—most significantly, technology and the Internet that make knowledge widely accessible for all—unschooling has never been easier, or more relevant.

Unschooling Tips

• **Create a literacy-filled and numeracy-rich environment.** Your important job as a parent is to ensure that your child is highly literate and numerate, but you don't need to follow a schooled paradigm to do it. Surround your child with books and mathematical concepts and create opportunities for literacy and numeracy to be revealed through everyday living and play. Taking frequent trips to libraries and museums, involving children in grocery shopping and commerce, playing board games, leveraging technology, and supporting emerging interests can all lead to proficiency in reading, writing, and arithmetic. These fundamentals can then act as a springboard for your child to explore other topics in a variety of categories, tied to his interests and passions.

• **Learn together.** An important part of unschooling involves our own process of parental deschooling as we rekindle a love of learning for the sake of learning. Find books and activities that interest you, and immerse yourself in these topics. Tackle a new skill, try out a new hobby, explore a new subject, and invite your children to watch as you learn, experiment, and improve.

• **Accept natural human variation.** Acknowledge a wide range in natural literacy and numeracy development. Question schooled defaults about when a child should know how to read and compute. Challenge linear curriculum frameworks and the myth that learning is hard.

• **Rethink formal academics.** Unschooling sets up young people to take charge of their own learning and to set their own goals, when supported by adults and their community. Often those goals may be linked to formal academics. If there is one thing that grown unschoolers reveal it is that unschooling does not preclude academic success in college and beyond. In fact, it could help to ensure it.

• **Don't overdo it.** Sometimes unschooling parents can become so committed that they begin to force "natural" learning. It sounds paradoxical, but daily "forced" baking, or games of Scrabble, or endless rounds of the ABC song—in the hope that literacy and numeracy will spring organically—will begin to feel more like a chore than an ordinary part of living. Go through your days mindful of the many ways we learn just by living, but don't turn what should be a naturally unfolding process into a forced objective.

6

Tech-Enabled Unschooling

*"Technology is nothing. What's important is that you have
a faith in people, that they're basically good and smart,
and if you give them tools, they'll do wonderful things
with them."*

—Steve Jobs[1]

ANDRE UHL IS A RESEARCHER at the Massachusetts Institute of Technology's famed Media Lab, which for over thirty years has served as an incubator for new ideas and pathbreaking technologies. Andre's primary research focus is artificial intelligence and ethics. Alternative education in general, and unschooling in particular, were unknown to Andre and his wife, Koko. She is from Japan where alternative education and homeschooling are quite rare, and he is from Germany where homeschooling is currently illegal. Wading into alternatives to school was not something the couple planned, but a glimpse into forced schooling changed their perspective.

When their older daughter, Bliss, got a spot in a public prekindergarten program in their city, they went to the visitation day to check it out. Bliss felt that she didn't want to go to the preschool without her parents there, at least initially. Andre and his wife found this reaction completely normal and understandable for a four-year-old child who had never been away from her family for a long period of time.

"We expected that we would help her build trust by getting to know the teachers and other families together during a transition period. I knew that my sister in Germany had stayed with her daughter for several weeks in kindergarten until her daughter finally told her that she was ready to stay on her own." Andre and Koko expected the same transitional experience here in the United States and were surprised when the teacher told them that they would have to drop their daughter off the next day. She said that there was no way they could stay with her because it was against the policies of the school. So Andre and Koko asked Bliss what she thought about being dropped off the next day, and she said that she wouldn't like it. The teacher overheard her remark and said very gently, "Don't worry, we have many toys to distract you." Bliss then replied, "But I don't want to be distracted, I just don't want to be sad."

Andre and Koko were astonished by the wisdom in their young daughter's words. They knew they should listen to and trust her, rather than dismiss her feelings. As Andre recalls: "The sad thing is that the people we met that day—the principal, teachers, parents, and kids— were all really nice people, and I could see that they all wanted the best for their children. However, there was this common sense that in order to ensure the best for your child, you've got to stick to those given rules, even if your child is screaming in fear." Andre and Koko truly believe that it wasn't the people, but the system of schooling itself "which deprived everyone of compassion." That day, the parents promised their daughter that they would provide her with a learning environment that would acknowledge and respect her feelings, not try to distract or ignore them. "And that's how we connected with local unschoolers," says Andre.

Now, Bliss spends most of her time learning from the world around her, pursuing topics that interest her, going to libraries and museums, taking a circus class, playing with friends. She also goes to the Macomber Center, a self-directed learning center for unschoolers. She tinkers in their woodshop, experiments in their music room, makes art in their craft room, plays with Lego blocks, and freely explores the woods and fields that surround the center with kids of all ages, from kindergarteners to teenagers. Classes on various topics are offered, often based on what the children are interested in, but none are required. Adult facilitators are available to help and offer support and comfort, but they don't decide what children should know or tell them how to act. The core of the unschooling mind-set is that children can and should drive their own learning and doing, when surrounded by resources and caring adults.

Learner-Directed Education

Bliss is thriving, and now Andre is shifting some of his research focus toward unschooling and the ways it can be expanded to more children. He's in the right place to do it. One of the founding faculty members of the MIT Media Lab in 1985 was Seymour Papert, a mathematician and artificial intelligence guru who recognized the extraordinary ways new technologies would alter education. Papert was heavily influenced by the ideas of Jean Piaget, the well-known twentieth-century Swiss psychologist, with whom Papert studied early on in his career. Piaget believed in a constructivist view of intellectual development, in which children build their knowledge over time through play and experimentation and the interaction of new ideas with existing mental models.

In his 1980 book, *Mindstorms: Children, Computers, and Powerful Ideas*, Papert writes, "Children seem to be innately gifted learners, acquiring long before they go to school a vast quantity of knowledge by a process I call 'Piagetian learning,' or 'learning without being taught.'"[2] Papert thought that the resources available to children to help them learn without being taught are of critical importance. In 1967 he invented Logo, the first computer programming language for children, arguing that the advent of technology, and its greater accessibility, could be key factors in helping children to continue the natural process of learning increasingly more sophisticated content without direct teaching. Papert became a critic of education models based on top-down instruction and passive learning. He believed that "the model of successful learning is the way a child learns to talk, a process that takes place without deliberate and organized teaching." So firm was his vision of the ways technology could facilitate natural learning, Papert foreshadowed the end of conventional schooling, believing that "schools as we know them today will have no place in the future."[3]

Over the last three decades, researchers at the MIT Media Lab have been inspired by Papert's early work and insights. They continue to create new technologies and inspire new thought on the ways computers and computer programs can facilitate children's natural learning in a noncoercive, noninterventionist way. One of the Media Lab's most well known recent inventions for kids is the Scratch programming language, a free, online coding program specifically geared toward children. My kids, especially my girls, love Scratch as a way to build playful, animated programs and games using accessible coding tools. Like other free, online programming languages for children, Scratch encourages creativity and collaboration through coding. It's artistic and engaging and offers opportunities to share with other young coders all over the world. Authentic programming tools and languages are introduced in the spirit of play and invention.

First launched in 2007, Scratch is the brainchild of the Media Lab's Lifelong Kindergarten research group. Mitchel Resnick, who leads the Lifelong Kindergarten lab, echoes Papert's vision that learning should be supported naturally throughout childhood and beyond—just as it is in early childhood: provide young people with support and resources to drive their own learning, leveraging their own curiosity and interests, and in the spirit of play. In his 2017 book, *Lifelong Kindergarten*, Resnick laments how today's education shifts from a more playful, organic process in early childhood to conventional instructional methods later on. He writes: "Students spend much of their time sitting at desks, filling out worksheets, and listening to lectures—whether from a teacher in the classroom or a video on the computer."[4] Resnick advocates injecting the four Ps of learning—projects, passion, peers, and play—into education to help shift the education model from passive to active and preserve creativity.

The Lifelong Kindergarten lab shares space with the Media Lab's Learning Initiative in a bright, wide-open room rimmed with Lego bins inside the enormous research center on MIT's riverfront campus. Led by J. Philipp Schmidt, the Learning Initiative explores questions about the ways in which humans learn, how learning can be better supported, and how information can be more accessible to assist in knowledge building. Schmidt cofounded Peer 2 Peer University (P2PU), one of the early offshoots, like Khan Academy, of the massive open online courseware (MOOC) movement. P2PU collaborates widely with public libraries to facilitate a web of free, noncoercive, online and in-person classes.

The promise of P2PU and other MOOCs, like edX and Coursera, that link free, quality courses to anyone with an Internet connection is that they help to make education learner-directed instead of teacher-led, with the learner deciding what she wants to know, when, and from whom. Technology can help to flatten the educational hierarchy. It can move us away from an archaic system of factory schooling to a more humane approach to education that supports self-development and fosters creative diversity. In 2008, two colleagues decided to teach a course on learning theory to students at the University of Manitoba in Canada that would extend beyond campus borders. Stephen Downes and George Siemens wanted to see if there was any interest in sharing information for free with the larger public, rather than only with their tuition-paying college students. They had twenty-five students enrolled in their course for credit—but another twenty-three hundred joined online, for no credit and no fee.[5] There was a clear interest in and a huge demand for openly accessible, online course content available to the public at no cost. MOOCs were born.

Since then, MOOCs have grown rapidly. The *New York Times* called 2012 "the year of the MOOC," as the Massachusetts Institute of Technology and Harvard University teamed up then to create edX, offering free, online courses to the masses. Additional universities later joined edX, and Coursera (which also launched in 2012) brought together more universities to provide free online programming. Udacity, also launched in 2012, was started by Stanford University professor Sebastian Thrun and others after Thrun's 2011 MOOC computer science class on artificial intelligence had over 150,000 enrollees.[6] Massive though they may be, many MOOCs offer an assortment of learning props, from video lectures to downloadable syllabi, reading materials, and assignments, and interactive, small group opportunities. A 2015 report on MOOCs found that the largest group of enrollees consists of "hobby learners," or self-directed adults seeking lifelong learning opportunities for their own interest and enrichment.[7] While "hobby learners" eager for new knowledge may be a MOOC's key constituency, MOOCs may not always encourage creativity and curiosity. In fact, Stephen Downes has said that unlike the "interactive and dynamic" platform of his initial MOOC in 2008, many modern MOOCs fall back on the "static and passive" approaches of conventional education.[8]

MIT's Schmidt and Resnick, along with their Media Lab colleague Natalie Rusk, have been experimenting with MOOCs to try to make them less passive. They write, "There is now a growing awareness that broadcasting short video content to larger numbers of people misses the things that are most important for learners: working on projects that they are passionate about, in collaboration with peers, within a playful environment that encourages experimentation."[9] There is a real opportunity with MOOCs to reimagine education, rather than falling back on the top-down instructional model of industrial schooling. It's easy to use new technology to replicate old patterns. The challenge is to realize the potential for new technologies to create new pathways for learning and doing that are driven by the learners themselves.

Using Technology to Learn

Even before the advent of MOOCs, the power of technology to propel learning without schooling, particularly for children, has been well documented. In 1999, Dr. Sugata Mitra and his colleagues began conducting computer literacy experiments in the urban slums of New Delhi, India. Mitra placed a computer with an Internet connection into the wall outside of his office. Any passersby could access this computer. No instructions or assistance were provided, and no adults gravitated to the computer. But the children, who were mostly poor and uneducated and who had no computer or English literacy, came in droves. They worked together, playing around with the different applications and programs, teaching each other, and making up their own language to describe various computer terms, like icon and mouse. Within this noncoercive, multiage space—in a safe, public area—the children gained remarkable computer literacy within just a few weeks.

Mitra and his colleagues were so encouraged by this initial success that they expanded these computers with Internet connections into various other urban slum and rural areas of India, with the same results. Mitra's studies became known as the "hole in the wall" experiments, and they consistently revealed how multiage groups of disadvantaged children throughout India could work collaboratively to teach themselves. Mitra coined this process "minimally invasive education." In some studies, Mitra created control groups, with some children (ages six to fourteen) learning computer literacy in formal, teacher-directed classroom settings and others learning through the "hole in the wall" experiments. The child-directed groups attained computer literacy skills at rates comparable to children in the teacher-directed control groups. Mitra described some of the potential implications of his research for education in general, explaining "that any learning environment that provides an adequate level of curiosity can cause learning among groups of children. Children's desire to learn, along with their curiosity and peer interaction, drives them to explore the environment in order to satisfy their inquisitiveness."[10]

In his powerful, award-winning 2013 TED Talk about his "hole in the wall" studies, Mitra described additional findings, including the ability of formerly illiterate children to learn to read, to teach themselves English, and to understand advanced scientific content (like DNA replication), simply by having access to an Internet-enabled public computer. The results were particularly profound when the children were connected with what Mitra calls, the "Granny cloud." He put out an ad for grandmothers to offer an hour of time a week for free to be available online if the "hole in the wall" children got stuck. The only things the grandmothers offered were encouragement and support—not instruction. Mitra concludes: "If you allow the educational process to self-organize, then learning emerges. It's not about making learning happen. It's about letting it happen."[11]

The technological advancements of today, including MOOCs, make unschooling and self-directed education more accessible and more relevant than ever before. Not only can more of us interact with the resources and information we need to ask and answer our questions, but the needs of our larger society are shifting toward innovation and away from acquiescence. We need drivers, not passengers, to steer the way. Mitra revealed how access to computers and the Internet, along with helpful adults, could support childhood learning outside of a classroom. Similarly, today's technology can help us learn almost anything.

My nine-year-old son, Jack, is a skateboarder. He discovered this passion at age eight when he saw skateboarders periodically passing along our city streets. He just had to know more. He played around with a cheap, used skateboard we had lying in our shed, practicing some moves and getting the feel for balance and motion. He became interested in the overall modern skateboard movement and some of its key figures. We watched a TED Talk together about Rodney Mullen, one of the sport's pioneers. He read magazine articles about skateboarding and visited various local skate parks. He spent hours watching YouTube videos about tricks and techniques, and then practiced them over and over and over again on his board. Eventually, we visited a local skate shop run by a young skateboarding enthusiast who also became passionate about the sport when he was Jack's age. We got Jack a real board and his skills took off as he spent as much time as possible at the skate park, trying new tricks, watching and learning from more experienced boarders, and gradually helping the newcomers. Skateboard culture is something special indeed.

Skateboarding is an interesting sport because, suddenly, in the mid-1980s the skill level of skateboarders soared. What happened? New VCR and VHS technology came on the scene, enabling experienced skateboarders to create instructional how-to videos showcasing the latest moves. Armed with this new knowledge, skateboarders practiced these new skills and adapted them through trial, error, and collaboration with other skaters at the park. In a *Forbes* article on this skateboarding phenomenon, contributor John Greathouse writes, "Even kids who didn't watch the videos were influenced, as their friends quickly mastered tricks that might have been impossible to decipher from still images in a magazine and showed them off at the local skate park."[12] YouTube is the latest technology platform to accelerate learning, making it particularly easy and enjoyable to learn how to do almost anything. Whether Jack is watching the latest skateboarding tricks, Abby is researching how to pin and preserve her bugs, my husband is trying to figure out how to fix the toilet, or I am learning the right way to chop celeriac, YouTube is a go-to source for today's knowledge-building.

In much the same way that the skateboarders learned from the action videos in the mid-1980s and Jack now learns from YouTube, new technologies support self-directed education. One of the reasons why schooling emerged as it did, dating back to medieval times, was that knowledge was scarce. Books were rare and expensive, and information on most topics was not readily accessible. Today, learning is much more egalitarian. Children and adults can learn what is meaningful to them in real time, using various tools and resources. When I observe Jack watching his skateboarding videos, or I see him explore different YouTube videos for tutorials on how to best draw people figures, or I watch him decide which free, online photography course to enroll in, I am struck by how discerning he is of his instructors. He quickly dismisses some of the videos and courses he finds, and gravitates toward others, often depending on the quality of the teacher or the clarity of the instruction. He is able to choose his teacher, choose his instruction, based on what resonates with him.

Unschooling and self-directed education do not mean that young people never learn from teachers or get instruction in various topics or go to formal classes, complete formal assignments, and take formal exams. It simply means they choose to do it—and choose not to do it if it doesn't work for them. I once signed up for an adult education class on a topic that interested me. I paid the full, nonrefundable fee, read the participation policies, and hoped for the best. In the end, I didn't think the instructor was particularly good or that attending the class was a valuable use of my time, so I left. Self-directed learners of all ages have similar freedoms: they can take classes or not, as long as their decision to stay or go does not bring hardship to others. Freedom, not license. Giving young people the ability to choose their teachers and instructors, or to not choose them, simply grants children the same respect and autonomy afforded to adults. With an abundance of free and accessible online learning tools, choosing among teachers and types of instruction is easy and expected. This alters conventional teaching-learning patterns. The ability to freely choose how you learn and from whom you learn it puts the learner at the helm. Learning and teaching become a more fluid process of seeking and sharing.

In many ways, this was Ivan Illich's vision of education in 1970 when he wrote *Deschooling Society*. Illich says, "The current search for new educational *funnels* must be reversed into the search for their institutional inverse: educational *webs* which heighten opportunity for each one to transform each moment of his living into one of learning, sharing, and caring."[13] The sheer growth in technological resources since Illich wrote those words, along with their greater accessibility to more people in more places, means that the time has never been better for a learner-directed education revolution. It's no wonder that a copy of *Deschooling Society* sits on a shelf at the Media Lab's Learning Initiative.

Reimagining Learning from the Ground Up

In 2006, educator and author Ken Robinson gave a TED Talk called, "Do Schools Kill Creativity?" At over fifty million views, it remains the most-watched talk in TED's history.

Robinson's premise is simple: our current education system strips young people of their natural curiosity and creativity by shaping them into a one-dimensional academic mold. This mold may work for some of us, particularly, as he states, if we want to become university professors; but for many of us, our innate abilities and sprouting passions are at best ignored and at worst destroyed by modern schooling. In his TED Talk, Robinson concludes:

> I believe our only hope for the future is to adopt a new concep-
> tion of human ecology, one in which we start to reconstitute
> our conception of the richness of human capacity. Our educa-
> tion system has mined our minds in the way that we strip-mine
> the earth: for a particular commodity. And for the future, it

won't serve us. We have to rethink the fundamental principles on which we're educating our children.[14]

The big question is can we fundamentally rethink education within the existing schooling framework? Can conventional schools shift entirely from a focus on teacher-centered instruction within a preestablished curriculum framework to a learner-centered philosophy of self-directed education where young people decide what to learn, when, how, and from whom? The answer is a definite "maybe, if." Maybe schools can rethink the fundamental principles of education, if they begin to look nothing like schools. Maybe schools can be transformed, and not merely reformed, if they eliminate all of the policies and protocols, regulations and agreements, curriculum and assessment practices, and teaching and learning theories that most schooling has observed for the past 165 years. Maybe schooling can look more like learning, if energetic and entrepreneurial parents and educators make it happen.

Fundamentally rethinking education is exactly what Alec Resnick and his team are doing as they launch a new self-directed public school. While studying at MIT as an undergraduate, Alec read *Deschooling Society*, which opened his eyes to the problems of forced schooling and the possibilities of alternative pathways for education. Illich's powerful message of the way that schooling leads to institutionalized thinking in many aspects of life and fuels a lack of agency resonated with Alec, who experienced what learning could be like for the first time while studying at MIT: passion-centered, project-driven, technology-enabled, collaborative, and fun. He began to read many more books, including those of Seymour Papert and John Holt, triggering an unrelenting urge to help transform education from teacher led to self determined. He and some colleagues launched an innovative after-school program for urban children just outside of Boston focused around technology and self-directed learning. The mayor of the city became increasingly enthusiastic about the after-school program and encouraged Alec and his team to launch a full-fledged school. They resisted, until finally after the mayor's prolonged insistence they began to sketch out a plan for what would become a fully self-directed, non-charter public high school called Powderhouse Studios.

The process was painstakingly slow, with delayed approvals and disparate ideas on the school's "shoulds" and "musts." To achieve the goal of a completely self-directed public high school that looked nothing like a conventional school, Alec and his team were convinced that they needed freedom from traditional public school policies and procedures. They applied for and received relief from the State of Massachusetts through its 2010 Innovation Schools legislation, granting Alec and his team the power to recruit and hire teachers, choose their own curriculum and scheduling approaches, and control their own budgeting practices without being tied to standard district protocols and collective bargaining agreements.

With state approval set, and district-level issues still being worked out, Alec and his team expanded their vision for Powderhouse. They still didn't have a location for the school, and there were many lingering details, but they were committed to its basic framework: Powderhouse would enable the city's young people, ages thirteen to eighteen, to learn together in an integrated, multiage space as they followed their interests, used the resources of their community, and had access to helpful facilitators when needed. The school would look more like a modern research-and-development lab than a conventional school, with wide open spaces and the freedom to come and go as the students wished. The school would be open year round, with students taking vacations or time off when it worked best for them and their family, just as adult workers do. It would also be open all day long, with students able to arrive and leave freely. Alec says: "We think the future of learning doesn't look anything like school. It looks much more similar to work: much more ambiguous, much more interdisciplinary." Teenagers would be responsible for designing, managing, and executing intense, in-depth, multiyear projects that lead to mastery in various subjects, but do so in a more authentic, hands-on way. There would be no assigned classes, no grades, and no testing. Project mastery, however, would be evaluated against Common Core curriculum expectations.

What about mandatory standardized testing? Massachusetts was one of the first states to impose high stakes testing and curriculum standards that later mirrored the national Common Core curriculum frameworks.

All young people enrolled in public schools are expected to take the statewide Massachusetts Comprehensive Assessment System (MCAS) exam as tenth graders, and a passing score is required for high school graduation. How will students in a fully self-directed learning environment, not tied to a traditional teach-and-test model, navigate the standardized testing hurdle?

Other public high schools have attempted to implement self-directed programs similar to Powderhouse, but often they become schools-within-a-school or are hybrid models with school time split evenly between self-directed activities and required academic content. They may also lean toward project-based learning or self-paced models, rather than embracing self-directed education that is fully driven by the learner, without external directives and assessment. In their book, *A School of Our Own*, Samuel Levin and Susan Engel share their experience of launching the Independent Project, a semester-long self-directed program within another Massachusetts public high school that students could take advantage of during their junior or senior years—after they met the statewide standardized testing requirement.[15] Powderhouse is different. Alec explains that he sees Powderhouse as a "partnership with parents." If parents want their children to take the MCAS, then he and his team will offer whatever tutoring and testing practice those students may need. If parents and students are not interested in MCAS, then the founders will help them to join the growing ranks opting out of high-stakes testing.

Alec and his team trudged along with their vision, slowly working their way through state and local red tape. The process was at times frustrating. They caught a break in 2016 when, in collaboration with their city, the Powderhouse team won a $10 million cash grant from XQ Super School Project, an organization focused on transforming high school education, whose board of directors is led by Laurene Powell Jobs, wife of the late Steve Jobs. With an influx of cash and a national media spotlight, the Powderhouse project accelerated. The team found a perfect location—a new, multiuse development about to be built that would combine workspaces, living spaces, and learning spaces in the heart of the city. The school is set to open in the fall of 2019.

At the construction site where I first met Alec, I can see that Pow-derhouse is, quite literally, being built from the ground up. It serves as an unintentional metaphor for what we need conventional public schools to become if they are to truly move from a schooling paradigm to a learning one. They need to be built entirely from scratch.

I am struck by Alec's clarity of purpose. He is passionate about this project and its potential for reimagining public education. Despite his mild manner and soft-spoken tones, Resnick is emphatic about the future he wants to help create. "It is very clear to me," he says, "that the world I want to live in is one where families have control over resources to allocate to their children, and have support to allocate those resources effectively." Equity is a big driver for Alec, who says he wants Powderhouse to reflect the current socioeconomic diversity of the city's traditional high school. He is using a weighted lottery system to ensure representative admissions. Integrating unschooling ideals into a public school is not without its hurdles. For instance, even though Powderhouse is exempt from many standard district policies, the founding team was urged by the superintendent to add "content specialists" to their staff. They must also map all student projects to Common Core competencies and high school graduation requirements, which could limit students' full autonomy. Still, Powderhouse could become a leading model for conventional schools hoping to reinvent themselves to become free and open community spaces committed to self-directed learning.

Modern Makerspaces

Just down the road from Powderhouse is another exciting learning space focused on unschooling principles. Located along a busy city street just outside of Boston, with the words LOTTERY and SPICES still visible on the red awning of this former convenience store space, Parts and Crafts serves as a fascinating and successful model of natural learning for urban children aged six to fourteen. Inspired by the burgeoning "hackerspace" movement, Parts and Crafts is a child-centered makerspace for unschool-ers, after-school students, and summer campers. Parts and Crafts founder Will Macfarlane left MIT after his freshman year and became interested in alternative education. He grew increasingly convinced that "school was most effective when it got out of the way and allowed informal learning communities and partnerships to form."

Much of Will's education worldview originated from his own experience in school. He didn't like school as a child. His mom was a teacher, but she recognized that school performance was not the full measure of one's abilities and talents. After leaving MIT, Will became interested in the Sudbury model of learning, with its emphasis on noncoercive education, personal responsibility, and democratic governance. He read A. S. Neill's *Summerhill* and worked for a while at a Sudbury school in Oregon, growing more committed to the ideas of freedom, autonomy, and community in education. He was also fascinated with tinkering and technology and the marriage of the two, and he taught himself computer programming, eventually writing software for an architecture firm.

Will's interests in computers, technology, democratic models of education, knowledge-sharing, and tinkering dovetailed with the burgeoning hackerspace movement of the 2000s. Hacker culture was nurtured in the 1960s and '70s at the MIT Artificial Intelligence Laboratory, where Seymour Papert was codirector before the Media Lab emerged. It spread slowly, often through small computer clubs where like-minded people would tinker with new technology. Modern hackerspaces first appeared in Germany in the 1990s, spreading more rapidly throughout Europe and the United States in the early part of this century. While their specifics vary, most hackerspaces are open, publicly accessible, collaborative spaces where community members gather together to share knowledge, tinker, and build with both manual and digital tools and machinery. Some of the key characteristics of hackerspaces, or what are now often called makerspaces, are autonomy, freedom, access, hands-on learning, collaboration, sharing of ideas and resources, and lack of hierarchy.[16]

Will was deeply inspired by the hackerspace and maker movements. He says, "I've always been involved in technology, yet also troubled by the tech industry." This idea of community-based, technology-focused spaces based on education, autonomy, and accessibility resonated with Will. He and a friend decided to merge their passion for technology and tinkering with their philosophy of noncoercive, self-directed education.

"We wanted to create open spaces where technical tools are available and people can use them." They started with a summer camp for kids. Camp Kaleidoscope ran for several summers with a simple premise: let young people make their own decisions. As Will says, "It's such a simple idea but it's so different from what we're used to."

Summer camp can be a place where kids are naturally allowed more freedom and autonomy, saving "real" learning for the school year. It can be easier for parents to dabble with unschooling ideas in summer or in after-school programs without making a full commitment to self-directed education. But some parents were so taken by Camp Kaleidoscope's approach to learning, as a self-directed hackerspace for kids, that they wanted it to extend beyond summer. These parents approached Will and Parts and Crafts cofounder Katie Gradowski, saying that if they made this a full-time option, then they would pull their kids out of school and send them there instead. Encouraged by parent-driven demand for a self-directed learning center, Will and Katie founded Parts and Crafts in 2008. Technically a private, nonprofit resource center for homeschoolers and unschoolers, Parts and Crafts is not a school but is certified as a state-licensed child care facility. Avoiding designation as a school means that Parts and Crafts avoids compulsory school attendance laws and curriculum requirements and can offer flexible enrollment options for its member families, from one day a week of participation up to five days a week. It also offers a popular after-school program for children throughout the community, vacation and summer camp programs, and year-round "open shop" hours where tinkerers of all ages can enjoy maker culture.

The center's philosophy hinges on open play, self-directed learning, and child autonomy within a makerspace of tools, resources, books, supplies, optional classes, and adult facilitators. Access and autonomy are fundamental aspects of its educational vision. As Katie says: "Above all, we believe that kids learn best when given the space to play, mess around, and be themselves. We spend a lot of time taking apart computers, programming in Scratch language, building kid-size hovercrafts, constructing, crafting, inventing, playing, and having a blast exploring the world around us."

Its camp and after-school programs fund much of Parts and Crafts's unschooling program, which they call the Center for Semi-Conducted Learning. Classes run in eight-week increments, with staff and unschoolers deciding together what should be offered. All classes are optional, and most are not what would be traditionally considered academic. Recent classes include dinosaur-model making, puppetry, 3D animation, video game analysis, building a computer, and cartooning. A child could spend the whole day avoiding classes and focusing on her own activities, whether that is reading in the comfy library corner, playing a board game, knitting or sewing, or tinkering with the many circuits and gears available. "Above all, we have a great community of kids and families," says Katie.

> Many of the kids who come through our programs have had negative experiences in school, and I would say that whatever place a child is coming from—whether they're a homeschooler, a camper, or a drop-in weekend workshopper—the real value of a program like ours is in creating a collaborative space for kids to engage (or re-engage!) with learning on their own terms. That's basically the goal—to create a friendly, supportive space where people are engaged in making, building, and doing cool stuff together.

My daughter Molly attends Parts and Crafts part-time, gravitating to classes centered around their woodshop, as well as anything to do with cooking, coding, and crafting. One term, she and several other kids chose woodworking for their morning class. Katie had a group project for those interested in some guided instruction, but Molly and another child decided to work on their own woodworking projects rather than the group one. (She was making wooden swords for her younger brothers.) This is the essence of self-directed learning: opportunities are made available, adults are available to help or offer assistance when needed, classes or formal instruction may be offered but are not required, and interests are nurtured within a supportive, cooperative, multiage environment. This could happen at home, in a community learning center, or in some type of noncoercive school—or perhaps all of the above.

Unschooling isn't about pedagogy or place; it's a framework. As Will says: "It's not really a pedagogical stance. It's a moral stance. It doesn't focus on teaching and learning, but more on how people should treat each other." Still, Will sees a definite role for parents and other adults within the self-directed education model. "We generate ideas and provide offerings for kids, but we don't force them to do them. There are things we know more about, and there are things they know more about. It's a relationship." Because it's a relationship, it's critical for both children and adults to have mutual respect and responsibility. If, for example, a child asks for instruction on a certain topic or wants to work on a specific project and an adult spends time and effort to prepare it, then it can be disrespectful to decide later not to participate. Autonomy and personal responsibility—or freedom, not license—can be the biggest challenge of unschooling regardless of where it takes places.

One of the primary goals of Parts and Crafts is accessibility, and the founders and staff are constantly seeking ways to make their programs more accessible to more families, particularly low-income and disadvantaged families in their city. They are disturbed by current trends that value "personalization" and "self-direction" for more well-off children while emphasizing "competency" and "outcomes" for more disadvantaged youth. Freedom and autonomy are often celebrated for more privileged kids, while skills and drills are reinforced for those with less privilege.

The idea that we increasingly have a two-tiered education system, with progressive and self-directed education more accessible to young people of privilege while children from more depressed backgrounds are stuck with more restrictive, drill-based, outcome-focused schooling environments, is deeply disturbing to the Parts and Crafts community. As Katie states:

> We believe that maker culture—the ability to think, create, and build with your hands—has a transformative capacity, one that should be available to all kids regardless of income, background, or socioeconomic status. From the beginning we've run all of our programs on a sliding scale and have made them available regardless of a family's ability to pay.

To help bring maker culture to the larger community, Parts and Crafts has recently assumed responsibility for running the city's fab lab, short for fabrication laboratory—a growing trend within the hackerspace realm. A key goal of fab labs is to make digital tools and technologies that are typically unavailable, or only limitedly available to the public, more accessible. Fab labs were another innovation springing from the MIT Media Lab, where professor Neil Gershenfeld teaches a popular class called "How to Make (Almost) Anything." Equipped with cutting-edge technology, such as laser cutters and 3-D printers, and a variety of computers, robotics tools, and digital design software, fab labs are the latest installment of the maker movement. Gershenfeld runs MIT's Center for Bits and Atoms and calls digital fabrication, or making (almost) anything using digital technologies, the next digital revolution.

Likening it to the early 1950s when MIT researchers successfully connected an early computer to a milling machine and watched as the computer controlled the machine rather than a human controlling it, Gershenfeld sees digital fabrication as a new frontier. When he first offered his "making anything" class he was surprised by how popular it was—with one hundred students (most of whom did not have technical backgrounds) showing up for a class that could accommodate only ten. They all wanted to make things. Reflecting on that inaugural class, Gershenfeld writes: "One made an alarm clock that the groggy owner would have to wrestle with to prove that he or she was awake. Another made a dress fitted with sensors and motorized spine-like structures that could defend the wearer's personal space. The students were answering a question that I had not asked: What is digital fabrication good for?"[17]

Community-based fab labs, now numbering in the hundreds across the globe, are seeking to answer that question in novel ways, driven by the interests and ideas of individual makers who may not otherwise have access to such sophisticated technology. Fab labs and makerspaces are often integrated into public libraries and other free and accessible community spaces. Miguel Figueroa of the American Library Association says that "makerspaces are part of the libraries' expanded mission to be places where people can not only consume knowledge, but create new knowledge."[18] Located in the basement of a public school, the community fab lab that the Parts and Crafts team runs is free and open to all members of the public during most weekday afternoons and evenings.

The first night Molly and I visited, she quickly became absorbed in their array of 3-D printers and laser cutters. Some community members were working on computer design projects, others were getting an overview of the vast capabilities of complex digital machinery. The overall space looks a bit like your middle school woodshop class, but the spirit was quite different. The room was bright and cheerful. A diverse group of people, of different ages and colors and backgrounds, worked on projects that were meaningful to them. They weren't there by compulsion. They weren't told what to do, what project to work on, or given limited choice among a few ideas. They were free to create whatever they wanted, with full access to the latest technological tools and enthusiastic and knowledgeable facilitators available to help and guide if needed. They were allowed to direct their own creativity, leveraging the energy of the space, the enthusiasm of their fellow cocreators, and the support of knowledgeable facilitators.

Gershenfeld discovered in offering his "making anything" class that students' learning was fueled by their own interests and their enthusiasm for sharing what they discovered with others. If someone learned a new skill or achieved a new level of digital functionality, they would eagerly share their experiences with their lab's cocreators. Illich's vision of community environments characterized by webs of "learning, sharing and caring" come alive in these high-tech makerspaces. These spaces promote "webs" of learning, tied directly to interests and needs, rather than the conventional "funnels" that Illich and others criticize. In his book *Fab: The Coming Revolution on Your Desktop*, Gershenfeld writes about the ways makerspaces and fab labs can facilitate self-directed learning: "This process can be thought of as a 'just-in-time' educational model, teaching on demand, rather than the more traditional 'just-in-case' model that covers a curriculum fixed in advance in the hopes that it will include something that will later be useful."[19] Moving away from a contrived curriculum and toward learner-directed education is perhaps the most fundamental shift in moving toward an unschooled society.

It's not surprising that a group like Parts and Crafts, inspired by both the maker movement and the promise of self-directed education, would also see the potential in community fab labs. Here, the members of the broader community can do some high-tech tinkering and make almost anything using the latest digital technology. They don't need a curriculum to tell them what to do, or a teacher to force them to do it; they simply need a space that supports their natural creativity, without compulsion, offering real-time instruction or guidance when needed. Parts and Crafts has been able to build, as they call it, "a scrappy community space at the intersection between hackerspaces, free schools, and the growing homeschool movement." Their original, technology-focused prototype of self-directed education can be a model not only for unschooled children but also for an integrated, noncoercive, community-based approach to self-directed education for learners of all ages.

Technology in Learning: Gift or Curse

"We shall soon be nothing but transparent heaps of jelly to each other," the journalist wrote. It's a common refrain about technology overuse and social media saturation. The rapid rise of technology in such a brief period of time leads to concern over how to manage its mounting influence. We worry, especially as parents of growing children, how technology impacts their physical, mental, and spiritual health. We worry about how technological tools designed to foster connection could instead make us more distant, or "jelly to each other." We worry that new technologies could be addictive, causing us to withdraw from the wider world. The quote could easily be said of today's near-panic around technology, particularly of children and technology. The truth is that it was written in 1897 by a London writer fretting over the latest technology threatening to rip apart human closeness. What was this evil technology? The telephone.[20]

Humans have long feared new technologies as potential threats to our collective culture. Prior to Bell's telephone, there were the printing press and mass book production that placed cheap paperbacks into the hands of the lower classes for the first time. Spurred by technological advancements in printing, serialized novels were the video games of the nineteenth century, with many critics spouting concern that such petty and distractive forms of entertainment would be our ruin. In 1845, a writer said of the rampant serializing of fiction: "Useful as a certain amount of novel reading may be, this is not the right way to indulge in it. It is not a mere healthy recreation like a match at cricket, a lively conversation, or a game at backgammon . . . It throws us into a state of unreal excitement, a trance, a dream."[21] In other words, novels were fine in small doses, but consuming vast amounts of them displaced other activities deemed to be more uplifting. Horace Mann, the nineteenth-century common school leader, was particularly wary of novels for their potential to corrupt young minds. For example, he wouldn't allow schoolchildren to be exposed to the fictional stories of his brother-in-law, Nathaniel Hawthorne, and even the books of Charles Dickens were off-limits.[22]

Similar concerns and criticisms surround technology today, especially for children. Warnings abound about the addictive potential of video games and social media. We see young people becoming absorbed in technology and also notice the ways we adults may be lured frequently to our Facebook and Instagram accounts. In their book, Screen Schooled, teachers Joe Clement and Matt Miles write about how their high school students are becoming technology addicts, with smartphones and social media causing kids to become dumber, more distracted, and more disconnected than ever before. The authors write:

> How much do you know about what goes on from the time your son or daughter leaves your home in the morning until he or she gets home in the afternoon or evening? If you're like most parents, not much. Teachers are the ones who know your child's school behavior best. And we've watched firsthand as young people have been profoundly changed by their technology, seemingly overnight.[23]

School teachers may know a child's *school* behavior best but not necessarily what their behavior might be without school. For schooled children, a smartphone or a Snapchat account can be a life raft in a sea of command and control. For young people in school, and particularly teens who are systematically cut off from the larger adult world in which they are meant to come of age, technology grants them some semblance of freedom and autonomy over their otherwise programmed lives. It is a tool for connection as they are increasingly disconnected from the "real world" by spending longer lengths of time consuming schoolstuffs.

Technology advocate danah boyd describes how technology and social media are the latest tools that young people use to try to connect with the wider world from which they are typically excluded. She finds in her research with teens that, contrary to the criticism, technology actually makes kids smarter, more focused, and more connected. In her book *It's Complicated: The Social Lives of Networked Teens*, boyd writes: "Most teens are not compelled by gadgetry as such—they are compelled by friendship. The gadgets are interesting to them primarily as a means to a social end. Furthermore, social interactions may be a distraction from school, but they are often not a distraction from learning."[24]

Concerns about today's technology, and particularly its potential overuse by young people, may again be an issue of *schooling* more than anything else. Technology may simply amplify the rift between the way children are schooled and the way they would otherwise naturally learn—by being immersed in their community, surrounded by peers and adults, following shared interests and passions. We may think technology is what is artificially altering our children when in fact it is schooling.

Much has been written about how certain technologies, especially video games, can be addictive to young people, but the latest research challenges that idea. In a large-scale 2016 study published in the *American Journal of Psychiatry* researchers found no clear evidence for video game addiction. In fact, they found that fewer than 1 percent of people experience any kind of Internet gaming disorder.[25] A 2010 study of children's video game play by Cheryl Olson of Massachusetts General Hospital found varied motivations for video game play, ranging from simple enjoyment and collaboration with friends, to opportunities to do things they otherwise would be unable to do, to challenge, competition, and escape. Olson concludes: "Compared with other media such as books, films, and radio, electronic games appear to have an unusually expansive appeal and serve a surprising number of emotional, social, and intellectual needs."[26]

Questions around the role of technology and whether or not to impose limits on screen time nag at parents of both schooled and unschooled children. We may project our own uneasiness with technology onto our children, wondering if we're all spending too much time online. In imposing limits that we think will be helpful, we may inadvertently make technology seem more appealing in its prohibition, preventing our children (and ourselves) from arriving at a natural saturation point. We may also be buying into the unproven idea that technology is damaging to our well-being. After all, I think most of us would agree that the printing press and the telephone have enhanced our intellect and our connections with others, despite the dire warnings of their critics.

Psychologist Peter Gray, who studies hunter-gatherer societies, explains that limiting children's computer time denies them access to one of our culture's most important tools. He writes:

> Why would we want to limit a kid's computer time? The computer is, without question, the single most important tool of modern society. Our limiting kids' computer time would be like hunter-gatherer adults limiting their kids' bow-and-arrow time. Children come into the world designed to look around and figure out what they need to know in order to make it in the culture into which they are born.[27]

Gray explains that hunter-gatherer children play with all the tools of their society, including dangerous ones; but he admits that elders will keep the poison-tipped arrows out of children's reach.[28] Today's parents can determine what our modern poison arrows are and keep those out of reach while making certain not to prevent children from playing freely with the essential tools of their culture.

Most of us admit that computers and technology have greatly improved our lives and our learning. The bigger question for unschoolers is how technology can facilitate self-directed education—empowering learners to educate themselves—without simply replicating the old teach-and-test framework in a new, high-tech way. Technology is a powerful tool. It can either help us to create a new model of education that places the learner in charge of her own doing and destiny, or it can disguise an old model of education under a digital veneer. Online coursework and degree programs—and increasingly high-tech K–12 learning software—frequently advertise their methods as embracing self-directed learning principles when in fact the more accurate term is self-paced. In most of these programs, the curriculum is set and the learning objectives and outcomes are given; the learner is simply able to move through the coursework at his own speed or in his own preferred sequence. This may be a step forward from lectures and rote memorization, but it is not truly self-directed learning—it is directed by someone else. Of course, if a learner chooses freely to take such a course, and can opt out of it at any time, then it lacks the coercion and compulsion characteristic of most conventional schooling. It is then a choice of a self-directed learner.

To achieve Illich's vision of educational webs and Papert's goal of transforming education through computers, we need to let go of the antiquated idea of being schooled in order to learn. Today's technology democratizes education, making knowledge and skill-acquisition more accessible than ever before. That knowledge is constantly changing, thanks to newer, faster, and better technologies. A static, top-down curriculum cannot possibly keep up with the evolving needs of a networked society. As the Media Lab learning team says, we need to move from "presentation to conversation," and from "courses to community."[29] For learning to be most meaningful and enduring, it must come from the learners themselves. Technology is just a tool; faith in people is the real breakthrough.

Unschooling Tips

• **Leverage technology.** Computers and technology have revolutionized the way we access information and acquire knowledge. Passive, classroom-based learning is no longer the default. Today, the Internet enables real-time, self-directed learning with an array of online courses, YouTube tutorials, and social networks. Technology-enabled learning eliminates outdated educational hierarchies, making information and resources more widely accessible to more people than ever before.

• **Provide access.** Let your children play with technology! Make it fully accessible to them, as they emulate the ways you engage with computers, technology, and social media. Connect them with the abundant, often free, educational programs developed for children, such as the online Scratch programming language (scratch.mit.edu) and other software tools. Encourage them to research answers to their questions, explore websites and videos, and offer to join them in their exploration. Discuss potential technology traps, possible dangers and risks, and the importance of source-checking information.

• **Negotiate limits.** Parents may want to impose some limits on technology based on how their child reacts to screen time or the family's overall value system. Just like some kids react negatively to too much sugar, some kids may respond poorly to too much screen time. Parents should trust their instincts. The key is to make sure limits are based on real effects, rather than imagined concerns around the role of technology in our culture. If a child has just come from a schooled environment, technology use may be an important part of her deschooling process, as she is granted more control over her time and actions. Once she realizes the full extent of her newfound autonomy, technology use may decline or shift as new interests emerge. Honest, frequent discussions between parents and children around technology may be the best approach to setting, and constantly evaluating, potential limits.

7

Unschooling Resource Centers

"As I inched sluggishly along the treadmill of the May-comb County school system, I could not help receiving the impression that I was being cheated out of something. Out of what I knew not, yet I did not believe that twelve years of unrelieved boredom was exactly what the state had in mind for me."

—Scout, in Harper Lee's *To Kill a Mockingbird*[1]

DAVID LANE HAS BEEN a teacher for over twenty-five years. He has worked with teenagers in a variety of classroom settings, most recently as a public high school teacher in a conventional district school. During his teaching tenure, he has found that conventional schooling has become more restrictive and less open to a child's individual needs. "If anything," says David, "we've doubled down on many of the techniques and approaches, rather than trying entirely new things. We think *more* will be better: more time in more required classes, more accountability, more standardization, more tests will get us better results." David tried to make changes from within, suggesting new or different ways to foster self-directed learning within his public school, but efforts were slow and resistance from school personnel was high. Frustrated by the growing standardization of conventional schooling and the unwilling-ness or inability for schooling to change to truly support young people's natural learning, David decided to create his own alternative to school. "Teaching is not the job it used to be," says David. "We have to admit that the job we went into ten or more years ago no longer exists. But almost none of us are."

David took the leap. In 2016, he launched Ingenuity Hub as a self-directed resource center for unschooling teens inside a business incubator space offered by his city. There, young people follow their own interests and work on their own projects, surrounded by peers and helpful grown-ups with full access to the larger community. Most of the young people who attend were formerly in school, and it can take a long time for them to deschool, or adapt to the freedom and autonomy that unschooling offers. "In our experience," says David,

> some of our kids go through a period of time where they appear to "do nothing." Sometimes they know what they want to do but are unsure how to get started. A few have really needed a lot of time and space to decompress from school. Some need time to work through the whole idea of being free from school. Others are so focused on what they want to do, and frustrated by school's attempt to prevent them from doing it, that as soon as they have the chance to spend as much time on it as they want, they jump right in and go. To me, this is deschooling too, just in a different direction.

The contrasts David has observed between the schooled kids with whom he has worked and the unschooled kids have been striking.

> Speaking in general terms, schooled kids' approach to almost everything is: "What's the least amount of work I can do to get the result (grade, for example) that is the lowest acceptable to me and my family?" But as kids become more comfortable with self-directed learning, I see things change. They begin to see the value in experimentation. They stop talking about "failing" at things. Instead, when something doesn't work, they decide what to do next, which sometimes includes abandoning that effort completely, or coming back to it later.

Naturally optimistic, and with great enthusiasm for the power of education, David doesn't think self-directed learning principles can be successfully integrated into conventional schooling. "There are too many power structures that depend on the status quo for their positions that it will take a very long time for the gatekeepers in the system to change it," says David. "I think we need many more thriving alternatives to school. Kids in every community deserve access to this approach."

Alternatives to school, such as unschooling resource centers, are spreading quickly across the country. More educators are growing weary of rigid, test-driven conventional schooling, and more parents are seeking new options that retain their children's natural curiosity. Unschooling centers support a hybrid learning model that can make self-directed education more accessible to more families and help young people gain the support and connection they need. These centers re-empower both parents and their children. Typically, parents register or self-identify as homeschoolers with their state or town, which provides the legal designation necessary to comply with compulsory schooling laws and puts parents in charge of overseeing their children's education. Then, young people are able to attend an unschooling center—which is usually a small fraction of the cost of a standard private school—on a part-time or full-time basis, depending on the center's offerings and the family's needs.

I hear from parents all the time who wistfully say, "Oh, I wish my kids could be unschooled!" Maybe one is a single parent, or a family with two working parents, and can't physically be there for their child during the day. Maybe a partner or family member is skeptical of unschooling and it presents an impossible barrier. Maybe a child has been in school for so long that the thought of a drastically different learning environment is unsettling. For these families, an unschooling center can provide the space and support for self-directed education that may be otherwise unattainable. Still other families may find that an unschooling center offers resources that they are not able to personally provide, like access to a range of musical instruments, or a woodworking studio with an array of tools and machines, or a fully stocked art room with crafting materials galore, or a troop of community experts and guest instructors who regularly lead demonstrations on interesting topics. The key tenets of all unschooling centers are freedom and choice, with resources available and adults accessible, and the ability for young people to opt out of most activities if desired. (I say most because often self-directed learning centers will have some community expectations, such as periodic participation in community meetings, required clean-up, or an assigned community role.)

Freedom to Learn and Create

The extreme nature of today's conventional schooling may be accelerating the proliferation of these unschooling centers nationwide, but the model has been around since the time of John Holt and homeschooling's modern revival in the 1970s. Holt's influential 1964 book, *How Children Fail*, was one of the first books that Peter Bergson read after graduating from Harvard in 1967, and it forever altered the way he viewed education and learning. Peter, a gregarious grandfather now in his seventies, opened the country's first self-directed learning center with his wife in 1978 in suburban Pennsylvania. It has since become a model for self-directed learning centers and alternatives to school worldwide.

In the Peace Corps right after college, Peter was assigned to work with Filipino math teachers to help them move from teaching "old math" to the "new math" that was all the rage at the time. What fascinated him most was not the latest curriculum fad or instructional methodology; it was that he realized what little conceptual understanding of mathematics he and his teaching peers had retained after all their years of schooling. Instructional methods that taught calculations instead of concepts led many adults to not only dislike math but also to lack broader mathematical thinking skills. It challenged Peter's ideas of learning and schooling. After the Peace Corps, he dove into research on learning theory and began to question the prevailing schooling model. This was Vietnam-era America, when radical educators and writers vocally challenged authoritarianism and institutional oppression by focusing more on child-centered learning. Peter became good friends with Holt. When he and his wife, Susan, decided to unschool their own four children, Holt's *Growing Without Schooling* newsletter served as an inspiration and guide to natural learning.

Peter and Susan decided to expand self-directed learning beyond their own home and family. They founded Open Connections in Delaware County, Pennsylvania, as a natural learning center for homeschoolers and unschoolers, and it has flourished for forty years. From modest beginnings in a cramped space for preschoolers and kindergarteners to a major expansion at a new location in 2000, Open Connections now serves children ages four to eighteen on a twenty-eight-acre historic farm site. Peter's grown unschooled daughter Julia currently runs the center, continuing the original vision of Open Connections as a place to nurture childhood freedom and creativity. Young people only attend the learning center two to three days a week, and on any given day there are over ninety kids on campus. I ask Julia why they only offer part-time attendance options. She says: "We are in partnership with families, but ultimately it is the parents who are driving the educational path. We feel that if we offered a full-time option, it would shift the responsibility for educating children from the parents to Open Connections."

As the center's mission makes clear, young people are granted the freedom to learn and create. Like many unschooling centers, classes on various topics are offered but are not required and young people decide which classes they want to take, if any. Younger children up to about age nine spend time in an open, fully self-directed play space. When I visited, four adult facilitators were engaged in structured projects, including sewing and art, with any children who were interested, but the majority of the kids played freely throughout the colorful, light-filled space brimming with books and games, art supplies and crafting materials, toys and Montessori-inspired manipulatives, and a fully stocked woodshop with real hand tools. Julia explained that as the children get older, they often start to crave more structured learning activities, so the center offers theme-based, adult-led classes for tweens and teens. Tuesdays emphasize arts/humanities and Thursdays focus on math/science. During my tour, a lively group of tweens, with a handful of enthusiastic adult facilitators, was dissecting fish in one of the center's sophisticated science lab spaces. A group of young teens was working with other facilitators on self-selected independent science projects for an upcoming symposium where they present their findings to the larger community.

Open Connections has a no-screen policy, except for the shared laptops and computers that the center offers. One teen was sitting on the couch using her laptop to research ancient water purification systems; another was exploring the impact of gender bias on perception.

The oldest teen group, assembled in a spacious and comfortable upstairs loft area in the center's elegantly restored barn building, was debriefing their latest fundraiser. Each year the oldest teens work on a self-selected group project and each year they always seem to choose a trip to a far-flung city. They then do all of the travel planning, reservations, rate negotiations, and fundraising to ensure that the trip is fully paid for all attendees. For their first fundraiser, the teen group wrote, directed, and produced a dinner theatre performance for the larger community that was a big success. When I visited, they were engaged in a dynamic brainstorming discussion to decide on their next fundraiser.

They key difference between self-directed learning centers like Open Connections and other progressive education options is that Open Connections is an alternative *to* school, not simply an alternative school. As registered homeschoolers, parents retain education autonomy and can take advantage of part-time programming tied to children's interests and free from compulsory schooling mandates around attendance, curriculum, and assessment. This grants young people the agency to learn what, when, how, and with whom they want without an adult-imposed agenda. Like adults, young people engaged in self-directed education have the freedom to choose. With the support of their learning community, children and teens are able to decide how to spend their time and to pursue topics that most interest them, sometimes in a structured, classroom way and sometimes not. Their learning is self-determined.

While his peers rest in retirement, Peter Bergson is not slowing down. He is working to expand the vision of unschooling and self-directed education to more families in more places. Now that Open Connections serves nearly one hundred families with twenty-five dedicated staff members, and is almost entirely self-sustaining with an endowment that Peter and his team have been building for over three decades, he recently launched the Natural Creativity Center in the Germantown section of Philadelphia. Peter has long believed that self-directed education should be accessible to all families regardless of socioeconomic background. "As much as I loved nurturing Open Connections into existence over the majority of my career," he tells me, "I always had it in the back of my head that I wanted to make self-directed education available to low-income and moderate-income families." While he has tried tirelessly over the years to make Open Connections accessible to all families regardless of ability to pay, he knew that bringing an unschooling center to the heart of the city was the best way to reach underprivileged families.

In January 2016, Natural Creativity opened in the rented education space of a local church. It currently serves as a natural learning incubator for about twenty young people from the surrounding neighborhoods, most of whom have subsidized tuition. Like Open Connections, all of the young people at Natural Creativity are registered homeschoolers, with the center serving as a part-time complement to the learning that they are already engaged in at their homes and in their larger community. Peter views unschooling resource centers as spaces that can augment an individual's personal learning process, but the responsibility for education rests with the individual child. As Peter explains: "Education is an internal process within the individual. I can't give you an education; it's not a product. I can't make you think, I can't motivate you. All of those things are the result of internal decisions and connections. Knowing yourself and what you want are largely neglected in conventional, structured schooling."

Natural Creativity focuses on facilitating the process of learning, with the "product" left up to each individual. Mountains of books and materials line the colorful walls. A gigantic set of Cuisenaire counting rods consumes the entirety of the coffee table at the center of the room, surrounded by plush couches. Hand-built wooden play structures filled with fluffy pillows and mats create quiet nooks for reading and resting. There is a room dedicated to messy science experiments, a full wood-shop with both hand tools and more advanced machines, and a large art room where a community artist frequently leads classes for those who are interested. When I first visited Natural Creativity, a big game

of Dungeons and Dragons (D&D) was underway in another room, facilitated by a young adult facilitator. A young girl was sitting on one of the
couches knitting with bulky purple yarn while another young person in
pink-socked feet worked at one of the nearby sewing machines. A small
group of kids was playing cribbage nearby.

A highly diverse team of adult staff members helps when needed.
During my visit, this help ranged from being available near the D&D
game, to helping kids assemble a giant crossword puzzle on the art table,
to searching for a young child's missing doll, to accompanying a group
to the downstairs gymnasium. A big barrier for some of the center's
young people, several of whom live in significant economic distress, is
transportation. When a city bus didn't show up, one of the staff members
drove to pick up a young person at her home and bring her to the center
so she could continue with the ongoing D&D game that captivated her.

Young people at Natural Creativity are fully in charge of their own
learning and doing, with resources and facilitators available to support
them. They can attend as they choose, participate in a classes or opt
out, and get immersed in a project without interruption. They decide
how they will spend their time, whether or not they need or want help,
and what their current and future goals may be. They are not graded or
assessed. Their learning doesn't fit into specific subject silos or content
areas to cover. They don't look to teachers to tell them what to do, what
to learn; they learn what and how they want, using the resources available and with grown-ups serving as mentors and facilitators. As Holt
writes in *Learning All the Time*:

> We can best help children learn, not by deciding what we think
> they should learn and thinking of ingenious ways to teach it
> to them, but by making the world, as far as we can, accessible
> to them, paying serious attention to what they do, answering
> their questions—if they have any—and helping them explore
> the things they are most interested in.[2]

In just a short time, Peter is already seeing a positive impact. One
girl arrived at Natural Creativity from public school at age fourteen and,
according to Peter, was "basically illiterate." The engaging learning space,

with helpful facilitators noticing her interests and connecting her to resources, enabled her literacy skills to dramatically improve in a fairly short time. Peter says, "Children will learn to read and figure out rules of phonics by seeing patterns in the words that have meaning to them." Once this teenager saw reading as a tool to help her explore interests that were personally meaningful, her literacy flourished. Another adolescent arrived at the center from a local public charter school after being bullied and beaten at school. This teen found a much more nurturing, compassionate learning environment at Natural Creativity, where individuality and originality are treasured.

Natural learning is authentic and empowering. It taps into the innate, self-educative capacity of humans to investigate and make sense of their world. For children who have never been schooled, their curiosity and instinctual drive to learn about their world continue into adolescence and adulthood. For schooled children who leave school and join an unschooling center like Open Connections or Natural Creativity, their creative spark can be relit. Once these formerly schooled children realize that they are, in fact, in charge of their own learning and doing, without adult coercion, they are inspired to learn without waiting to be taught. As Peter says: "We see what gets traded off with the 'teach-em, test-em' approach, and we place a higher priority on the self-directed learning approach and the creative process."

Learning Is Natural, School Is Optional

While Peter Bergson and his wife were expanding Open Connections in the early 1990s, Ken Danford was growing increasingly disillusioned with his role as a teacher in a public middle school. Teaching eighth-grade social studies, he knew there were deep issues with conventional schooling, but he initially clung to the belief that if only certain conditions were met, then things would get better. If only the school had more money, if only they had better curriculum, he thought, then school wouldn't be so bad. While he was waiting for schooling to improve, a colleague urged him to read Grace Llewellyn's book *The Teenage Liberation Handbook: How to Quit School and Get a Real Life*. Ken resisted at first because it was related to homeschooling, but once he sat down to read it he had a major revelation:

I read it in a night and it was magical. Here were kids who
don't go to school and they thrive. I couldn't believe that kids
could actually learn without teachers like me. I realized that the
major issue was that my students didn't want to be at school.
I was forcing them to learn and do things that they didn't want
to learn and do. As teachers, we were making kids' lives worse.
I really started to question it.

Ken decided to leave his teaching job in 1996 and launch North
Star, a self-directed learning center for teenagers in western Massachusetts. Along with his colleague Joshua Hornick, who also left his job as
a public middle school teacher, Ken opened the center as a community
resource to help kids quit school and homeschool instead. "It's really
unschooling," says Ken, "but homeschooling is the legal designation
that makes self-directed learning possible." The founders envisioned
North Star as a community center where kids could gather, hang out,
take trips together, and participate in classes or tutoring if they wanted.
There would be no grades, no attendance taking. Teens wouldn't be
compelled to be there and wouldn't be forced to do anything in particular while there. Ken knew that he wanted the center to be a part-time
resource for families and teens—not a full-time alternative school. As
local teens filled the space, many of them spent their non-center days
in jobs and internships throughout the community, in interest-based
activities and community athletics, or taking community college classes
and auditing classes at several local colleges and universities.

Ken began to see profound changes in many of the teens who came
to the center. Often deeply unhappy and feeling trapped in conventional
schooling, these teens began to regain their creativity, individuality, and
enjoyment of learning once they were provided with freedom and a
coercion-free community. "It's the power of the unschooling approach,"
says Ken. "It's treating people with basic respect, asking them what they
want to do—and taking no for an answer. This shouldn't be particularly
revolutionary, but it is. Once the teens are happy, they start considering
what they want to do, what risks they want to take. Happiness precedes
accomplishment."

Ken finds that the teens intuitively understand this process; it's the parents who often need more hand holding. He recalls several occasions where parents pulled their teens from school and enrolled them at North Star. Ken says: "They'll say to me, 'You've saved my kid! Thank you! Our family is so much better now; you're awesome! So . . . now what about math?'" He typically responds by telling these anxious parents that it's only been a few months; they should try to relax, trust the natural learning process, and give their child abundant time to deschool from years of forced education. Sometimes parents can do this and sometimes they can't. Many of the educators I spoke with indicated a wide range in parental commitment to unschooling and self-directed education, with some parents really embracing it and others not. For those parents who don't, they often use a self-directed learning center as the "unstructured" activity of the week, replicating school and pushing formal academics on other days. It's not surprising that the parents most resistant to the philosophy of unschooling are the ones most likely to reenroll their kids in a conventional school.

Since its opening, North Star has worked with over five hundred teens as an alternative to school. Many of them have gone on to successful and fulfilling lives and careers, often being accepted to some of the country's most competitive colleges and universities. As Ken learned: "Kids don't need schools. School is an outmoded concept." The center's motto—learning is natural, school is optional—reflects this belief that schooling is not the only way to be educated. In 2007, North Star hosted its first weekend workshop to share its innovative education model with others. These workshops grew and expanded over the following years and ultimately led to the creation of Liberated Learners, a nonprofit organization that works with parents and educators to launch North Star–inspired self-directed learning centers in their own communities. These new unschooling centers are now sprouting worldwide.

Learn Life

Driving along the highway in 2013, George Popham spotted a sign: North Star: Self-Directed Learning for Teens. He knew nothing about this place but made the quick decision to swerve off at the next exit to see what it was about. A public school teacher, George was dismayed by what he saw in school and wanted to help create a new educational space for adolescents. He wasn't sure what he could do or where to look for answers. "So many otherwise bright, talented students I worked with hated the schooling process and many developed an active aversion to learning," he tells me. "I was also very disturbed by the toxic power relations between students and teachers; so much of the job required rigidly controlling students. It was clear to me that the whole thing was killing students' natural creativity and intrinsic enthusiasm, and I thought there just had to be some other way of doing education."

When George pulled off the highway to visit North Star and learned about Liberated Learners, he was captivated. He quit his teaching job and in 2014 launched Bay State Learning Center with an initial cohort of over twenty young people, ages ten through nineteen, in the rented education space of a large suburban church. With a motto of "Learn Life," Bay State has grown and expanded from a part-time alternative to school to up to five days a week for those families that need a full-time option. Like other self-directed learning centers, the young people who attend Bay State are registered homeschoolers whose parents assume responsibility for their child's overall education.

During one of my visits to the center, a group of kids was working together in the makerspace, using tools and technology—including the center's new 3-D printer—to create and invent. Some kids gathered for a class on dystopian literature led by one of the adult facilitators. I sat down on a well-worn couch and chatted with some of the teenage boys who were playing the Minecraft video game on their phones or gaming on their laptops. At this center, there are no limits on screens and young people are free to spend their time however they choose. For the young people who come from conventional schooling, this freedom can seem almost too good to be true.

According to George, the deschooling process for formerly schooled young people can take a long time. The process varies by individual, frequently tied to how much trauma schooling may have caused, but George finds a common pattern. First, the young people are typically very quiet and withdrawn, with an obvious suspicion and distrust of adults. "It's as if they are just waiting," he says. "They are wondering: 'OK, when do you start messing with me? When do you start running my life? How long?'" They gradually see that this is not an alternative school; it is not a school at all. They can sit around and do nothing, play on their phones, nap, and no one will try to stop them.

Next, says George, as they emerge from their schooled stupor they start socializing with the other young people at the center. They will sit on the couch with their phone, but they will talk more and more to the other kids. This could go on for months, says George, much to the astonishment of many worried parents. Gradually, the social piece builds to become a primary part of a young person's day. Then a group of the kid's peers will get up and go to one of the many optional classes offered at the center. One day, the previously withdrawn kid will go with them. She will begin to see that she is, in fact, the one in charge of her own life and learning and will start to trust adults. "They discover they can have a relationship with an adult that's not a power relationship," say George. "They realize that here are adults who are genuinely interested in them as people."

The deschooling process typically extends to the child's home life, where relationships with parents and other family members dramatically improve. "There is generally less conflict at home," George says. "Some of this is due to less pressure from school, fewer calls from the principal, less wrangling with parents over homework and how a kid spends his time. Some of it is that the child is less reactive, less stressed. Often parents can't see the kinds of pressures that school exerts."

The Bay State team is getting good results. Some of the young people begin taking community college classes and doing internships as they get older, shrinking their time at the center to just a couple of days a week. Some of them get immersed in complicated, in-depth projects that they initiate independently, like a sixteen-year-old boy who shared with me the science fiction film that he and his peers wrote and produced. Some of them get so immersed in the content of the optional classes offered that they explore and read more about the topic on their own. Several of the center's attendees have now gone on to college and careers, taking with them a renewed sense of control over their own future. One fourteen-year-old boy I spoke with said that coming to Bay State three years earlier was a significant improvement over school. He said: "At school, I was forced to learn stuff that I wasn't interested in, stuff I already knew. Here, I have the freedom to learn how I want, when I want, whatever I want with teachers who are more like friends than superiors."

Self-directed learning centers help to make unschooling a realistic option for more families and provide an important stepping stone from a schooled life to an unschooled one. Each center I visited throughout the country has its own community culture, and its own requirements and expectations. Some, like Open Connections, have a no-screen policy, while others like Bay State allow unlimited screen use. Natural Creativity is in the heart of a major city, while North Star is more rural. Despite their nuances, each unschooling center shares a commitment to cultivating natural learning within a noncoercive, supportive, resource-rich environment. Their founders also understand that parents are the ones most responsible for overseeing their children's education. These centers can assist parents in facilitating self-directed learning, but it's the parents who are empowered. For some families, this complementary support is just what they need to make unschooling work; for other families, a full-time "unschooling school," like those described in the next chapter, is a better option.

Unschooling Tips

- **Investigate self-directed learning centers near you.** Connect with your local homeschooling community to explore various co-ops and collectives or check out the Alliance for Self-Directed Education (http://self-directed.org) for an updated list of learning centers and unschooling schools worldwide.

- **Start your own!** Take the initiative to create a community-based, noncoercive learning space in your neighborhood. Decide on your vision, investigate local regulatory requirements, determine community interest, gather founding families, scope out a space, and put up your shingle!

Organizations like Liberated Learners, Inc. (http://liberatedlearners.net) and Agile Learning Centers (http://agilelearningcenters.org) can provide start-up guidance and direction.

• **See it as a resource, not a replacement**. A self-directed learning center should ideally complement your child's unschooling lifestyle. It may offer a consistent social group, access to certain classes and materials and mentors, and a neutral space for learning and growth, but it should not replace the immersive learning your unschooled child is able to do within the larger community. Unlike schools, learning centers are resources for recognized homeschooling families who assume the full responsibility for a child's education.

8

Unschooling Schools

"There is no greater education than one that is self-driven."

—Neil deGrasse Tyson[1]

"NINE-YEAR-OLDS ARE POWERFUL," ANNOUNCES A boy in socked feet carrying an iPad as I walk into the foyer of the Agile Learning Center in New York City (ALC-NYC). He meant it. Powerful is an apt description for the kind of unschooling happening at ALC-NYC. Located on the top floor of the one-hundred-year-old Church of the Good Neighbor building in Harlem, ALC-NYC is a warm and welcoming space where kids ages five to eighteen take responsibility for their own education.

Unlike the self-directed learning centers described in the previous chapter, where young people are legally recognized as homeschoolers and may attend full- or part-time, ALC-NYC is a full-time, licensed independent school. In New York, that licensing means that the school complies with simple health and safety requirements, provides immunization reports, conducts periodic fire drills, ensures there is no asbestos on the property, and tracks attendance to be in compliance with state compulsory schooling laws. Beyond these administrative requirements, unschooling schools like ALC-NYC are free to operate however they choose, determining their own education plan and being exempt from state curriculum directives and testing requirements. For ALC-NYC, that plan is curriculum-free and entirely self-directed, with young people deciding how to spend their time each day. Very little is required of attendees except for basic community responsibilities like participating in school meetings and helping to clean up the space at the end of each day. In fact, before enrolling their child, parents must read and accept the following statement to make sure they understand what self-directed education really means:

> I understand that the ALC provides a real-world learning environment for students to develop self-direction, self-motivation and self-knowledge and as such never requires students to attend specific classes or produce specific work. The school will support students' requests for learning, but does not direct learning activities according to any curriculum. The School Meeting may make certain activities mandatory for the smooth operation of the school. Currently these are: morning meetings, end of day meetings, clean-up, fire drills, and appearing when a complaint has been filed. Beyond these, the choices are up to each child.

I wander around the light-filled, comfortable urban space. In one room, kids are building a fort out of pillows from a nearby couch. In another, kids are on one of the desktop computers or a handheld device playing Minecraft or a similar video game. In the room designated as the library, a girl is reading in a cozy corner. No one is wearing shoes and everyone is free to roam. There is a lot of laughing and chatting and playing, but nothing seems chaotic or loud. A math class is taking place in a sunny room with a long table. An adult is facilitating the class, using a mix of resources including Khan Academy. As I pop in and out of the handful of rooms, making my way toward the large, open kitchen area nestled in back, I am struck by a single thought: This looks just like unschooling at my house—pillow forts and all.

In his 1987 book, *Free at Last*, Daniel Greenberg describes what the Sudbury Valley School he cofounded is like. He writes: "The place doesn't look or feel like a school at all. The standard 'school cues' are missing. It looks more like a home, with many persons going about their varied activities in a determined, yet relaxed, manner."[2] ALC-NYC has this same feeling, reminding me of how my kids go about their daily activities, sometimes taking classes or doing what looks to others like "academic" work, but often just playing, talking, exploring, eating, reading, crafting, and creating. The language is also different from conventional schooling. The term "teacher" doesn't exist here. Although they may lead classes on specific topics, adults at ALC-NYC are referred to as facilitators or staff members or simply grown-ups. Kids call them by their first names.

I sit down with Melody Compo, one of the facilitators, at the kitchen table. In the room with us are a few kids sitting on a nearby couch, reading or playing on a smartphone. One facilitator sits at the table eating lunch, while another reads a book in a nearby chair. Young people come in and out, sometimes with questions for the adults or to share something cool they are working on, and sometimes to grab a seat at the table to eat their lunch or chat with a friend.

While talking with me, Mel whittles a snowflake pattern onto a small wooden block that she holds in her hand. She talks about her own ongoing deschooling process since coming to ALC-NYC. Mel first became interested in John Dewey and his progressive education ideas in college, but she then took a job in corporate America that she found to be unrewarding. At a party, she bumped into a former college classmate and current ALC-NYC staff member and learned that the school was hiring. Eager for a new challenge, and to reengage with her earlier interest in alternative education, she enthusiastically accepted the job offer that followed. "It's been a big deschooling process for me," says Mel. "I was raised in a system of right answers. I am learning here that there is often not a right answer." Not long before coming to ALC-NYC, Mel had come out as queer and was questioning much about the way she was taught about the world. The conveyor belt of school to college to job began to seem empty and unfulfilling. "I checked every box, got good grades, made the dean's list, had a good job, but I wasn't happy," says Mel. "I felt failed by the system in a way that I hadn't before in my life."

Joining the ALC-NYC community reinvigorated Mel and helped her to see that self-directed education—allowing young people to be in charge of their own life and learning—was an essential component to ensuring a happy and fulfilled life. "It is a very healing place," she says.

"We see it with our parents and our new students. There is this sense of really seeing people for who they are, really knowing them. There is no rush, no right answer. The work we are doing here is really important." At first, Mel didn't know how to work in such a space. She kept waiting to be told what to do, asking for permission to do things. It took her a while to realize that, like the young people who attend ALC-NYC, she was empowered to be self-directed. One day, she decided to rearrange and improve the library. It became her first mission, something she tackled with great energy and joy, realizing that she could engage in activities at ALC-NYC that mattered to her. "I had this ownership! That was the first moment that I really got what this place is all about."

From there, Mel threw herself into other activities that she found personally rewarding and reconnected with many buried interests. She read aloud some of her favorite books, like *Lord of the Rings, Harry Potter*, and the *Golden Compass*, to kids who wanted to listen. She watched Star Wars movies with them, played board games, chatted about current events and cultural trends. She now offers various optional weekly classes, ranging from printmaking to creative writing. She accompanies kids who want to go on field trips around the city to museums, parks, and historical sites. She helps to coordinate some of the other classes that are offered each week at ALC-NYC. These classes are frequently taught by outside volunteers with a special interest or expertise, such as Japanese language or fermentation.

While Mel and I chat, kids come in and out of the kitchen. Some grab their coats and head to the park around the corner. Others go to their favorite deli a couple of blocks away to grab lunch. I ask Mel about this freedom to come and go. She explains that each parent decides for his or her child what level of supervision and off-campus freedom to allow. The facilitators don't make the rules, but they will respect whatever expectations the parents have for their child. Regardless of supervision expectations, there is a lot of off-campus time for most kids, with facilitators frequently accompanying them to nearby parks or going on subway trips to various city destinations. Learning in and from the city is a main priority for the ALC-NYC staff as well as for the kids and parents.

Ryan Shollenberger, the school's codirector, tells me a bit more about the role of adults at ALC-NYC. He talks about the unschooling spectrum: the wide interpretation of A. S. Neill's idea of "freedom, not license," or what they at ALC call "maximum support with minimum interference." On one end of the spectrum is no influence on children's learning and doing, and on the other end is more direct influence on their learning and doing. Ryan says ALC-NYC strives to be in the middle. "We try to balance the freedom of the individual with the needs of the community," he says. Ryan explains that at ALC-NYC kids are free to do whatever they want, within the community agreements that they accept. For instance, Ryan recalls how one child wanted to do fire play. He wanted to learn to start fires and watch various things burn. License would be to let the child go with no influence. Freedom, not license, involved allowing the child to find a way to play with fire that wouldn't violate building codes and threaten the safety of other community members. The child took his fire play outside on the school's expansive fire escape, with plenty of water available and an adult facilitator observing nearby.

Young people at ALC-NYC—and adults—are encouraged to be continually mindful of personal goals, or intentions as they call them, to make sure that they can be fully supported by the community and the facilitators. ALC-NYC strives to be a noncoercive learning space, while acknowledging that adults do have an important role in supporting kids' learning and development. "Kids have thousands of influences on them every day outside of school—television, billboards, relatives, and so on. We do make suggestions, we do have class offerings based on what kids are interested in. We don't think that standing back and avoiding suggestions or offerings is doing them a service." The most critical feature of the unschooling philosophy, however, is the ability to say no, to opt out. Ryan and the ALC-NYC team take noncoercion very seriously. Aside from the key community tenets around respect and responsibility, which all young people know about when joining, there are very few rules or requirements. "Facilitators are available, resources and classes are offered, but if they're not interested, that's cool," says Ryan. "It's all about relationships," he adds.

Agile Learning Centers are a rapidly growing network of self-directed schools and homeschool collectives throughout the United States and around the world. Two of the organization's founders, Tomis Parker and Nancy Tilton, who lead a bustling ALC school in Charlotte, North Carolina, are among a growing group of Agile Learning facilitators who help other parents and educators launch similar communities in their hometowns. They provide the vision—an intentional community of self-directed learners—and offer start-up guidance, marketing materials, and suggestions on building a like-minded tribe. ALCs share the same underlying pedagogical foundation, while the tools and practices are designed to continuously evolve and adapt to meet the needs of each community using them. Some function as part-time self-directed learning centers for homeschoolers, while others, like ALC-NYC, are full-fledged schools. Initially introduced in New York by Arthur Brock, the ALC educational model is inspired by the democratic/free school and unschooling movements, intentional communities, and the agile software movement. Beginning in the 1990s, and soaring throughout the 2000s, agile software development embraced a set of practices and principles that sought to replace a rigid, linear, static process of software creation with a much more dynamic, collaborative, and adaptive model. These theoretical agile practices are integrated into the Agile Learning Center model, encouraging ongoing intention-setting, teamwork, and continuous reflection. Agility is key.

For many of the ALCs, their intention-setting is closely linked to making self-directed education more accessible to more families. Located in the heart of Harlem, ALC-NYC is demographically reflective of their neighborhood and offers tuition support through a generous sliding scale. Unschooling schools and self-directed learning centers are typically a small fraction of the cost of traditional independent schools, showing that high-quality education can be offered at low cost. Still, ALC-NYC charges tuition, and even the minimum of the tuition scale—$4,500 a year—is prohibitively expensive for some families. The ALC-NYC team tries to find creative ways to raise money to offset tuition costs and support their sliding scale, but the price tag remains steep for some. As Mel explains, "It's hard to make self-directed education accessible because it's not free, and it's not free because we don't take money from the state, because we don't test, because we are self-directed."

There lies a major reason why self-directed education and unschooling are generally outside the purview of public schooling. Conventional evaluation and accountability measures, and a schooling model based on teaching specific content according to a specific curriculum, are often incompatible with a self-directed education model that puts young people in charge of their own learning. Incorporating unschooling ideals into a forced schooling model presents a real challenge, as an earlier generation of education reformers discovered.

The Education Counterculture

During the 1960s and '70s, a flurry of progressive educators sought to integrate more freedom and self-direction into the public schools. Fueled by the countercultural ethos of the time, largely in response to American involvement in the Vietnam War, progressive education ideas and practices gained traction. The open classroom, which educator Herb Kohl writes about in his book by the same name, was an effort to change the structure of schooling to make it less authoritarian. Classroom walls were removed, desks were rearranged into groups over rows, young people were given more freedom, learning was made more interactive. In Philadelphia, Pennsylvania, in 1967, the city's public school system launched its Parkway Program, sometimes known as the "school without walls," in which young people were able to select their own classes and learn throughout various spots across the city, including private businesses, museums, local universities, and public spaces. The Parkway Program embraced the progressive education idea that young people must be intrinsically motivated in order to learn best. High schoolers were given great latitude in their learning, no grades were offered, and assessment was loosely defined. In 1970, the *New York Times* called the Parkway Program "one of the nation's boldest experiments in public education," noting that over ten thousand students applied for only five hundred available slots.[3] Similar education efforts were underway in other cities throughout the country during that tumultuous epoch, with high hopes that schools could revolutionize themselves and alter society's course. Alongside these public school efforts, hundreds of private "free schools" also opened, founded on principles of self-direction, participatory governance, and noncoercion.

Throughout the 1970s, as the counterculture faded and the political climate shifted, many of these progressive education programs fizzled. Classrooms reerected their walls, desks were pushed back into their rows, and the Parkway Program gradually became absorbed into the traditional curriculum of the larger school district. The political energy of the counterculture weakened and the status quo reemerged. A new principal, who previously ran a traditional high school, ultimately took the reins at Parkway and made it virtually indistinguishable from the district's other schools.[4] Even most of the independent free schools folded throughout the 1970s as the Vietnam War ended and the counterculture's momentum waned. Ron Miller writes in *Free Schools, Free People* that "when, in the 1970s, American politics stabilized and hippie fashions, rock music, natural foods, and other trappings of the counterculture were transformed into commercial commodities, the tension between consciousness and politics, between personal wholeness and social change, developed into a split, and radical pedagogy was largely divided into its constituent elements."[5]

Many efforts to restructure learning around less coercive education ideals died amid a "back to basics" push, but a few survived and thrived. In Colorado, the Jefferson County Open School is a public school that was founded in 1969 on the open classroom ideals of self-directed learning, choice, autonomy, and nonstandardization. Now almost fifty years later, the school continues to practice these values, serving as an inspiring model for conventional schooling alternatives within the public school system. Also in 1969, the Albany Free School in New York opened as an independent school and has endured, paving the way for other modern free schools across the United States. Similarly, the Sudbury Valley School celebrated its half-century anniversary in 2018. Founded in 1968, Sudbury Valley now acts as a beacon for parents and educators eager to create new, self-directed, self-governing schools, with dozens of Sudbury-inspired democratic schools operating around the world. Finally, and perhaps most significantly, homeschooling and unschooling began their contemporary revival and expansion in the wake of the counterculture movement, as parents sought more sustainable, family-centered alternatives to conventional schooling.

A major criticism of the free schools that sprouted during the 1960s and '70s—and to some extent today—is that they remain available only to the privileged few. As progressive education reformer Jonathan Kozol wrote in his 1972 book, *Free Schools*: "In my belief, an isolated upper-class rural Free School for the children of the white and rich within a land like the United States and in a time of torment such as 1972, is a great deal too much like a sandbox for the children of the SS Guards at Auschwitz."[6] Many of today's free school leaders take great efforts to challenge that criticism, seeking ways to make noncoercive, self-directed education available to as many young people as possible.

Where Children Are Free

Located in a classic brownstone on a busy, tree-lined street, the Brooklyn Free School (BFS) in New York City balances unschooling ideals, democratic decision-making, and an unrelenting commitment to education for social justice. Their numbers reflect their efforts: During the 2017–18 school year, over 90 percent of BFS's eighty students were on sliding-scale tuition, and 50 percent of the students were African American, Hispanic, Asian, or multiracial. School administrators say that more than one-quarter of the children, who range from pre-K students to high schoolers, would be placed outside of mainstream classrooms in conventional schools due to learning differences. Sixty percent of the school's staff members are nonwhite. A licensed independent school, BFS was founded in 2004 by Alan Berger, a former public school assistant principal. It was influenced by the philosophy and practices of the Albany Free School, the country's oldest urban free school, as well as other self-directed democratic free schools. Until BFS opened, there hadn't been a free school in New York City since 1975, when the Fifteenth Street School shuttered.

At BFS, like at Agile Learning Centers and the other unschooling schools and centers described in these pages, there are no required classes, no tests, and no grades. Classes are offered, sprouting from the kids' own interests. Kids come and go as they please, and much of their time is spent outside of the school at local parks, on field trips around the city, doing internships, and engaging in external community service activities. Despite not offering a standard curriculum and letter grades, BFS graduates have not had trouble getting accepted into colleges of their choice. When I asked my young tour guides, who both came to BFS from more conventional schools, what they like most about their school they replied almost in unison: "Freedom." Indeed, the school's motto is: "Where children are free."

Age mixing is not only encouraged but expected and treasured. The overwhelming attitude among unschooling and self-directed education advocates is that allowing for natural, unforced interactions among children of different ages leads to the most powerful learning. Segregating young people by age is a product of the factory schooling model, designed for efficiency and order. Conversely, age mixing allows young people to interact with others more naturally, often tied to shared interests and compatibility. Unschoolers reject the idea that five-year-olds should only play with other five-year-olds and middle schoolers should only interact with their same-age peers. These arbitrary distinctions don't exist within a natural learning framework. Just as I don't interact with only other forty-one-year-olds, children shouldn't be forced to interact with only those who share their birth year. Peer learning cannot be so neatly boxed. At BFS, the little kids learn from the older ones, not in a top-down, instructional way but by simply being around them, observing and imitating and asking questions. The older students likewise learn from the younger ones, recognizing their natural place as role models and regulating their behavior accordingly. Older kids don't see younger kids as a burden, and younger kids don't see older ones as intimidating. They learn together, in community.

During my visit to BFS, I sat down with Noleca Radway, the school's director. Noleca's background is in progressive education, but it wasn't until she was searching for a school for her own daughter that she discovered self-directed education. Her daughter began attending BFS in 2010, and Noleca soon joined the staff as a counselor and later became the executive director. One of the real strengths of the school, according to Noleca, is its focus on democratic principles of self-governance. The students and staff members have equal votes and all decisions around school governance, hiring, firing, policies and procedures, classes offered, and expectations and responsibilities are decided through weekly town meeting–type discussions and democratic voting by all members of the school community. This is not the "student council" model that I remember from public school. This is true democratic self-governance, where all rules, decisions, and practices are made jointly by students and staff. As she became more involved with the school over the years, Noleca observed a real disconnect. "We had this diverse group of students, but the staff was all white." She and others began to ask: "How are we practicing democracy if we're not talking about power and privilege?" The message resonated, and the school members began to marry the ideals of democratic free schooling with social justice work. They hired a highly diverse group of staff members and committed to tackling larger social justice issues within their school community, as well as more globally.

Even though they vote equally through their democratic decision-making process, adults still play a vital role within the BFS community. As Noleca says: "We are in partnership with young people. This idea that adults don't have a role in self-directed education is irresponsible. We offer a suite of courses, we respect teachers and educators, we offer suggestions." Noleca explains that parents are ultimately responsible for their children's education. The school works with parents to ensure that young people are highly literate and numerate, within a model of self-directed, noncoercive education. "If we have a kid who says he wants to go to NYU," says Noleca, "then we'll say OK you need to know math." As in any democracy, the BFS community has its occasional conflicts, but the members work them out through discourse and compromise, believing strongly that young people can only learn how to live in a free and democratic society if they have been allowed such an opportunity throughout childhood and adolescence. In conventional schooling, most young people only learn how to live under authoritarianism. In an unschooling environment focused on freedom and personal responsibility, true democratic ideals can be practiced. As Noleca emphasizes: "Democracy has to be flexible. Rigidity is the opposite of freedom."

Because Life Is Not Standardized

Ben Draper was unschooled until he was eight. It was the early 1980s and Holt's *Growing Without Schooling* newsletter had been instrumental in supporting the expanding homeschooling movement. Ben's mother, Carol, had read Holt's *How Children Fail* years earlier when she was in college studying to be a teacher. It painted a vision for how learning could be, should be, and revealed the ways that conventional schooling practices frequently fail children. She worked as a fourth-grade and sixth-grade public elementary school teacher, trying to inject Holt's philosophy of child-centered, interest-led learning into her classroom, but she became increasingly frustrated by the rigidity of conventional schooling. Ultimately, she left teaching and unschooled her kids, drawing on inspiration from *Growing Without Schooling* and Holt's other writings. Ben remembers visiting Holt in his Boston office alongside his mom, who was seeking advice on how to convince her husband that unschooling works.

Unschooling suited Ben for much of his early childhood, but by the time he was eight, many of his homeschooled peers had gone off to school and he was getting bored. His mom took him to visit the Sudbury Valley School in Framingham, Massachusetts, and he was enchanted. It was a great fit for him, and he felt immediately comfortable in this type of self-directed learning environment. He spent the remaining years of his childhood and adolescence there, while his mom drove him an hour and a half each way every day. At Sudbury Valley, Ben pursued his interests. Nothing was forced and a child was free to do whatever he chose, as long as his freedom didn't impede on anyone else's. Ben skateboarded a lot and played the guitar. He started painting. He was a late reader, not becoming interested or proficient in reading until his teen years. He later graduated from Sudbury Valley, got easily accepted to various colleges, attended Tufts University in Boston, and became an accomplished artist—with some of his paintings appearing in the contemporary art wing of Boston's Museum of Fine Arts and other galleries.

Today, Ben runs the Macomber Center, a self-directed learning center for homeschoolers located near the Sudbury Valley School in Massachusetts, where he strives to create a free, noncoercive, supportive learning space like the one he so deeply valued as a child. Ben says:

The radical idea that kids need to be handed complete control of their own education is foreign to most parents. Our mission is to make sure that the families who really do want to give their kids freedom have a rich, vibrant community where their kids can thrive. I also feel that it is my responsibility to provide encouragement and support to those parents who are courageous enough to take this leap into the unknown.

Inspired by his years at Sudbury Valley, Ben incorporates many of the school's ideals into his own work at the center and in his own parenting of two young children. A primary ideal of self-directed education is simply letting children be who they are rather than molding them to become something else. It is about supporting young people's natural gifts and emerging interests, not using these as a launching pad toward some amorphous future. It is about now, not later. Daniel Greenberg writes about the graduates of Sudbury Valley: "Our greatest gift to them was to let them be. By not robbing them of what was truly their own, we did more for each one than an army of more 'helpful' people could ever have done."[7]

In 1986, researchers evaluated the outcomes of Sudbury Valley School graduates. Their survey findings, published in the peer-reviewed *American Journal of Education*, reveal that despite no curriculum or assessment or adult-driven expectations whatsoever, Sudbury Valley graduates do well in the "real world." Those who wanted to went on to higher education and, despite having no transcripts, record of academic work, or test results from Sudbury Valley, they managed to get accepted to college and pursue graduate school study if they chose. For some of these Sudbury Valley School graduates, college may have been their first exposure to formal classes and exams; yet, according to the survey results, none of these graduates noted any difficulty adjusting to the formal structure of college classes. The survey also found that Sudbury Valley School graduates pursued a wide variety of careers in many different industries and professions. Many of the respondents indicated that these careers were directly tied to their interests, and that they had a jumpstart on their current careers owing to the ample time they spent pursuing their career-related interests as students at Sudbury Valley.[8]

Two additional reports of Sudbury Valley School graduates, conducted by the school itself in 1992 and 2005, revealed similar findings.[9] Without conventional schooling, when fully supported in self-directed learning environments, young people can thrive.

The Sudbury Valley School continues to offer an education framework that appeals to both parents and educators. Across the globe, Sudbury-inspired schools have sprouted, focused on non-compulsory learning and democratic self governance. For Melissa Bradford, a former public school science teacher, the Sudbury model seemed like an ideal learning environment for her two young children. When they were toddlers, she created a small, Sudbury-style school. She later unschooled them, forming an unschooling co-op with dozens of other local families. In 2008, when her children were thirteen and eleven, she founded the Tallgrass Sudbury School in suburban Chicago, Illinois. Her kids remained at Tallgrass through their teen years. Now in their twenties, her daughter works at a university and her son is training to be a nurse.

Located directly across the street from the town's public junior high school, Tallgrass is nestled in the spacious and inviting education space of a quaint church building. The sign by the entrance announces its vision, that learning shouldn't be standardized "because life is not standardized."

On my first visit to Tallgrass, I arrived at nine in the morning, but many of the young people didn't stroll in until after ten. To be in compliance with state compulsory schooling statutes as a recognized independent school, Tallgrass students, who range in age from five to eighteen, are expected to attend school for at least five hours a day, five days a week. Much of that time, however, can be off-campus, exploring the surrounding neighborhood, going to the public library or a local restaurant or park, or trekking into the city for the day. Unlike at ALC, where parents determine the level of off-campus privileges allowed for their children, at Tallgrass the community decides together. Kids are "certified" by other kids and staff members, with various levels of unsupervised, off-campus privileges. These levels range from being able to play on the outside grounds of the school unsupervised, to going off-campus to various approved locations, to the highest level of going anywhere they want, without restrictions—including to downtown Chicago.

A key tenet of the Sudbury model of self-directed education, and of democratic education in general, is self governance. The young people have just as much of a say in how the school runs as the staff members, and all decision making occurs at a weekly school meeting. All school members are asked to attend the first five minutes of the meeting, but after that they are free to leave if they choose. At the school meeting I observed, the members shared subcommittee reports on various topics, ranging from finances to admissions to marketing. They reviewed reports of the school's judicial committee, an elected group of students and staff that meets several times a week to address any interpersonal conflicts or rule breaches and to issue any reprimands. All members of the school community set the rules, and new students must agree to them when joining. Enforcement is also community driven, and all warnings or punishments are governed by the judicial committee. Democracy can be hard, and places like Tallgrass believe that the best way to teach democracy is to have young people live it, becoming fully immersed in democratic decision making and self governance.

Another agenda item at the school meeting I observed was the issue of classes. Tallgrass, like similar unschooling schools, downplays the importance of classes, acknowledging that classes are often tied to a schooled idea of how people learn, and not a more organic learning approach. The large calendar in one of the main gathering spaces lists weekly classes in Spanish and math led by Tallgrass staff members. They, like nearly everything at Tallgrass, are always optional and community initiated. Occasionally volunteers from outside the school offer classes in various topics, such as architecture and costume design. At the school meeting, the group talked about how these volunteer-run classes tend to be hit-or-miss, with some of the classes quite popular and well attended and others not so much. The group had a thoughtful discussion about the need to be respectful toward volunteers who are offering their time and expertise, while also ensuring that learning is noncoercive. A key decision was to be more discerning when suggesting class offerings and to be more candid with potential volunteer instructors about expectations and the ideals of noncoercive, self-directed learning.

After the meeting, the young people scattered to one of the many rooms and cozy corners available to them in this relaxed and inviting space. Some kids played video games together in a room set up with a gaming console. Some kids read books in the library or the art room. Some kids sang with the karaoke machine that one girl brought from home. Some kids did cartwheels on the rubber mats they laid out on the floor of one of the larger, wide-open rooms. I sat down in the kitchen with several of the younger girls who had gathered to eat lunch. They were talkative and welcoming, with none of the aloofness that tweens sometimes display. They asked about my research, about unschooling, and told me more about the culture of their school. Freedom was a common denominator, with the girls sharing how they spend their time in the building and off-campus during the day, following their own interests and learning in community with others.

I noticed, too, that the adult staff members clearly had a role among all of this self-direction. The young people talked to the adults easily, asked questions, sought assistance, laughed, and joked. One boy walked in and sat by himself for a while with his winter coat still on, eyes turned downward. A staff member approached him, sat beside him and gently put her arm on his shoulder, speaking in soft tones. After checking in with him, she left. Soon, the boy was joined by another young person who joked with him, and eventually the boy took off his coat and settled in. Elizabeth Lund, one of the adult staff members explained: "The role of adults varies. I would say that half the time we are focused on administration, making sure the school is running. The other half of the time we are a resource for the kids, not necessarily for teaching, but sometimes that is a part of it. Mostly, we answer questions, help with problems. A kid might say: I have this problem. How should I handle it?"

Elizabeth's view on the role of adults is consistent with unschooling in its many forms, whether in homes or in self-directed centers or schools. Adults spend part of the time keeping everything running smoothly, and part of the time acting as a resource for learning, exploring, and problem solving. Adults hold the space for natural learning by tending both the space and the learners within it. They do this without judgment, without coercion, in a spirit of community and care. Another Tallgrass staff member, Michael Kaiser-Nyman, adds: "There is no dynamic here of 'I have power over you.' Kids and staff members have shared power. That's also why we don't have bullying. There is no power struggle."

This last point is particularly interesting and represents a common theme in unschooling circles. Bullying is practically nonexistent in learning environments free from coercion. It makes sense. If people—young or old—are placed in environments where they have little freedom and control, this can trigger bullying behaviors; and if those who are being bullied can't freely leave, then hostility may continue indefinitely. Author Kirsten Olson refers to bullying as "an expression of the shadow side of schooling." She writes: "If we create school systems in which compulsion, coercion, hierarchy, and fear of failure are central features of the academic experience, and essential to motivating and controlling students, then the energy from those negative experiences will seek expression."[10] Conventional schooling environments built on compulsion and power fuel bullying. Psychologist Peter Gray reinforces this point, explaining that bullying is rampant in institutions where people are powerless to leave, such as schools and prisons.[11] If compulsion is removed, bullying is far less likely to occur because those being bullied can simply walk away. Similarly, there is less reason to bully others in a noncoercive environment because the would-be bullies are also free. There is nothing to fight against, nothing to try to control. Freedom is a powerful social stabilizer.

Freedom and Responsibility

With freedom comes responsibility. The myth that unschooling and self-directed education create a *Lord of the Flies* culture of chaos and savagery simply doesn't exist because of the emphasis on responsibility—to oneself and others. In a diverse, multiage space, with the support and experience of adult facilitators, the freedom to learn is balanced with a commitment to community. At the Houston Sudbury School in Houston, Texas, their motto of "freedom and responsibility" is etched throughout the school, from their signs to their T-shirts. Everyone takes it seriously. Cara DeBusk is one of the school's founders. A former schoolteacher, she unschooled her daughter for many years before joining with other unschooling parents to create a school inspired by the Sudbury model. The founders wanted a dedicated, neutral space where the young people could create community. Located on a sprawling acre of land in the heart of the city, framed by old horse stables and animal stalls, Houston Sudbury is located in a quirky single-family home leased by the school.

During my visit I spoke with Aryeh Grossman, one of the adult staff members. As a child, Aryeh attended a conventional public school for his elementary years before his mom sought an alternative for middle school. She had discovered A. S. Neill's book *Summerhill* while she was in college studying to be a teacher and its ideals stayed with her. Later, Aryeh's uncle opened the Jerusalem Sudbury School, a government-funded but independently operated Sudbury school in Israel. As Aryeh finished fifth grade in public school, his mom looked for more inno-vative education options. She found the Fairhaven School, a Sudbury school in Maryland that was an hour-and-a-half drive each way. The family made the commute every day for two years until they finally moved closer to the school.

In his book *Like Water* Fairhaven School staff member Mark McCaig writes about the unschooled philosophy—the idea that learning happens naturally, continuously, in both complex and obvious ways rooted in our daily experiences. He says: "While students sometimes engage in tradi-tional academic classes—they've studied Algebra to Zen—most learning is informal and experiential. Our students learn about their lives by taking charge of them and living them fully. In the relative absence of formal classes, life itself becomes the curriculum."[12] For Aryeh, Fairhaven was an extraordinary gift. "It was fantastic," he recollected. "There is no other word to describe it. My whole life in school up to that point had been about other people telling me what to do. Now, that wasn't the case. I was in charge of my education."

Young people find their own interests and talents through self-directed education, and Aryeh gravitated toward the democratic deci-sion-making process and school-meeting approach that is central to the Sudbury model. During one of his first meetings as a student at

Fairhaven, the community was discussing the possibility of banning pocket knives because there were concerns that some members were being unsafe with them. This was revolutionary to Aryeh, who had been one of the safety patrols in his public school charged with taking away any potentially dangerous objects from other students. "This would have been unheard of in public school," says Aryeh of the pocket knives at Fairhaven. The school community voted initially to ban the knives, but Aryeh worked to create an internal certification process that emphasized safety practices and Boy Scout–approved training approaches. With this certification process developed, the school community ultimately voted to once again allow pocket knives. For Aryeh, it was a powerful example of democratic decision making, leadership, and initiative, and the balance of freedom and responsibility. "When people are given that amount of freedom, they own it and they naturally take up the responsibility because they deeply care about the community. It's never chaos."

Aryeh graduated from Fairhaven and began taking community college classes and online courses. "I hadn't had any formal academics since fifth grade," says Aryeh, "but I didn't find my classes to be the least bit difficult." His coursework focused on creative writing, philosophy, and math. Within six months of beginning his coursework, he went from pre-algebra proficiency to college level math. "When you are determined to do something, you can sit down and do it," says Aryeh. As his interest in college-level coursework built, Aryeh's mother lost her job. He put his college classes on hold and got a full-time job to help support his family. He moved to Texas and was working in retail when he heard about a new Sudbury school opening in Houston. He began volunteering. Now a full-time staff member at Houston Sudbury, Aryeh is back to taking part-time college classes in topics that most interest him, particularly writing.

I tell Aryeh that the book I am working on is primarily a parenting book, sharing unschooling ideas from a parent's perspective. What advice does he have for anxious parents who may be uncertain about embracing unschooling for their own children? "Your kids will be fine," he replies. "You won't screw up your kids. That is a parent's main concern—and it is completely valid! If parents don't have that concern, then they might be doing something wrong. They want what is best for their children. I want parents to be totally critical when coming here or exploring these ideas." Aryeh then points to the compelling research on self-directed education and the empirical data on how Sudbury alumni thrive. These findings reinforce that unschooled young people will not only be OK, they may well become deeply happy, skilled, and fulfilled in adulthood. What parent doesn't want that?

Unschooling Tips

• **Check out unschooling schools.** The Alternative Education Resource Organization (www.educationrevolution.org) provides plentiful information on alternative schools (some self-directed and some not) around the world, including programs to help you start your own. The International Democratic Education Network (www.idenetwork.org) offers global resources on self-directed schools.

• **Find like-minded families.** Many unschooling schools begin when a group of committed people gather together to create an alternative to school for their own children. Find others in your community who may want to take this leap with you.

• **Do your homework.** Starting and operating a full-time unschooling school is a lot of work, often with little financial reward or guarantee. Many founders spend years planning and preparing before taking the leap into running a school. Research and visit other unschooling schools that inspire you, and that may be able to help you get started. For example, the original Sudbury Valley School has an extensive online bookstore and starter kit for prospective Sudbury school founders (www.sudval.org).

9

Unschooled Teens

"Collecting data on human learning based on children's behavior in school is like collecting data on killer whales based on their behavior at Sea World."

—Carol Black[1]

CHILDREN OF ALL AGES DESERVE and benefit from the freedom to learn, but unschooling may arguably be more important for teenagers than for any other group. Largely excluded from the authentic world in which they are designed to come of age, most schooled teens crave independence and autonomy. Instead, they are treated like tots, with their daily movements and actions controlled by others. Why should we be surprised that in search of connection to the larger world, many teens gravitate to their smartphones and social media accounts? They long for freedom and community. When we instead restrict their freedom and mandate their participation in a contrived community, we create the conditions for what is widely known as teenage angst: the defiance, moodiness, and risky behavior that we accept as normal adolescence. But it's not normal. Adolescence is not the problem; schooling is.

In his compelling book *Teen 2.0: Saving Our Children and Families from the Torment of Adolescence*, researcher and former editor in chief of *Psychology Today* Dr. Robert Epstein explains that adolescence is largely a social construct. "Driven by evolutionary imperatives established thousands of years ago, the main need a teenager has is to become productive and independent," Epstein writes. "After puberty, if we pretend our teens are still children, we will be unable to meet their most fundamental needs, and we will cause some teens great distress."[2] Some of this distress may be what we accept as the typical tumult of the teen years, but increasingly this suffering manifests in skyrocketing rates of anxiety, depression, and suicide for adolescents. Unlike adults, who have suicide spikes during the warmer months, suicide rates for children and adolescents drop during summertime. Once school resumes in the fall, the suicide rate for young people jumps.[3]

A recent study confirms a high correlation between school attendance and suicidal thoughts and actions. The 2018 study published in the journal *Pediatrics* analyzed hospital admissions data at thirty-two children's hospitals across the country from 2008 through 2015. During that time period, researchers found an alarming increase in hospital admissions for suicidal tendencies and self-harm for children ages five to seventeen, with the largest rise among teenage girls. These suicidal tendencies peaked during back-to-school time each fall.[4] The study's findings shed more light on the rising suicide rate among children, suggesting that school attendance may play a large role. Data from the CDC reveal that between 2007 and 2015, suicide rates doubled for teen girls ages fifteen to nineteen and rose by over 30 percent for teen boys.[5] Particularly alarming is that the suicide rate among ten- to fourteen-year-olds also doubled since 2007, with girls in that age group experiencing the sharpest rise in suicides.[6]

In a separate study on adolescent strife, the American Psychological Association found that school is a main driver of teenage stress, and that teenagers are even more stressed out than adults. The report was based on 2013 survey results of over one thousand teenagers, ages thirteen to seventeen. According to the study, teenagers reported that their school-year stress was significantly unhealthy, with 83 percent of teens saying that school is "a somewhat or significant source of stress," and 27 percent of teens reporting "extreme stress" during the school year. By comparison, the teens' summertime stress levels were strikingly low.[7]

According to Dr. Epstein, teenage distress—whether mild or severe—is a distinctly American phenomenon. He writes: "In more than a hundred cultures around the world, teens have no such difficulties—no depression, no suicide, no crime, no drug use, no conflict with parents. Many cultures don't even have a word for the period of life we call adolescence. Why are American teens in such turmoil?"[8] Epstein goes on to suggest that much of this teenage angst results from the "infantilization" of teens as they are confined and enclosed for much of their adolescence and their actions and thoughts are managed by others.

The term "adolescence" comes from the fifteenth-century Latin word *adolescere*, meaning "to grow up or to grow into maturity." But it wasn't until 1904 that G. Stanley Hall, the first president of the American Psychological Association, coined the term "adolescence" to identify a separate and distinct phase of human development. Hall's fourteen-hundred-page *Adolescence: Its Psychology and Its Relations to Physiology, Anthropology, Sociology, Sex, Crime, Religion and Education* struck a chord with policymakers and educators hoping to expand mass schooling. The book's biggest fans included education policy makers eager to extend the upper limit of the compulsory schooling age.[9] The expansion of compulsory schooling statutes, particularly for teenagers, enclosed young people in schools for much more of their adolescence and may have contributed to the rise of the "typical teenager" stereotype that persists today.

For George Popham, who runs the Bay State Learning Center described earlier, freedom for adolescents has proved to be a potent remedy for teenage strife. Many of the parents and young people who arrive at his center never previously considered unschooling or self-directed education. These were unknowns. Schooling seemed the obvious and accepted path of education. They found Bay State when mounting anxieties or depression brought on by conventional schooling reached an untenable peak. George says:

A huge number of the new students who come to us are presenting some kind of anxiety disorder, and we find that almost all of them are significantly improved within weeks of joining the center. I get calls from therapists asking what we have done! I think

the real story is in what we haven't done. We haven't made all
their choices for them, we haven't structured all of their available
time, and we haven't coerced them into unnaturally regimented
patterns. Everything changes when you take coercion out of the
picture. Teenagers are actually quite happy people by nature.

We assume that teenagers are naturally inclined to behave the way
they do, rather than question the unnatural conditions we create for
them. Teenagers are not innately troubled. The key is to support their
natural development by removing them from restrictive, artificial institutional environments while reintroducing relevant pathways toward adulthood. While it is critically important to help teenagers struggling with
school-related anxiety and depression, it is worth considering the evolutionary mismatch between forced schooling and adolescence. Designed
to be fully immersed in real-world experiences and productive work,
dictating their own thoughts and actions—while surrounded by both
adult mentors and peers—teenagers are instead cut off and controlled,
drugged and disciplined. Freedom may be their best medicine.

Leaving School

Nick Eberlin was bored. He was a good student in his public school system, consistently earning a place on the honor roll. But after his junior
year of high school, he chose to leave school for unschooling. "I decided
that I wanted to pursue an education, not schooling anymore," Nick tells
me. It was something he had been considering for a while. He started
refusing to bring home any schoolwork, using class time to complete
assignments that he found to be mostly irrelevant. "Most of what I was
learning in school," says Nick, "I'd forget in a month if not sooner. It felt
like a complete waste of time." He also saw how the game of school was
impacting himself and his peers. He imposed some self-help measures,
like homework refusal, to lessen the burden, but he saw his classmates
struggling under the weight of forced schooling. "I think school is negatively affecting teens for sure," says Nick. "Each individual should have
a personalized education experience that prepares them for the life that
they want to live. Instead, we are all given the same schooling that highly

praises rote memory learning (which I feel is useless in today's world with the resources available) and encourages whatever it may take to receive the A, whether that means putting your health at risk or going so far as to cheat on tests. I think that the school system is manufacturing students who all more or less act and think the same."

Nick knew that schooling was deeply flawed and he began to investigate alternatives. He came across the idea of self-directed learning and immediately gravitated toward the unschooling philosophy. It seemed to resonate with his view that interest-based, self-driven learning—not tied to some arbitrary curriculum or bureaucratic requirement—was the best kind of education. He left school and joined Ingenuity Hub, an unschooling center for teenagers described previously. Many people discouraged him from quitting school, saying "you only have one year left!" But he was determined. As an unschooler, Nick was able to pursue his passions authentically, embedded in the real world, doing real work that interested him, in community with others who supported his self-directed efforts.

Nick was always interested in technology, beginning his first blog when he was just eight years old. Then he started building websites, teaching himself various programming languages such as HTML, CSS, and JavaScript from online courses, documentation, and web tutorials. Leaving school allowed Nick the time and space to dig deeper into technology and improve his skills and knowledge. He wanted to learn more about advanced web design techniques, as well as the French language, entrepreneurship, and current events. Spending his days as a teen unschooler, with resources and mentorship available through the local self-directed learning center, Nick was able to build a successful web design business with several well-paying client contracts. "Getting away from school allowed me to focus more on what was going to help me in the real world," says Nick. Now eighteen, he is incorporating his business and taking necessary steps to make it his career. Nick has some advice for other teens: "If you truly feel that leaving school is the right choice for you, do it! Don't let others' opinions influence your decision because in the end, your happiness is what matters and will allow you to live a fulfilled life."

An important part of teen unschooling is connecting with other teens. Adolescents in general crave connection with peers, in addition to opportunities to do purposeful work tied to their interests and facilitated by adult mentors. Friends matter. For Nick, the self-directed learning center he used in what would have been his senior year of high school provided peer connection, access to resources, and helpful adults. A physical building is a nice feature, but it is not the only way to nurture teen development and meet adolescents' very real and essential need for social interaction. Other out-of-the-box resources for supporting teen unschooling include online peer networks, teen summer camps, world travel opportunities, and apprenticeship programs.

Supporting Teen Connection

Jim Flannery was in his first year of teaching physics at a public high school in a socioeconomically depressed district. As a science guru and self-proclaimed "metaphysical junkie," he was excited about sharing the mystery and awe of the universe through physics. He felt that adolescents, in particular, would benefit from seeing the world in a new way, exploring various scientific principles and allowing curiosity to guide experimentation. Jim says, "Science is all about discovery and understanding and asking meaningful questions and predicting outcomes. It takes our world around us and puts it through a really exciting lens that asks 'What is our reality?'"

Jim's enthusiasm soon flattened. The day before school started, he was handed a standardized test and told that the students' graduation was linked to passing the test. All of the joy and promise in sharing his love of science with teenagers didn't matter. His job was to get kids to pass an arbitrary test that he didn't believe in and that he felt was in no way reflective of what science is really all about. He knew that he was stuck, so he began the semester with as much hope as he could muster. He also vowed to give his students as much freedom as possible. "My class became the 'bathroom class,'" remembers Jim. "I refused to tell kids they couldn't use the bathroom. So other teachers began telling their kids, 'Wait until you're in Mr. F.'s class and then you can use the bathroom; he lets everyone.' It was crazy. I actually got reprimanded for letting too many kids use the bathroom." Jim tried to make the best of his teaching job, but the controlling, test-driven environment and the overall condescension and lack of respect toward young people proved too frustrating. He left and began plotting how to help teenagers get out of school.

Jim discovered unschooling and the philosophy of self-directed education and he was instantly captivated. He wanted to build a technical platform that would help kids to leave school and be supported in their self-driven learning. Initially, he envisioned a tool like Khan Academy, where teens would create their own content and teach other teens; but as he built the platform and invited unschoolers to join, he realized that what these teens really wanted was a more informal, socially oriented forum for communicating and sharing. For example, he realized that teens didn't want a peer to *teach* them how to do XYZ; they really wanted a platform to talk about how to *learn* XYZ. He created Peer Unschooling Network, or PUN, to facilitate peer learning over peer teaching. As Jim says:

> What I see in PUN is this: it is a place for unschoolers to get together and socialize. In some ways, this could be a place for them to be "learning" from one another in a formal fashion. If someone is trying to learn something, a teen on PUN could either tutor them directly or share with them a link to a useful resource. But ultimately, the goal isn't for this to be a "learning platform." When I've interviewed unschoolers, they've specifically said they wish there were more unschoolers and that there was a way to find and connect with the ones that already exist. I think PUN serves that purpose.

PUN makes unschooling real for teens who may be just beginning to wonder about alternatives to school or who are convinced they want to leave school and are unsure where to go. Through PUN, these teens meet other teens who are taking charge of their own education in meaningful ways. "It's not a hypothetical thing happening in a distant land," says Jim. "These are real teens who can speak directly about their unschooling experience." He hopes that parents will support their teens in leaving school for unschooling, but he also sees PUN as a way to empower the teens themselves to take the necessary steps to make the case for unschooling. "In the absence of active and involved parents, I hope kids can lean on one another for support," says Jim. "Peer support, mutual support, could be the key to helping many kids bridge that frightening gap of unlocking from the school system and creating their own self-directed learning communities."

Not-Back-to-School Camp

Jim's idea has precedent. For years, unschooling advocates have been designing and implementing programs to help teen unschoolers connect with one another. Some of these efforts have involved helping young people who feel trapped in school to create an exit strategy; others have focused on connecting unschooled teens with each other. One early unschooling advocate who inspired Jim's current work is Grace Llewellyn. In 1991, Grace published a book that would change the course of many teenagers' lives over the coming decades. A former middle school English teacher, Grace grew increasingly unsettled by the rigidity and control that defined schooling—even in the small, private school where she had most recently taught. She read Holt's books and began to agree with him that schooling was the problem, regardless of how frilly and dressed up that school might be. Grace quit her teaching job and penned *The Teenage Liberation Handbook* as an unschooling resource written directly for teenagers, with advice on how to leave school and pursue a self-directed education. While aimed at adolescents who felt trapped at school, the book spoke to many teachers as well—including those featured in these pages—who ultimately left teaching to start self-directed learning centers and unschooling schools. "How strange and self-defeating that a supposedly free country should train its young for life in totalitarianism," writes Grace in the early pages of her book.[10] Liberation is a powerful message—for both teens and adults.

The impact of *The Teenage Liberation Handbook* was immediate and far-reaching, with more teenagers deciding to leave school for unschooling and more educators choosing to quit teaching to create alternatives to school. While she was pleased with the book's influence, and often corresponded with readers through the mail, Grace felt that there was more to do. Speaking to a group of teen unschoolers at a conference in the mid-1990s, Grace had a thought: What if she could help to create a space for unschoolers to connect in a more intentional way? She noticed that some of the unschoolers already had a community of like-minded peers with whom they connected, but many didn't have any such community. She began to brainstorm ideas on how to get these teenage unschoolers together. A weekly overnight summer camp for teens seemed a perfect beginning.

Not-Back-to-School Camp emerged in 1996 as a way to foster community and connection for teen unschoolers. Now, over two decades later, the camp continues to thrive, expanding to more locations and bringing together more teenagers than Grace ever could have imagined. Focused on unschooling principles, the structure and content support interest-based, self-directed learning within a close-knit community. "Most of what happens is completely optional, except community meetings," says Grace. There is an orientation meeting that explains guidelines for mutual respect and consent and that details chores and community responsibilities. The remainder of the program is focused on a blend of fun excursions and activities such as dances, talent shows, and art exhibits; various workshops offered by other campers and staff members; and some intense trust-building activities that foster sustained empathy and connection.

Grace's initial goal of connecting teen unschoolers to each other in a meaningful and enduring way has been a huge success. Campers, ages thirteen and up, often attend every summer and stay connected throughout the year through technology and social media, as well as planned visits and other gatherings. Many former campers have chosen to live with other campers in a particular city, often becoming roommates or neighbors. Some campers remain with the program, becoming junior camp counselors and full-fledged senior staff—taking time out of their work schedule each summer to devote to the camp that they found so uplifting. Not-Back-to-School camp is now entering a new stage, with children of former campers beginning to attend. The long-term relationships that sprout from Not-Back-to-School

Camp are the most personally gratifying for Grace. "We have long-time staffers who were first campers. I still really enjoy connection with campers, but more deeply meaningful to me are the colleagues and friends who have become some of the most important people in my life."

Sophie Biddle is one of those people. In her public middle school in Phoenix, Arizona, Sophie was miserable. She was a top student, but she hated the social dynamics of the school: the bullying and the teasing because she was smart. "I was getting straight As, but I hated it," says Sophie. The one bright spot of her week was the community theater program she participated in outside of school. There she met a friend who was sixteen and who had been unschooled her whole life. "Emily calls herself a pre-K dropout," says Sophie of her friend. "I was totally enchanted by her." During their theater time together, Sophie confided in Emily about how much she disliked school and how depressed she was that this schooled life was to be her destiny until high school graduation. Emily suggested she read *The Teenage Liberation Handbook*. Sophie ordered it, read it in a day, and created a detailed PowerPoint presentation to share with her parents on why she should be allowed to leave school and become an unschooler.

Her parents were understanding but suggested that Sophie finish up the final few weeks of eighth grade and then attend an arts-focused public charter school the next fall. If after a couple of months at the charter school Sophie still wanted to leave, her parents would relent. Sophie agreed to give the new school a try. The social dynamics at the charter school were better for Sophie, but she was bored and unchallenged. After two months she asked her parents again if she could become an unschooler and they said yes. In the beginning, her parents had some specific expectations for Sophie, like asking that she take at least one math class per semester at the local community college. She enrolled in a math course there at fourteen and liked college much more than high school. Gradually, as her parents went through their own deschooling process, including their own reading of *The Teenage Liberation Handbook*, the schooled expectations diminished. Sophie continued to do theatre and the math class at the community college, and she also got a job working at a nearby organic farm, helping to care for hundreds of chickens and preparing for the weekly farmers' market. She participated in a local homeschool group that consisted mostly of unschoolers and found a solid cohort with which to connect.

The summer of her first unschooling year, Sophie went to Not-Back-to-School Camp in Oregon. Her friend Emily had attended the previous summer and was returning. Sophie was eager to join her. At fifteen, Sophie would be gone for two weeks to camp—the longest she had ever been away from home. She was anxious but excited. "It was so amazing," Sophie says of that first camp experience. "I felt valued and connected to that community so quickly. I left camp and felt fundamentally seen and witnessed in a way that made unschooling much clearer to me going forward." She returned home with a drive and focus unlike anything she had ever known. "I came home and told my parents: Look, I am going to start taking American Sign Language classes, get more serious about dance, stop doing swimming." Her parents rolled with Sophie's newfound clarity of purpose. The community college math requirement fell by the wayside, and Sophie began to live a fully self-directed, interest-led unschooled life.

That fall after camp a lot happened for Sophie. She and her family moved to Portland, Oregon. As soon as their bags were unpacked, Sophie flew to Kansas City to spend Thanksgiving with twenty Not-Back-to-School Campers who gathered at three local unschooling families' homes for the holiday. Back in Portland, she found the robust city bus system to be a lifeline for her unschooling, enabling her to travel independently all over the city to take classes or go places tied to her interests, which remained dance, theatre, and sign language. From some unschooling friends, Sophie learned that a well-respected, self-directed free school was nearby. She enrolled there as a student to see what it was like, but after two months she decided to leave. "I loved the philosophy and loved the staff, but arbitrarily being at school all day, with people I didn't really connect with, didn't jam with me," recalls Sophie. A few months later, she contacted the school to volunteer in helping with the younger kids and developed a burgeoning interest in working with young children. At sixteen, she worked as a nanny for a local family with a toddler and a preschooler—a role she would keep for the next five years.

During her remaining years as a teen unschooler, Sophie continued to cultivate her interests, work with young children, and attend Not-Back-to-School Camp every summer. She took classes at a community college and decided that she wanted to pursue a four-year college degree, with a specific interest in science, so she upped her community college math classes. From community college, she transferred to Portland State University's honors college as a sophomore and graduated at twenty-one with a degree in sociology and elementary science education. Today, Sophie lives in Seattle, Washington, with some other Not-Back-to-School Camp alumni and works at the University of Washington in education outreach focused on youth empowerment. She takes time off each summer to work as a staff member at Not-Back-to-School Camp.

As Sophie reflects on her teen years as an unschooler, she is grateful for the many ways that her parents were deeply involved in her life and learning but also trusted her and let go. "My mom likes to describe her role as 'bumpers on a bowling alley,'" says Sophie. "They did such a good job of letting me go all over the place but not have it be a free-for-all." Trust yourself and trust your kid, is her advice to unschooling parents. "Trusting young people is one of the most radical notions in our society, but childhood and human development are not linear paths. Really, it's a journey."

For Evan Wright, a former teen unschooler and long-time Not-Back-to-School Camp staff member, the unschooling journey was life altering. School was not a good fit for him. "I was someone who was really interested in learning but had a hard time in school," he recalls. At age twelve, he was diagnosed with Attention Deficit Disorder (ADD) and placed on Ritalin so that he could focus better on his schoolwork. By fifteen, he was miserable and knew that he desperately needed to leave school, but he didn't know how. Serendipitously, he was browsing in a bookstore one day and came across *The Teenage Liberation Handbook*. "At first I thought it was just some snarky joke," he remembers, "but at some point while reading I realized this isn't a joke, this is serious. I really responded to a lot of the ideas and possibilities, both for myself and for education." Grace's book validated Evan's feelings and detailed how to present his case for leaving school to his parents. "As you may expect, they were not thrilled," he says.

His parents hoped it was just a fleeting idea, but Evan was persistent. His parents recognized how unhappy he was at school, and through a series of conversations, they ultimately decided to allow Evan to leave school at fifteen for unschooling. "It was important for me to communicate to them that this wasn't just the absence of school, but the presence of a different kind of education that I wanted for myself," he says. At first, the compromise with his parents was to have an in-home tutor and do school-at-home; but after only a few months, Evan's parents saw the change in him and allowed him to stop the tutor and fully embrace unschooling.

> I stopped taking Ritalin. I realized that the same characteristics that were problematic in a classroom were strengths in the rest of my life. For me, ADD presented as having difficulty focusing on things I wasn't really interested in. Outside of school, that translated into being able to focus very clearly on things that I am interested in. For others, ADD may show up in other ways, but for me it was really only an issue within the classroom and not outside out of it.

Evan began exploring his city, going to museums, reading a lot, and riding his bike everywhere. He started volunteering at a nearby homeless shelter. He also spent much of his time deschooling. "I spent a significant chunk of my time in those early days of unschooling just decompressing from school. My confidence in myself, in my intelligence, and in my ability to learn had taken a lot of hits in the years before. Having time to take a break was really important."

Evan and his family moved to California, and he started volunteering at a local marine rehabilitation center for injured and orphaned sea animals. He also began connecting online with other unschooled teens and discovered Not-Back-to-School Camp. "It was a profoundly affirming experience," he remembers of going to camp at seventeen. "It was inspiring to see what other unschooled teenagers were doing with their lives. There were a hundred teen unschoolers there. I got a sense of what was possible for teenagers, given all this freedom, and how they went about learning things." Like Sophie, Evan left Not-Back-to-School Camp with clear intentions for taking greater control of his life and education. Back in California, he got an internship at a marine sanctuary, in partnership with National Geographic and the National Oceanic and Atmospheric Association (NOAA), where he was able to learn more about ocean and marine animal health from some of his top scientist idols. Also in the wake of camp, Evan began traveling independently. He lived for a month on his own in Costa Rica, assisting with research on sea turtles and exploring the rainforest, and he explored much of the California coast—experiences he doubts would have been possible if he was in school.

Now thirty-seven and living in Seattle, Evan leads Not-Back-to-School Camp and helps to connect teen unschoolers throughout the year. He also works for a nonprofit organization focused on leadership development for LGBTQ adults. He attributes much of his adult fulfillment to his teen unschooling experience. "The whole idea of education and schooling has been collapsed into each other," says Evan. "We need to begin separating them. Schooling is just one form of education. Education is much broader than schooling."

World Schooling

Lainie Liberti discovered just how broad education could be. The financial crisis of 2008 hit her hard. She was a single mom living in California with her nine-year-old son, Miro, where she owned her own business doing branding work for eco-minded clients. The economic downturn that followed the bank bailout led to the loss of some clients and an overall uncertainty about the future. Rather than be victims, Lainie said, she suggested a radical shift. She stalled her business, sold all of her possessions, pulled Miro from school, and the duo took off to Central America for what she thought would be a short-term hiatus from capitalism gone awry. Friends tried to dissuade her, colleagues told her she was committing professional suicide, but Lainie knew it was time for a big change, where she and her son could break away from the work-and-consume cycle that they felt characterized so much of American society. Ten years later, Lainie and Miro are still traveling the world, grateful that what seemed like a rotten twist turned out to be such a fulfilling life change.

When they were eight months into their trip, living slowly and stress-free off of their small savings, Lainie and Miro decided not to return to the United States. Lainie began to investigate homeschooling and quickly discovered unschooling as the educational approach that described the life learning she and Miro were experiencing. More than unschooling, in fact, they were "world schooling." The pair was learning Spanish, with Miro nearly fluent. They explored cities and villages, got to know the local people, and became immersed in the fabric of small communities. Following their curiosity, they explored the history and culture of the places they visited. "We learned to say yes to everything," says Lainie. "We came to see the world as our classroom, that there are no limits to imagination and learning. Taking learning outside of the classroom creates an opportunity to be present both at home and in the world, and it teaches you compassion."

Miro and Lainie spent their first years in Latin America, feeling at home in the language and culture of the cities, towns, and villages in which they lived. They lived simply, with few belongings for basic needs. Lainie began to do some freelance consulting work on the side, but mother and son had no interest in returning to the United States to live and work.

When Miro was fourteen, he and his mom were invited to speak at an unschooling conference in the United States. For the first time, Miro was immersed in a community of like-minded peers, and he was elated. Here were kids just like himself, learning without school, following their own interests, free to live and explore without the typical restrictions of today's adolescents. Returning to their world schooling, Miro became depressed. He knew he loved living and learning in and from faraway places, but he desperately craved more peer connection. Miro and Lainie brainstormed various options, including returning to the United States and settling in an area thick with unschoolers, but neither of them wanted to do that. Instead, they launched Project World School.

"We realized that there was no one place with unschoolers that we could move to, so we decided to bring the unschoolers to us," Lainie recalls. "We were learning so much. The focus of our lives had become learning and learning together with others. We wanted to share that with other unschoolers." That first Project World School pilot program brought a group of six unschooled teenagers to Peru for six weeks to become fully immersed in local living within an intentional community. "We loved the world and we wanted to live in community with all these other people and all these places," says Lainie. "After that pilot, we were able to figure out what worked and what didn't work and focus on the core foundations of our program, which center around community-building, team-building, trusting, and learning to say yes to new experiences."

Now in its sixth year, Project World School brings together unschooled teenagers for two- to four-week trips in varied locations. In 2017, their world schooling journeys included stays in Bali, South Africa, Mexico, Peru, Greece, and Thailand. Groups typically include fifteen teenagers who, through consensus-building and negotiation, are able to cocreate what is often a life-changing experience. "We'll accept anyone as long as their focus is on community and self-directedness," says Lainie. Recently, they had several schooled teens join their world communities and it created some challenges. "Because I am the perceived adult, they immediately placed me in a position of authority, and waited to be told what to do. It took constant reminding that we are not telling them what to do, but deciding together as a community what to do," says Lainie. "Many of the schooled kids had less motivation to share their own viewpoints, to be cocreative. It took a lot of time for them to do some basic deschooling." On a post-trip evaluation, one of the schooled teens wrote that he wished there was more age segregation and didn't like that thirteen-year-olds learned alongside eighteen-year-olds. "He didn't really get the unschooling and world schooling ethos," says Lainie. Learning from a varied assortment of people and places, with community and self-direction as core tenets, is the heart of Project World School's mission.

Now eighteen, Miro is taking a more central role in running the organization and leading the trips, along with other co-facilitators, giving Lainie a well-deserved break from seven months a year with teens.

Project World School has offered Miro the authentic peer connection and lasting friendships with other unschoolers that he craved, while enabling him to live and learn around the world in community with others. "I didn't realize how beautiful the world is, how diverse it is," says Lainie as she recollects life before world schooling. "I think about kids forced to go to school, following someone else's dream of what will make them happy. Learning is not schooling," says Lainie. "A diversity of experiences is what makes life rich, not a spoon-fed education that is meaningless." Opening the world to others, especially teens, has been an important part of Miro and Lainie's personal unschooling journey. Letting go of the limitations and expectations characteristic of a schooled life can lead to new discoveries and unexpected opportunities. For Lainie and Miro, unschooling led to an entirely new way of living and being in the world, and new economic opportunities that they could never have imagined while living a schooled existence. When we move education beyond the four walls of a school classroom, and gradually deschool our thinking, we may begin to wonder about other enclosures in our lives.

Apprenticeships

Work may well be one of those enclosures. Industrial schooling of the nineteenth century created an efficient mechanism for training young people to become obedient workers. Individual interests and enthusiasms were squelched on the assembly line of forced school to factory work. Not much has changed. Today's conventional schooling continues to diminish childhood curiosity and dismiss creative passions, setting young people on an often debt-laden path of school to college to less-than-fulfilling work. Ideally, work should be meaningful and connected to our talents and passions. If it's not—if our work is more menial or mundane—then hopefully our creative passions have not been destroyed by mass schooling and they are what truly define and inspire us. Cultivating those passions may ultimately lead to work that is more fulfilling. Author and global strategist John Hagel writes:

> One of my key messages to individuals in this changing world is to find your passion and integrate your passion with your work.

One of the challenges today is that most people are products of
the schools and society we've had, which encourage you to go
to work to get a paycheck, and if it pays well, that's a good job,
versus encouraging you to find your passion and find a way to
make a living from it.[11]

Teen unschoolers reveal alternative pathways to adulthood, tied to
their passions. Unfettered by the regimentation of conventional schooling, unschoolers chart their own course. Often this path may include
college. Many of the grown unschoolers I spoke with chose to take a
few community college courses in adolescence and ultimately enrolled
in four-year degree programs and graduate studies. Some chose to delay
college for work or travel or community service projects and pursued
higher education once they had a real purpose for doing so. For many
unschoolers, college isn't the default. It is chosen or not based on
how it connects to an individual's current interests and future goals.
Unschooled for most of her childhood in rural Virginia, Carsie Blanton
moved across the country to Oregon when she was sixteen. She lived in
a house with other young adult unschoolers, whom she met during her
summers at Not-Back-to-School camp. She chose not to go to college
and instead built a career around her creative passions. Now thirty-two
with a successful career as a musician and songwriter, Carsie looks back
on her teen unschooling experience out west:

> I think moving out at sixteen was a very "unschoolerish" move.
> I joined two bands and immersed myself in music, played gigs,
> wrote songs, went on tour. I also started writing a book, wrote
> a bunch of bad poetry, and went to poetry slams. I don't think I
> could have done any of that if I had been in school, at least not
> at that age, and all of it turned out to be instrumental (no pun
> intended) in my career and creative life. Unschooling was the
> perfect education for me for the same reasons that being a full-
> time writer and musician is the perfect job for me.

The "college or bust" idea that pervades much of our society can
funnel young people into college tracks that are expensive and undefined

and lead to careers by default rather than choice. I often say that college is not an end goal that I set for my children. If they want to go to college because it will help them in whatever path they want to take in life, then good for them; but it is not the capstone of our unschooled approach. College should be one of many options for teens as they move toward adulthood and decide on careers. As Paul Goodman writes: "Our aim should be to multiply the paths of growing up, instead of narrowing the one existing school path."[12] In *Compulsory Miseducation*, Goodman goes so far as to suggest giving money directly to adolescents "for any plausible self-chosen education proposals, such as purposeful travel or individual enterprise."[13]

Apprenticeships can be a valuable, time-tested approach to connecting adolescents with the authentic, practical experiences of the adult world. First appearing in the later Middle Ages, apprenticeships became an opportunity for young people, usually between the ages of ten and fifteen, to gain practical skills and on-the-job training from a master craftsman. These adolescent apprentices came of age surrounded by real life experiences and adult mentors. The growing disconnect between today's teenagers and the real world from which they are removed may be one factor contributing to alarming rates of adolescent turmoil. Psychologist Robert Epstein writes, "A century ago, we rescued young people from the factories and the streets; now we need to rescue them from the schools."[14]

Holed up in schools, separated from the adult world except for an occasional after-school job, most teenagers have very little opportunity to work alongside masters in their field or craft. They have little exposure to real work and varied occupations, and they often go to college because that is what is socially expected, whether it's right for them or not. Adolescent apprenticeships, and even teen part-time jobs, are increasingly becoming remnants of a bygone era. According to the US Bureau of Labor Statistics, teen labor force participation has plummeted from a high of 58 percent in 1979 to just 34 percent in 2015, with a projected rate of only 24 percent by 2024.[15]

For Isaac Morehouse, this pattern is troubling. Homeschooled as a child, Isaac had the freedom to play and explore his interests and talents.

He also learned the value of real work. Growing up in a family with a disabled father meant that Isaac and his siblings took on many household responsibilities. These weren't just childhood chores; they were essential jobs for keeping the family cared for and the home running smoothly. Still, there was a lot of time to play and Isaac spent much of his childhood engrossed in his Lego toys.

When he was a teenager, Isaac decided to try high school. He wanted to see what it was like, but the novelty soon wore off. "I hated having my schedule planned by someone else. I didn't like that I had to wait to work." He told a teacher that he was considering leaving for community college. The teacher scoffed at the idea, suggesting that Isaac wasn't yet mature enough for that. Isaac left anyway and enrolled in community college at sixteen. College was better but not ideal. "I still thought that most of the classes were silly and wasteful. I had the sense that no one wanted to be there but you had to do it if you want a job," says Isaac. He eventually graduated from a four-year university, but he found that most of his learning happened outside of the institution's walls. He also began to understand that diplomas and degrees and other types of credentialing are merely signaling mechanisms. Bryan Caplan writes about this signaling factor in his book *The Case Against Education*. He says, "Even if what a student learned in school is utterly useless, employers will happily pay extra if their scholastic achievement provides *information about their productivity*."[16] It is not that a piece of paper proves your intelligence and worth; it's that employers rely on these documents as a way to filter prospective employees.

What if, Isaac thought, he could create an alternative signal? What if he could help connect people to interesting jobs while satisfying employers' needs for sifting and sorting to find the best workers? Inspired by this possibility, in 2014 Isaac launched Praxis, an apprenticeship program for older teenagers and young adults that provides essential training and mentoring while connecting apprentices to eager employers. Praxis comes from the Greek word for "doing," and captured Isaac's vision for modern apprenticeships. Homeschooled and unschooled teens are often his most enthusiastic and successful apprentices. However, he gets a fair amount of people who are in college but are unhappy and debt-ridden, or have recently left college and still don't know what they want for a career. At Praxis, apprentices go through an intensive, online, self-paced training program where they learn common workplace software (such as Excel, PowerPoint, and Trello) and other skills related to business communication and theory. More important, according to Isaac, apprentices-in-training learn how to identify their own skill sets and interests, present those skills and interests in a way that appeals to prospective employers, and then find employers who like what they see. After the initial apprenticeship training, Praxis connects all apprentices with willing employers in a variety of industries, who pay the apprentices for their work while also exposing them to real-life careers. Praxis continues to offer support and mentoring during the apprenticeship to help ensure success. Most of these apprentices go on to get full-time job offers from their employers, or use the apprenticeship as a launching pad to another job or career venture.

A criticism of apprenticeships and job-training programs is that they can create a two-tiered society, with more privileged teens moving along a college-bound path and those with less privilege funneled into lower-paid, less-skilled work that doesn't require a college degree. Proponents of apprenticeships disagree. They believe that apprenticeships can help to combat inequality and create opportunity. In his book *The Means to Grow Up: Reinventing Apprenticeship as a Developmental Support in Adolescence* Dr. Robert Halpern writes that

> youth apprenticeship experiences set the foundation for and in some instances actually create more nuanced and grounded post-secondary pathways for many youth, across social class. What might at first glance seem a strategy for reproducing inequality—an academic pathway and extended adolescence for the most advantaged youth, a more vocational pathway and a push into the adult world for the less advantaged—is one means for addressing it.[17]

Isaac and his wife now unschool their own four children, providing them with ample time and space to play and discover, to reveal interests and gifts, and to become engaged in real work with real people throughout their community. Isaac says: "The sooner you can learn to be self-directed in your life and in your education, the better. The more we can break from that schooled mind-set—that conveyor belt approach—the better. With our apprentices, we try to build as much of that agency as possible, instilling that self-directed mind-set." Isaac not only wants to help build other pathways toward adulthood and meaningful work, he also wants to help people to build their own signals, rather than relying on hollow pieces of paper to determine their self-worth. Isaac asks: "Why does everyone go to college? Because they think they have to in order to get a job. Why does everyone go to high school, to middle school?" By challenging these societal defaults, and offering other options for teenagers and young adults, Isaac hopes to help more people become active, self-directed leaders of their own lives and livelihoods.

When teenagers are free from the fetters of conventional schooling and allowed to become more immersed in the genuine culture of their community, they can thrive. The stress and anxiety and depression so characteristic of today's adolescents often disappear when kids are granted the freedom to pursue their own interests and develop their own talents, and when they are supported and mentored. Whether through self-directed learning centers for teens that provide access to resources and encouragement, through community college and online networks, world travel, work and apprenticeships—or all of the above—teenagers can become active members of the adult community rather than remain confined in coercive classrooms. Teenagers are incredibly capable and competent and, by nature, often happy and enthusiastic when given freedom and respect. Our job is to stop treating teens like toddlers and start welcoming them to the wider world.

Unschooling Tips

- **Don't believe the stereotype.** It's a myth that teenagers are naturally aloof, unpleasant, moody, and unmotivated. Look first at their environment before assuming that their angst is normal. Confined and controlled, just when they should be emerging more fully and independently into the real world, many adolescents need freedom to thrive. Give it to them.

• **Understand teens' need for connection and community.** Most adolescents crave peer interactions, ample social time, and the opportunity to be fully recognized, valued members of their larger community. Help to facilitate these connections, both real and virtual, by connecting your teens to their broader community and helping them to navigate entry into adulthood.

• **Be open to possibilities.** Without the constraints of forced schooling, the world can truly be your teenager's classroom. Look outside of your immediate geographic area for opportunities for your teens to pursue their interests, connect with like-minded peers, find mentors, and discover meaningful work. In addition to Project World School (www.projectworldschool.com), Unschool Adventures (www.unschooladventures.com) is another world schooling travel organization for unschoolers led by self-directed learning advocate and author Blake Boles. Unschool Adventures also hosts popular writing retreats for unschooled teens throughout the year. Worldschooling Central (www.worldschoolingcentral.com), launched by a family that sold their house to unschool and travel the world, is an online community connecting traveling families who want to use the world as their classroom.

• **Question the conveyor belt.** Maybe college is the endpoint of your teenager's education, and maybe it isn't. As lifelong learners, unschoolers often take an ad hoc approach to higher education, pursuing it when and if it is personally meaningful or helpful toward a goal, but not viewing it as an essential expectation of a life well lived.

10

Out-of-School Unschooling

"Play is often talked about as if it were a relief from serious learning. But for children, play is serious learning."

—Fred Rogers[1]

CHILDHOOD USED TO BE MORE self directed. Growing up, I spent hours after school, on weekends, and throughout summertime playing with the neighborhood kids. From an early age, we went off on our own, away from the watchful eyes of grown-ups. We climbed trees, played hide-and-seek, rode bikes with bare heads, built forts, had acorn fights. We fell down, scraped our knees, and got back up. We negotiated the web of social interactions, sometimes as leader and sometimes as follower, sometimes as the one left out and sometimes as the one leaving out others. We always knew we could go home.

Today, childhood is orchestrated. It unfolds under constant surveillance and within structured activities, on rubber playgrounds and in sterile classrooms. To give our children the same freedom and independence we enjoyed requires a calculated effort and an ongoing vigilance. For many parents, slowing down the accelerating pace of childhood is a major reason they choose unschooling. To allow for a more natural, play-filled, autonomous childhood, parents choose to opt out of the mainstream push for earlier academics, longer school days, and more enrichment activities. They avoid the dizzying speed of today's childhood, methodically carving out the time and space for wide open, unstructured play and the disappearing act of daydreaming. Preserving self-directed play is increasingly an act of resistance.

When we moved to our new home a few years ago, it coincided with a spurt of young children filling our city neighborhood. The sounds of children playing together on the street in the afternoon, moving the hockey net to the side each time a car passed by, gave me hope that childhood wasn't lost. With four kids and a house centrally positioned in the middle of an urban side street, our home became a focal point for neighborhood play. Then one day we got a note in our mailbox. It was from the neighbors across the street. They were graduate students in their early twenties studying at nearby Harvard University. The note acknowledged an increase in the afternoon noise level on our street since we moved in, making it difficult for the students to study. They wanted to know if we could give them our weekly play date schedule so they knew precisely when to expect the children's play. We politely said no, indicating that we hadn't violated any city noise ordinances and would let the children play, outside and unscheduled. They left us alone after that, but we later learned that they were getting their graduate degrees in urban planning! A generation of kids deprived of free play grow up to become the parents and policy makers of tomorrow. Fiercely protecting childhood free play must be a priority for all of us.

How did we get here? Lenore Skenazy, in her popular book *Free-Range Kids*, catalogs many of the varied forces that have led to a steep decline in childhood free play and independence over the last three decades. After she let her nine-year-old son ride the New York City subway alone in 2008, the national media dubbed her "America's Worst Mom." Granting children freedom and responsibility—much like what many of us enjoyed—now carries at best a social stigma and at worst a visit from child protective services.[2] We may publicly deride the "helicopter parents" who hover over and micromanage their kids, blaming them for a generation of weak and dependent young people. Societally, though, we prefer these intrusive parents over their more hands-off opposites. Childhood is on trial.

Skenazy, an accomplished writer and activist, explains that much of the reason childhood freedom and autonomy have disappeared stems from unfounded fears and changing social norms. Media sensationalism makes us think the world today is less safe than it was when we were kids, despite crime data showing the opposite. Working parents are often too busy to get to know their neighbors. New products and gadgets claim to make our children safer, leading us to assume that they are otherwise in danger.[3] All of this has contributed to a dramatic shift in childhood play patterns.

But it's not too late to bring back free, child-directed play. Unschooling parents and educators have quickly joined this bandwagon, seeking out and creating play-filled spaces for children and allowing them to taste the freedom and independence that many of us enjoyed as kids. For parents who can't choose unschooling, or who don't have access to an unschooling resource center or self-directed school, there are a growing number of ways to embrace the unschooling principles of freedom, interest-based learning, and childhood play. Self-directed summer camps and after-school programs, as well as community-based, child-directed play initiatives, are expanding, providing parents of conventionally schooled children—as well as unschoolers—more opportunities to reclaim childhood.

Not Your Typical Summer Camp

At Camp Stomping Ground in upstate New York, children are free. Unlike most weeklong overnight summer camps, Stomping Ground challenges the dominant idea that children need to be directed and instead allows children to wake up each day and determine what they want to do. Summer camp is arguably one of the few remaining venues where childhood freedom and play are acceptable, yet even summer camps are increasingly caught up in a cultural tide demanding more academically focused, adult-structured activities for young people. Camp Stomping Ground firmly rejects that trend, pushing beyond even the most liberal of summer camp models to fully embrace unschooled ideals.

Living and learning collaboratively, a mixed-age group of Stomping Ground campers and adult staff members engage together in meaningful summertime experiences that are entirely camper led. There are no required activities, no demands on what children should do and when. "Radical empathy" is a cornerstone of the Stomping Ground vision, and young people and adults work together to ensure that everyone is safe and respected within an entirely self-directed model of interaction. Learning freedom also means learning responsibility. As camp founders and directors Laura Kriegel and Jack Schott say:

> We live in arguably the most exciting and important time in human history. And yet, in a world that's never been more full of possibility, our children's lives have become more and more programmed and restricted. How can we prepare kids for happy lives in this world brimming with possibility if they aren't permitted to see that it exists?

To that end, Laura and Jack make sure that campers decide for themselves how to spend their time, whom to be with, and where and what to explore. For parents and children without access to full-time unschooling programs, maximizing out-of-school unschooling can be a priority. Self-directed camp programs like Stomping Ground provide children the opportunity to learn in self-directed, noncoercive ways.

At first glance, the structure of Camp Stomping Ground looks fairly typical of camp, with meals provided at regular times, a large indoor recreation area, expansive fields and woods in which to play, an inviting waterfront, and trained camp counselors. "The difference is that everything is optional," says Jack. In morning and afternoon blocks, various activities are offered, including photography, archery, canoeing, fire making and primitive skills, swimming, scavenger hunts, Dungeons and Dragons, theatre, ukulele, and so on. Campers can choose among these activities, or choose instead to hang out in the recreation area or out in the fields. They also have the ability to quit. If a kid tries archery and it's not her thing, she can opt out and do something else instead.

Some may wonder, won't kids just do nothing then? If they are not required to participate in certain activities at certain times, won't they just loaf around? Camp Stomping Ground has no restrictions on screen time for young people, though their rural location means that connections are only available in the main recreation area. Won't kids just sit around on their digital devices all day? "Parents are worried about screen time," says Laura. "Often we find that the parents who are most worried about screens are the ones whose kids are on them a lot at home, but these are the kids who quickly avoid screens once here. These are often the kids who are most active, most rambunctious, and they just want opportunities to play." Jack adds: "Some kids may be on their screens initially when they get to camp as part of their own 'deschooling' process, and then they see outside the window a huge shaving cream war. Who wants to miss out on that?"

Surrounding campers with a wide variety of fun and optional activities and resources can make screens less appealing, particularly for kids who crave free childhood play in a world in which that is rapidly disappearing. Most kids won't choose to do nothing when there is so much to do that is enjoyable and meaningful to them. Laura and Jack also don't share society's larger paranoia with screens. "Technology can be a community builder for kids and can be a shared experience, particularly for kids on the autism spectrum. There can be great connection in two kids watching a video on an iPhone and laughing hysterically," says Laura. "We honestly don't find it to be a big draw at camp, though. Three to four kids may play video games for an hour a day, but everyone else uses screens very sporadically if at all. There is too much else going on."

The founders first stumbled upon the idea of unschooling in their early days of visiting camps across the country before launching Stomping Ground. On one trip, they met an unschooling dad who ran a summer camp in his community. He shared books and resources and a new way of thinking about education that inspired Jack and Laura. Camp Stomping Ground sprouted from that inspiration. Now, they believe that summer camp can be a powerful springboard for many families to leap into unschooling principles and practices all year. About half of the campers at Stomping Ground come from a self-directed or unschooling background, while the remaining half are conventionally schooled. Jack and Laura want to fundamentally transform the ways in which the majority of children learn by helping families shift their thinking from *schooling* to *learning*. "We're reimagining a world where kids have a chance to learn differently," says Jack. "I'm hopeful for the future. We talk to more people who say this camp was attractive because of its self-directed nature. I think there is more and more restlessness about school being inadequate."

The goal for Jack and Laura is to help extend freedom and play for children beyond summer by educating others about the intense and authentic learning that occurs through unschooling. In addition to educating parents, the camp founders are committed to cultivating a new crop of educators who understand and embrace the unschooling philosophy. They make it an important part of their mission to recruit and train camp counselors in the tenets of self-directed education, and they remain dedicated to their counselor alumni group, in the hope that former counselors become engaged in unschooling beyond camp. According to Jack: "It's very fresh in the counselors' minds how awful school can be and there is so much energy in that eighteen-to-twenty-five age group around what more is possible."

Many parents would like to integrate more unschooled ideas into their lives but often don't know what to do or where to start. The Camp Stomping Ground founders, for instance, frequently talk to parents who want to choose self-directed education for their children but can't make unschooling work and don't have access to a nearby self-directed learning center or unschooling school. What can they do? First, unschooling is, at its heart, a frame of mind. It means putting schooling in its historical place and recognizing its role and limitations in our modern society. For some parents, adopting an unschooled way of thinking may simply mean taking schooling less seriously. It may mean joining the growing ranks of parents advocating for the elimination of homework or opting out of high stakes testing for their children. It may mean fighting for more recess and more free play in schools. It could also include simplifying children's out-of-school schedules, opting for fewer extracurricular activities and more unstructured, unsupervised play time for children to do their own thing. It might mean spending more time together at museums and libraries, places that already facilitate self-directed, non-coercive learning guided by interests. It could include a grassroots effort to resurrect neighborhood play. Or maybe, it's all of the above.

Community-Based Free Play

Disappearing childhood play was a major motivator for Janice O'Donnell, longtime director of the Providence Children's Museum in Rhode Island and founder of Providence PlayCorps, a summertime adventure playground program for inner city children. "Kids learn through play, but now they're not playing!" laments Janice, who has seen a dramatic decline in self-directed childhood play over the last four decades. Her interest in unschooling ideals began back in college when she first read A. S. Neill's *Summerhill.* "It sang to me, this idea of self-directed learning. It just made so much sense," she said. "I always knew school was not where I was learning. I did what I was supposed to do, got good grades, but I always knew that my real learning was happening outside of school." That book led to her mounting interest in the overall progressive education movement of the 1960s and '70s, as she devoured books by educators like John Holt and Herb Kohl, as well as George Dennison's *The Lives of Children* and Jonathan Kozol's *Death at an Early Age* and *Free Schools.* At the same time, she was watching her own young child learn and grow in the most fascinating ways, following her own self-educative instincts. Janice helped to start a parent cooperative school focused on self-directed learning ideals and began working at the new Providence Children's Museum in 1979, eventually serving as its director from 1985 to 2014.

Over the years as Janice helped to shape the museum, making it more hands-on and experiential for children, she became frustrated by the evaporation of childhood play. The advent of core curriculum frameworks and high-stakes testing meant that children's museums emphasizing play over academic content weren't as highly valued. Kids were spending more time in structured, adult-led after-school and weekend programming and were less able to enjoy wide open time at the museum, freely exploring whatever activity interested them most. She and her team decided to stop pandering to school groups, which she felt were never a great fit for the museum and became particularly problematic when driven by school competencies. "Museums aren't at their best with school groups," says Janice, noting that large groups with tight schedules make it difficult for kids to linger at something they enjoy. "Real learning happens when you want to learn about something," she adds.

The museum continued to welcome school groups but stopped courting them and bending to their curriculum needs. Instead, Janice and her team doubled-down on family-centered, child-focused learning through play at the museum. They also expanded outreach programs beyond the museum's walls, assisting with play-based after-school programs in low-income areas of the city, working with foster children, and collaborating with local libraries and other organizations that allowed more flexibility and more focus on genuine play and exploration. From this process, Janice and her museum colleagues decided to take a stand on play. "We decided to take back the word play," she said. "We boldly declared that play is what we are about. Our message is that children's play is valuable. It is critical to their learning and lack of play is really hurting children."

During the early 2000s, as Janice firmly committed to preserving childhood free play, she grew increasingly unsettled. Her museum was about play, and children had great freedom to explore within its walls, but it was a destination. It required, for the most part, young people to be brought there by an adult, for an excursion. Janice saw the need to rekindle neighborhood play, the kind that she remembered from her own childhood and that was now nearly gone. She began to learn more about the adventure playground movement, recognizing it as a possible way to help today's play-deprived kids.

Like unschooling, adventure playgrounds are not new but there is new interest in them. The first adventure playground opened in Denmark in 1943. Coined a "junk playground," that name has come to classify many of today's adventure playgrounds. They are often filled with scrap materials, tools and nails, building equipment, cardboard boxes and recyclables. The idea is to allow young people of all ages a space where they can build and tear down, create and destroy in a more unstructured, self-directed play area than sterile playgrounds often allow. Carl Theodor Sørensen was the landscape designer who built the first adventure playground. He found that kids were much more interested in playing in all sorts of other spaces than the planned playgrounds he built. Children could see right through their artificiality and craved something grittier and more genuine for their play.

Adventure playgrounds spread throughout Europe during the second half of the twentieth century, with now over one thousand of them worldwide. Most of these playgrounds are outside of the United States, but the movement is growing here too. Janice was intrigued by the adventure playground model and did an extended stay in London visiting a popular adventure playground in the city's low-income East End neighborhood. She was encouraged. Here was a space, right in the children's urban neighborhood, where they could come and go freely and that allowed for fully self-directed play with a range of scrap materials. Trained playworkers ensured children's safety but never directed their play. Like unschooling parents and educators, the playworkers hold the space for self-directed learning, identifying and facilitating interests without interrupting a child's personal play mission. "Playwork is the art of supporting children's play without directing," says Janice. In describing playworkers, she uses an analogy of a lifeguard at an ocean beach, saying that the lifeguard is there to help if there is real, serious danger, but he might also see that a child is building something with sea shells and may let the child know that there is a great sea shell spot around the bend. Playworkers protect and facilitate. They don't interfere or instruct.

With renewed enthusiasm in her endeavor to preserve and promote childhood free play, Janice returned home and got to work to bring the adventure playground model to the children of Providence. The museum had been offering various "pop-up adventure play" programs in city parks that attracted several hundred people at these daylong events, but Janice wanted something more permanent and consistent. She teamed up with the city of Providence to create an adventure play summer program called PlayCorps. In collaboration with the Providence Children's Museum, the city's Healthy Communities office, and the parks department, PlayCorps launched in the summer of 2014. At several public parks and playgrounds across the city, mostly nestled in low-income areas flanked by public housing developments, young people can gather each summer weekday to play with a wide assortment of junk materials, tools, cardboard and duct tape, old sheets and cloths, balls and rope, paints and chalk and water, and other fun supplies in a fully self-directed play space. They come and go to the park freely. PlayCorps is staffed by grown-ups trained in playwork practices and who also distribute the federal free- and reduced-lunch program at these summertime parks. With a total price tag of $100,000, serving over thirty-five hundred kids all summer long, PlayCorps shows that a little can go a long way. Most of the cost goes to paying the PlayCorps staff, who are frequently college students or recent college graduates, many of whom grew up in the PlayCorps neighborhoods. Funding comes from a blend of public and private sources.

While PlayCorps is an important step forward in promoting play and allowing more children access to the ideals of self-directed learning, Janice is not complacent. "I'd like it to go further," she says, explaining that a year-round program with a designated neighborhood space would be the next step in elevating community-based, self-directed learning through play. She says that while the summer program is beneficial in being so centrally located to children's homes, it also has its drawbacks. Sharing public spaces can get tricky, such as when local day care programs arrive at the playground and have very different rules about play and supervision than the PlayCorps team. A permanent adventure playground, free and accessible to all of the city's children all year long is Janice's vision—not just for the city of Providence but for cities and towns throughout the country. "We have people in their twenties who have not played, and now they will become parents. The most important thing is to spread the value of self-directed play, and explain how our children are hurt by missing it," says Janice.

If You Can Make It Here, You Can Make It Anywhere

In New York City, another summertime adventure playground has emerged, sharing Janice's commitment to play. Called play:groundNYC, it is located on Governors Island, a 150-acre, uninhabited former military island base just a short ferry ride from lower Manhattan and Brooklyn with a striking view of the Statue of Liberty. The playground itself encompasses fifty thousand square feet and was offered by the city through the nonprofit Trust for Governors Island, charged with redeveloping the island for community use. On weekends from spring to fall, children can come for free to the junk playground, which is filled with remnant materials, spare parts, hammers and nails, and other leftovers and recyclables that create an ideal play space for kids. Weeklong summer camp programs on the island subsidize the cost of the weekend adventure play, allowing it to be free and open to the public as often as possible. As play:groundNYC is a destination spot, with the ferry ride making it difficult for kids to come and go on their own, parents usually accompany their kids, but they are not allowed in the playground itself. Instead, staff members trained in the principles of playwork ensure safety without direction. A family adventure playground space for parents and younger children to play together is adjacent to the main playground space, which is for children around ages six and older.

Not surprisingly, play:groundNYC was the brainchild of two New York City unschooling parents. Alexander Khost and Eve Mosher met at a kids' birthday party and struck up a conversation about free play and adventure playgrounds. They found many similarities between self-directed play and the self-directed childrearing they were practicing. "It's really about trusting kids and stepping back to allow them to have the space and time to make decisions," says Alex, who is a certified K–12 art teacher in New York. After that initial discussion, Alex and Eve threw themselves into the world of playwork, learning more about adventure playgrounds, finding like-minded collaborators at a local university, hosting pop-up junk playground events at city parks, establishing a nonprofit organization, and launching a crowd-funding campaign. In the year prior to their opening, the play:groundNYC team also joined with the Brooklyn Children's Museum, hosting an adventure play exhibit that drew hundreds of visitors.

In May 2016, play:groundNYC opened with great enthusiasm and support. Today it is thriving, with goals for expansion on the island and in additional locations throughout the city, making it more accessible to more children. "Play:groundNYC is a wonderful place for showing that, yes, this can happen. If you can do it in New York, you can do it anywhere," says Alex.

After-School Unschooling

When he's not at the playground, Alex also devotes his time to the Brooklyn Apple Academy. Apple Academy is a resource center for unschooling families who typically enjoy its offerings up to three days a week—although it is open full-time. Located in a bright, inviting space above a tavern in the heart of Brooklyn's South Slope neighborhood, Apple Academy features a woodshop, fully stocked kitchen, and a wide open main gathering room rimmed with board games and play mats. Two smaller rooms branch off the kitchen area, one a library with computers and a well-worn couch and the other the art room, with a large table and crafting supplies. When I arrived for my first visit to Apple Academy, Alex was facilitating the space. Some kids were involved in a serious board game of Risk in the art room, where a couple moms joined in on the fun. Two other boys were in the computer room, playing some games on their devices. Soon, with Risk over and the screens losing their luster, the kids gathered in the main play area, wrestling and running around. Alex suggested heading out to a playground or to the nearby skate park to release some energy, but the kids decided they wanted to get into another board game on that chilly afternoon. Soon, the after-school kids would be arriving, getting a much-needed self-directed break from an otherwise structured day.

Noah Apple Mayers started Brooklyn Apple Academy in 2010 as a part-time self-directed learning center, offering various classes and field trips for unschooling kids in the city. It expanded over the years, ultimately settling in to its current location and widening its offerings beyond the unschooling community. Noah first got a glimpse of alternative education when he was homeschooled for one year in the eighth grade in rural Maine. "Looking back, it was the best year of education that I ever had, including college," he says. As an adult, he moved to New York and worked at the Brooklyn Free School, followed by a "micro-school" started by some New York City homeschooling parents who wanted a blend of schooling and unschooling for their kids. Noah eventually started Brooklyn Apple Academy as a dedicated space for supporting self-directed education.

In addition to their weekday unschooling program, with optional classes offered but not required, Brooklyn Apple supports an after-school tinkering program based around the center's woodshop. The kids work on their own tinkering projects, with adults available if they want help, but everything is self directed. "A lot of the kids in the after-school program are completely scheduled," says Noah. "They are more scheduled than I could possibly imagine as a kid. It's the norm now. When they come here, they are decompressing from school." He finds that the kids may spend an hour or so in the woodshop, then they might spend an hour reading comics on the couch, and an hour playing board games. While technically a three-hour after-school tinkering class, the self-directed philosophy of the space means that the kids are free to follow their own interests and initiative during that time. "Freedom should be available to all," says Noah, who is actively exploring ways to make unschooling and self-directed learning more accessible to more families, whether as an alternative to conventional schooling or as a supplement to an otherwise schooled life.

Self-directed after-school programs can be a lifeline for young people who spend the majority of their days in structured, adult-led activities with little room for play. In Houston, Texas, self-directed after-school programming meets adventure play at the Parish School. Parish is a private school for children with communication and learning disabilities. Many of their students have diagnoses of autism spectrum disorder, ADHD, sensory processing disorder, dyslexia, and so on. In 2008, the head of the school decided to create an innovative after-school program accessible to students of the school as well as to other children in the larger community. On a three-acre parcel behind the school, an adventure playground was born. Since its inception, the Parish School's after-school adventure playground has been run by Jill Wood, who serves as the school's librarian during the day. The kids, ages six to twelve, have the run of the space, where they collaborate and construct, encounter difficulties, and resolve conflicts with as little adult intervention as possible. Just like kids used to do.

Jill's role within the school during the day gives her a particularly powerful perspective on the way unstructured, free play can be transformative for children. "There is a real connection between librarianship and playwork," Jill tells me during my visit, swapping her indoor shoes for rubber boots as she switches into playworker mode. "Librarians are fierce defenders of freedom, information, choice, non-censoring, and nonjudgmental environments for learning." Children who may have a hard time in the structured, teacher-led environment of school thrive in the after-school space, building essential confidence and skills that are difficult to cultivate in a classroom. The space attracts unschooled kids and others from the larger community, but it also serves many students from within the Parish School. "Children are so incredibly capable," says Jill of the children in the adventure playground.

> If we step back, they will make magic. This is no exaggeration. We cannot believe what the kids create here. And we are dealing with a population that many people believe struggle with play. We believe that so many things that are problems in a classroom aren't problems out here. If a child is having a difficult time, we adults ask ourselves how we can change the environment to better suit the child's need, not how we can change the person; whereas in the classroom more things are disruptive because of the structure of the environment.

I arrive at the Parish adventure playground on a warm winter afternoon, the sun beating down on bits of metal, large PVC pipes, tin cans, old tires, plastic bottles, bent hula hoops, wooden pallets, stacks of lumber, discarded holiday wreaths, tattered sheeting, and elaborately built play structures—all assembled and decorated by the kids. There is an overturned metal shopping cart on one side of the playground, an old suitcase on another. The bottom of a ceramic bird bath lies nearby. "Can I start building now?" asks the first child to arrive. She pulls the heavy top of an old plush, pastel-painted hobby horse, its wooden rocker missing, across the grass to a play structure nearby. Soon more children arrive, running into the space, many screaming at the top of their lungs. You can tell that being here is a release, an opportunity to let go of all the "shoulds" and "musts" and "don'ts" that have filled their day up until that point. "Screaming is therapeutic," laughs Jill.

Parents are not allowed in the after-school adventure playground, which is open four afternoons a week throughout the academic year, at a cost to parents of $450 a month for the full-time option. "Parents would make this space dangerous," says Jill. Admittedly, I am taken aback by this statement. Parents causing danger? Parents protect from danger, right? As I observe the young people play, I begin to understand what she means. Jill and her colleague, Wes Hamner, are trained in the practices of playwork. They know how to observe without interfering, how to facilitate without controlling, and—perhaps most important—how to distinguish hazards from risks. This is the part that can be tricky for parents. There were moments, I confess, when I saw kids climbing on high structures or playing in certain ways when I had to catch myself from saying "Be careful!" If it were my kids at those heights, I likely wouldn't have shown restraint.

As parents—even those of us who are mindful of the importance of self-directed play—we can't help but worry about our children and their safety. Sometimes this worrying can make self-directed play less safe. I am quite sure that if my parents saw my autumn acorn fights with the neighborhood kids, they would have, at best, told us to be careful and likely would have made us stop. But they didn't see us, and so we played. In the process of playing, we learned how to self-regulate and become responsible for our actions. We learned how to accurately assess risks, test our limits, and push ourselves within boundaries we set for ourselves. We learned to rely on our own judgment and to work collaboratively with others toward common goals. We hit roadblocks and argued. Sometimes we got hurt and cried. This is the piece of adventure play and playwork training that Jill finds so important. The minute a child thinks an adult is in charge of the space, and in charge of determining risks, setting limits, and managing conflicts, the play space can become both more sterile and more dangerous. In such instances, the responsibility for safety rests outside the child. Jill points to the fact that the adventure playground generally has fewer injuries than a nearby conventional playground.

Both Jill and Wes feel sorry for modern parents. Wes, who also coleads community Parkour programs for city youth, recalls:

> Growing up, we went in my dad's scrap pile and toolbox to play, but today kids aren't raised with that freedom because of the strictness of modern society. Society as a whole has changed. Parents

are reported to police for letting their kids play in the street. They are expected to have their kids in every structured activity—that's what "responsible" parents do. It makes it harder for the child not to look to the parent to always assess risk for them.

Jill adds, "There is so much pressure on parents. We are the in-between. This isn't opening the back door and letting your kids run in the woods for five hours, but it is freedom."

In many ways, it is a sad commentary on contemporary culture that we now need designated, staffed spaces to allow for something akin to the unsupervised, self-directed play many of us enjoyed as kids. But for many children—particularly those who live in cities like Providence, New York, or Houston—an adventure playground may be one of the few remaining opportunities for childhood freedom. As I sat in the Texas sunshine watching children play in ways that have been nearly forgotten, several questions persisted: Why isn't there an adventure playground in every community in America? Why can't we reinvent existing after-school programming to grant young people, who must otherwise be in conventional schools, at least some afternoon freedom and self direction? Why can't unschooling-inspired, play-filled summer camps and community summer programs expand to support children all year long? Why don't children spend the majority of their day in play, rather than the minority?

The answers to these questions rest with us. As parents, we are the ones who decide what is important for our children and our communities. What we value will emerge. What we prioritize will get done. Our community programs and public spaces directly reflect our values and priorities. The real question is, do we care enough about childhood freedom and self-directed play to catalyze change?

Unschooling Tips

- **Maximize out-of-school unschooling**. Recognize the importance of free, unstructured play to children's health and developmental well-being. Seek, or create, unschooling summer camps and after-school programs that emphasize self-directed learning through play.

• **Transform your neighborhood**. Take back childhood play in your own community. Work with local officials to block off streets for car-free afternoon and weekend play. Connect with neighbors who fondly remember their unstructured, unsupervised youthful play and brainstorm ways to re-create this environment for contemporary kids. Host a pop-up adventure play event in a local park. Build an adventure playground, or help to convert an existing after-school or summer program into a space that showcases the importance of playwork.

• **Connect with community resources.** Libraries, museums, and local parks departments can be great allies in expanding and supporting self-directed play and out-of-school unschooling. Many already do.

11

An Unschooled Future

"I was made for the library, not the classroom. The class-room was a jail of other people's interests. The library was open, unending, free."

—Ta-Nehisi Coates[1]

WE NEED AN EDUCATED CITIZENRY but we don't need a schooled one. The patterns of conformity, obedience, and authoritarianism that are cultivated by mass schooling limit our ability to effectively address our society's present and future challenges. More significantly, these schooled patterns prevent the full realization of human potential. A relic of the Industrial Age, conventional mass schooling crushes creativity, hampers exuberance, stifles natural curiosity, and halts invention. These human inclinations—creativity, exuberance, curiosity, inventiveness—are essential qualities for the new Imagination Age. The good news is that we don't need to teach these qualities; we simply need to stop destroying them. They already exist in every child. Our job is to nurture these qualities and support our children in being the most creative, exuberant, curious, inventive beings they can be. They already have these gifts. Let's not take them away.

We may have left the Industrial Era for the Imagination Age, but our dominant education system remains fully entrenched in factory-style schooling. Enclosing children in increasingly coercive, standardized, test-driven schooling environments for most of their formative years is incompatible with the needs and opportunities of the Imagination Age. In her book *Now You See It* Cathy Davidson says that 65 percent of children entering elementary school will work at jobs in the future that have not yet been invented. She writes, "In this time of massive change, we're giving our kids the tests and lesson plans designed for their great-great-grandparents."[2]

In a changing world, where robots increasingly perform the assembly line jobs of previous generations of humans, retaining children's natural curiosity and supporting their incessant drive to explore and invent are key priorities. Unschooling provides the educational framework to maximize human potential in a post-industrial age. According to a 2016 World Economic Forum report on the future of jobs, many of the careers and skills that are most in demand today did not exist a decade ago—or even five years ago.[3] A one-size-fits-all model of mass schooling, with a static curriculum and predefined competency expectations, is woefully inadequate to meet the needs of an innovation-based economy. How can we possibly train young people on what they need to know when we ourselves don't know what they will need to know only a few years from now? Instead, we can help them to direct their own education, to become masters of their own competencies, by immersing them in the authentic world around them and allowing them to explore the interests that emerge from that exposure.

Some education reformers advocate for more out-of-the-box thinking to enhance conventional schooling for the demands and values of contemporary society. They may push for a more child-centered curriculum, less testing, and a more holistic schooling environment. But out-of-the-box thinking isn't enough. Since the beginning of compulsory mass schooling, many progressive educators have tried to tweak and tinker with the forced schooling model, but by many accounts conventional schooling has become even more restrictive. We need to reject the box altogether and create an entirely new geometric shape. Schooling is the box. What does learning look like?

Fortunately, we already have successful models of learning without schooling, some of which I have described. More families can opt out of school for unschooling. Self-directed learning centers and unschooling schools can be scaled and expanded to reach more young people. Self-directed summer camps and after-school programs that reflect unschooling ideals can be offered full-time and year-round. Teen immersion and apprenticeship programs can grow. Adventure playgrounds and other efforts to prioritize community-based, self-directed play for children can sprout in neighborhoods across the country. We can welcome children back into our public spaces, rather than enclosing them in structured, adult-led activities and schoolstuffs. Supporting these self-directed opportunities is the vast technological platform that defines the Imagination Age, offering unprecedented access to knowledge and information for all.

Beyond these examples, there are other ways in which our communities can support self-directed, noncoercive education for everyone. In many instances they already are. By looking more closely at the quality public resources of our cities, towns, and neighborhoods, we may reveal new ways to support natural learning without forced schooling. By supporting educators who are disrupting the status quo and creating entirely new public schools that look nothing like schools, we may be able to move away from coercion and toward self determination in education. By encouraging entrepreneurship and investing in innovative education models, we may uncover new possibilities that have yet to be imagined. The blueprint for an unschooled but well-educated society is right in front of us. We need to be brave enough to bury the industrial schooling experiment and seek out alternatives to school that help learners to educate themselves for the Imagination Age and beyond.

Community Resources

When you first walk into the building in McAllen, Texas, what you notice is its size. At 123,000 square feet, the one-story structure is gigantic, but warm and welcoming. New windows, bright walls, modern lighting, colorful carpets and chairs, and soft couches make the space inviting despite its massive size. There is a blend of open space and quiet nooks, 116 computer labs (including ten just for kids), a full-service café and volunteer-run bookstore, meeting rooms with state-of-the-art video-conferencing capability, and a 180-seat auditorium. And it is all free and open to the public seven days a week, 354 days a year. What is this extraordinary place?

The McAllen Public Library.

Renovated in 2012, the library is in a former Walmart store repurposed to meet the needs of the local community. Patronage has more than doubled with the new building, as it provides more space and more resources for learning, connection, and community engagement.[4] Libraries are public education at its best.

Even as many of their budgets get slashed, public libraries across the country are offering more with less, transforming into dynamic, free, and open learning spaces for all members of the community. By doing much more than lending books, public libraries are increasingly meeting the varied educational needs of their community with many other services. In Sacramento, California, the public library lends sewing machines, ukuleles, cameras, and board games. In Ann Arbor, Michigan, public library patrons can borrow telescopes and microscopes. In Grand Rapids, Minnesota, patrons can borrow fishing rods; in Biddeford, Maine, it's snowshoes; and in North Haven, Connecticut, it's cake pans.[5]

When trying to envision what an unschooled future might look like, public libraries are ideal examples. Publicly funded, sometimes supplemented by private donations, libraries are free, self-directed learning spaces in the truest sense. Unlike public schools, they do not discriminate by age. Patrons are not required to be there under a legal threat of force. There are no regulations on what or how to learn. Aside from some basic health and safety rules, community members are free to explore and use the library as they choose, with experienced librarians and volunteers available to help when needed. Many libraries host classes or activities, such as lectures, computer classes, English-as-a-second-language lessons, and librarian-led story times and book clubs. These events are available to all members of the community and are entirely optional. There is no coercion, no one telling others what they must learn or do. In some communities, the public library assumes summertime distribution of the federal free- and reduced-lunch program, helping to nourish children all year long.

In cities and towns across America, the public library is an elegant and efficient example of a taxpayer-funded, free and fully accessible, year-round self-directed learning space. Resources and classes are provided, knowledgeable staff facilitate natural learning, and community members of all different ages and experiences learn together, freely and without compulsion. Industrialist and philanthropist Andrew Carnegie declared that a library "outranks any other one thing that a community can do to benefit its people. It is the never failing spring in the desert."[6]

As a poor Scottish immigrant who came to the United States in 1848 at the age of thirteen, Carnegie had little access to formal schooling and was largely self educated, with books his primary teacher. Carnegie biographer David Nasaw explains that "Andy took his own self-education seriously. He wanted to read widely because that was what a man and citizen did, whether artisan or mechanic, clerk or merchant, Scottish or American."[7] Books in mid-nineteenth-century America were not cheap or readily accessible, but Carnegie caught a break when, in 1850, Alleghany, Pennsylvania, businessman Colonel James Anderson established his city's first quasi-public library. Colonel Anderson allowed local boys to borrow a book from his library each Saturday and return it the following week.[8]

Anderson's gesture deeply influenced Carnegie and served as the inspiration for Carnegie to dedicate a substantial portion of his acquired wealth toward establishing more than twenty-five hundred public libraries. The Carnegie libraries were often the first free public libraries in cities and towns across the country, and they set the precedent for the "open stack" library model, where patrons searched for books on their own rather than waiting for a librarian to retrieve them. Beginning in the early twentieth century, Carnegie libraries also featured some of the first designated children's rooms. Many served as vibrant community centers, housing bowling alleys, music halls, billiard tables, swimming pools, and gymnasiums.[9] Carnegie wrote in his autobiography, "It was from my own early experience that I decided there was no use to which money could be applied so productive of good to boys and girls . . . as the founding of a public library in a community which is willing to support it as a municipal institution."[10] The enduring and expanding legacy of public libraries as dynamic centers of self-directed education provides an important prototype for noncoercive learning without schooling.

Libraries are not the only existing examples of free and accessible, community-based, self-directed learning hubs. Many museums across the country highlight what can happen when abundant resources and opportunities are made publicly available to all members of the community. The Smithsonian Institution in Washington, DC, for example, blends both public funding and private donations to create a vibrant center of learning and discovery. Founded in 1846, the Smithsonian features nineteen museums and galleries plus the National Zoo—most of which are entirely free of charge and open 364 days a year (Christmas Day being the exception). At the Smithsonian, like other freely accessible museums, patrons can explore exhibits at their own pace, lingering in areas that most interest them and avoiding those that don't. Talented curators, staff, and volunteers are available to answer questions and explain content. Optional lectures, demonstrations, and hands-on activities are offered throughout the day with patrons welcome to participate or not. Imagine if, like public libraries, every community also had a public museum to support and encourage self-directed education.

Public libraries and public museums, along with other resources like public parks and beaches, public community centers, and public transportation, demonstrate the difference between public goods and coercive institutions. One is voluntary, openly accessible, and non-compulsory; the other is not. I overheard a conversation recently between a mom and her elementary-school-age daughter. The young girl was complaining about another child who sat next to her on the school bus that day and who was being mean to her. The mom tried to reassure her daughter, saying some days you get to sit next to people you like on the bus and some days you don't. "It's just like the city bus," the mom said. Except it really isn't. On the city bus, there are new and different people alongside you every day and, crucially, you can press the button and get off at the next stop. Compulsory schooling is inherently coercive.

By moving away from forced schooling and toward a model of education as a noncoercive public good—broadly defined and diversely offered—we can facilitate the creativity, exuberance, curiosity, and inventiveness of all our citizens. As Paul Goodman writes in *Compulsory Miseducation*: "On the whole, the education must be voluntary rather than compulsory, for no growth to freedom occurs except by intrinsic motivation. Therefore, the educational opportunities must be various and variously administered. We must diminish rather than expand the present monolithic school system."[11] Our public libraries and public museums, as well as many other public goods, reveal the power of freedom over force.

Educators

Freedom is what drove a team of veteran public school teachers to build a radically different kind of public school focused on many unschooling principles. Clear in their mission that simply removing walls and desks, giving kids some choice, and making schooling a little less unpleasant isn't enough, Scott Evans and Gabriel Cooper are part of the California team that created UnSchool San Juan, which opened in the fall of 2017. There are no grades, no tests, no homework. Students aren't referred to as freshmen or sophomores; they interact in multiage, interdisciplinary groups based on interests and goals. There is a large makerspace in the school, and abundant tools and technology. Community members are a vital part of UnSchool San Juan's internal learning environment, and outside apprenticeships are valued and sought. Like the Powderhouse School outside of Boston described earlier, UnSchool San Juan has teacher union support for their bold experiment in shifting from schooling to learning.

Scott and Gabriel each have about twenty years of experience within the district. Year after year, their frustration mounted. "Many kids are failing in the system and it's not the students' fault—it's the system," says Gabriel. The team was approached by the district's superintendent to create something new, and they devised their unorthodox plan: build a self-directed public high school that would allow young people to explore their own interests, pursue their own projects, and be surrounded by helpful resources and mentors to support them in whatever path they choose. The superintendent has been supportive, willing to take a chance on a project that attempts to overhaul both the structures and attitudes of conventional schooling.

Some modern public schools have implemented software or systems that allow young people more personalized choice and control, but they still operate under a set curriculum and standard assessment practices. They may be self-paced, allowing a student to move through the material on her own time and in her own chosen order, but the content is directed by the school—not the child. UnSchool San Juan is trying to push beyond that, while still operating within a conventional school district. "Coming to the UnSchool is the hardest place to get an education," says Scott, explaining how following the passive, teach-and-test approach of conventional schooling is in many ways easier than taking command of one's own learning and doing—even if that learning and doing remain loosely connected to district requirements.

Scott and Gabriel don't see any negatives if students participate in statewide standardized testing, but they plan to let students and parents decide whether or not to opt out of testing. If students want to earn a high school diploma from UnSchool San Juan, then they need to meet certain expectations related to core content areas. "Our students will still need to get credits for traditional core subject requirements in the district," says Gabriel. All UnSchool San Juan students work on projects connected to their interests, but to meet subject requirements the projects must be mapped to larger core competencies. Students decide how they want to show learning and mastery. The goal is for this to happen as naturally as possible, with advisor support. For instance, one student at UnSchool San Juan wants to build a ballista, an ancient catapult. The student will determine his own learning goals, but he may look at the historical, mathematical, and physics-related concepts throughout the course of his project and demonstrate sufficient understanding of content. While they are more loosely interpreted, and directly tied to a student's personal learning goals, the subject requirements create some constraints around content and assessment that unschoolers outside of conventional school districts avoid. Gabriel is not too concerned about this. "Learning is not without structure," he says.

Even with these few constraints, young people at UnSchool San Juan are granted much greater freedom and autonomy than their conventionally schooled peers. According to Gabriel and Scott, young people in school have been trained that a certain credit equals a certain outcome. It's a predictable, linear process. Moving from that conventional model to a more self-directed, interest-driven one requires a major mental and emotional shift. The founding team witnessed a predictable deschooling process in their students, similar to what other unschoolers go through when leaving traditional schooling environments. "They sit for months and then the lightbulb comes on," says Gabriel. They realize that they are much more in charge of their own education. It is up to them. Parents are often the ones who witness the most dramatic changes in their child's beliefs and attitudes. "Parents say they have never seen their kids grow so much as a human," says Gabriel. "They are amazing people now."

Along with their students, Scott and Gabriel say they continue to go through their own deschooling process. They catch themselves when using the language of typical schooling, like referring to students by level or talking about grades. It's a big learning curve—for adults and kids alike. "Never in my career have I been so outside of my comfort zone. Sometimes, I am in the danger zone," says Gabriel, who was an educator for eighteen years and is now the principal of UnSchool San Juan. "Stretching yourself to engage in this process is super scary. Your worst fear is to harm students' dreams. I am really honest with parents. I say I am not sure that this is going to work—but I am also not sure that conventional school will work. This is a roller-coaster ride, but then so is life."

As a new endeavor within the conventional public schooling system, UnSchool San Juan shows what could be possible. If eager educators are supported, if innovative ideas are embraced, and if learning over school-ing is allowed to prevail, there is hope that conventional schools could reinvent themselves as unschools. "Time will tell," says Gabriel. "The Greek root of the word 'school' means leisure. It was supposed to be enjoyable. The current system is broken, but maybe we can go back to what learning is all about—interests and discovery." UnSchool San Juan is a test. Will these educators be allowed to continue with their vision for a self-directed public school? Will traditional curriculum and account-ability metrics eventually exert more pressure? Will student autonomy be able to endure within an otherwise traditional school district? It remains to be seen whether UnSchool San Juan succeeds in ushering in a new era of public schooling, or if, like many of its predecessors, it gets reabsorbed into the dominant school system. As Gabriel says: "We feel like we are standing on the edge of a cliff and we don't know if we will be pulled back or allowed to leap."

Entrepreneurs

Educators like Gabriel and Scott are hoping to reform conventional schooling from within, but others are looking to build something entirely new outside of the prevailing system. Constructing a new education model that empowers parents and teachers alike is what drives entrepreneurs like Manisha Snoyer. Back in 2009, Manisha was a teaching artist and wanted to earn some extra money, so she started a foreign language school for adults. She loved teaching and working closely with her students but found that marketing and billing and other administrative functions consumed much of her time and energy. She wanted to focus on teaching and learning, not paperwork. She also met many other talented teacher-friends who wanted to launch similar educational programs but lacked the marketing tools and start-up savvy to make it work.

During this time, Manisha was also a host for Airbnb, renting out her New York City apartment at various points over the previous four years. "I started to wonder," says Manisha, "what if a marketplace could do for education innovators what Airbnb does for hosts: take away the marketing and payments processing so they can focus on building an incredible offering?" She launched CottageClass to do just that—and in 2017 secured angel investing from Airbnb cofounder Nate Blecharczyk and VP of Trips, Joseph Zadeh, both of whom have young children of their own. CottageClass now supports teachers and parents in creating and delivering a variety of education programs for children. It manages all of the administrative functions for these "edupreneurs" and helps to connect them to interested families and learners in the larger community. Just as Airbnb has reshaped the short-term lodging industry by working within the sharing economy, CottageClass and similar ventures can help to transform education. As Manisha says, "We built

CottageClass to make it easier for families to find grassroots learning initiatives and to make it easier for teachers and parent organizers to start new ones."

Manisha finds that the parents she works with are often frustrated by rigid, overcrowded, test-driven conventional schooling. Many, she says, never before considered alternatives to school but became so frustrated by mass schooling that they had no choice but to look elsewhere. According to Manisha, "There are increasing numbers of what you could call 'mainstream families' who normally wouldn't break the mold but are considering alternatives to the status quo—out of sheer desperation more than anything else. They are opting out of standardized tests or opting out of the traditional school system." CottageClass helps to connect these families with schooling alternatives in their community and very often leads these once "mainstream" families to become true alternative education zealots. "Inevitably," says Manisha, "they all become passionate about alternative education when they see the positive effects on their children and the wonderful communities they become a part of."

CottageClass is free for teachers and learners to join, enabling educators to create exceptional courses and families to explore various offerings without a financial commitment. If learners enroll in a course using the CottageClass platform, the company gets a percentage of the enrollment fee. Current offerings include workshops, one-off courses, child-care shares, summer camps, after-school and preschool programs, self-directed learning centers and "microschools." One of their offerings is Dida Academy, a self-directed learning center and mentoring resource for teens located in the heart of Brooklyn, New York. Dida cofounder Danielle Levine explains that CottageClass has been instrumental in helping her to build the Dida brand, get initial students, create community with other like-minded educators, and manage billing and enrollment. CottageClass also provides general liability insurance and property damage insurance for its member organizations, something Danielle says is rare and a huge bonus for small, upstart learning organizations. The full-time learning centers that CottageClass represents are generally half the cost of a typical private school and pay their teachers 20 percent more, showing the possibility for higher-value, lower-cost education when driven directly by parents and teachers.

CottageClass does not control or manage the content of any of their courses, so while not all of their offerings reflect unschooling values, many do. The educators offering programs have complete freedom when creating and delivering content. "When you give people that much freedom," says Manisha,

> you inevitably attract people who believe in freedom and self-direction. It's our belief that every child (and every human) has a natural curiosity, a biological thirst to learn and grow. As educators and caregivers, it's our job to provide children with their basic needs (food, shelter, love) and to support them in what they do best—learn.

Manisha's vision for CottageClass is bold. She hopes that this decentralized model re-empowers parents and teachers and fundamentally reshapes American education. Already CottageClass has served over four hundred families. Currently based in New York City, the organization is expanding to other cities and has already received inquiries from twenty-five hundred teachers from seventy-seven cities around the world. As CottageClass grows, Manisha finds a common thread: eager educators who feel stifled in a standardized, conventional system and frustrated parents hoping for something better for their children. "We want all parents to be able to guide their child's education as they see fit, and choose from a diverse variety of courses, schools, and activities," says Manisha. "Our mission is to rebuild our education system from the ground up by the people who know it best—teachers, parents, and kids."

Parents

It all comes down to parents. It will be parents who decide whether or not we move toward an unschooled future. It will be parents who determine whether or not to reclaim their child's education. Will conventional schooling, as bad as it is, still prevail? Is an inadequate babysitter still better than none? If everyone else uses her, isn't she good enough? Parents will choose whether or not to settle for good enough. Parents will decide whether to keep funneling more than $600 billion into K–12 conventional US schooling every year, or to invest in noncoercive, self-directed education options for all young people. Education can be disentangled from schooling.

The apparatus to support an unschooled but highly educated society exists. Unschooling families, self-directed learning centers, unschooling schools, out-of-school unschooling resources—and the grown alumni of each—show that young people can and do retain their curiosity, passion, and excitement for learning when allowed to grow without school. Community resources and technology provide an existing framework to expand self-directed, noncoercive education to more young people, in ways already available to adults. Public libraries and museums have long been examples of taxpayer-funded but non-compulsory hubs for natural learning and lifelong education. Educators and entrepreneurs are inventing new opportunities to facilitate unschooling and provide greater education freedom and choice.

Children are not widgets. They do not need to be placed on an assembly line when they are tots and worked on for over a decade to become shiny and learned. Education is a natural process of absorbing and synthesizing content and culture. It can be supported in numerous ways without destroying the curiosity and imagination that drive human learning. An unschooled future envisions the simple but revolutionary idea of noncoercive, self-directed education for all young people. It leverages real and virtual resources to support natural learning, and relies on adults who facilitate more than teach. Moving beyond schooling, to embrace education as a broader societal good, opens up many new possibilities for learning. I have shared some of these examples, and there are likely many others that have yet to be built. As parents, we decide whether we stay mired in an industrial model of conventional schooling or instead welcome an unschooled future that nurtures curious, well-educated children. Unschooling ourselves is an important first step.

Acknowledgments

THANK YOU TO MY HUSBAND, Brian, and our wonderful children, who gave me the time and strength to tackle this project.

A special thanks to my agent, Jill Marsal, who spotted the potential in this book idea and found it an ideal home with the great team at Chicago Review Press.

With gratitude to my mother, Joanne McDonald, who read draft after draft; to my friends Susan Koechner and Rachel Chaney for their early edits and insights; to Tali Richards for her research help; and to Walter Grinder, Charles Hamilton, and Lawrence Reed for their ongoing encouragement and mentorship.

Thank you to Peter Gray and my colleagues at the Alliance for Self-Directed Education who work tirelessly to promote unschooling ideals and to make this educational philosophy more accessible to more families.

Finally, to the parents, educators, and unschoolers featured in these pages, I am deeply honored to share your stories and visions of learning without schooling.

Additional Resources

Books

A White Rose: A Soldier's Story of Love, War, and School, by Brian Huskie
Art of Self-Directed Learning, by Blake Boles
Better Late Than Early, by Raymond and Dorothy Moore
Better Than School, by Nancy Wallace
Big Book of Unschooling, by Sandra Dodd
Challenging Assumptions in Education, by Wendy Priesnitz
Creative Schools, by Ken Robinson
College Without High School, by Blake Boles
Compulsory Miseducation and the Community of Scholars, by Paul Goodman
Deschooling Our Lives, by Matt Hern
Deschooling Society, by Ivan Illich
Dumbing Us Down, by John Taylor Gatto
The End of School, by Zachary Slayback
Free at Last, by Daniel Greenberg
Free-Range Kids, by Lenore Skenazy
Free Range Learning, by Laura Grace Weldon
Free Schools, Free People, by Ron Miller
Free to Learn, by Peter Gray
Free to Live, by Pam Laricchia
Growing Up Absurd, by Paul Goodman
Guerrilla Learning, by Grace Llewellyn and Amy Silver
Hacking Your Education, by Dale Stephens

Home Grown, by Ben Hewitt
Homeschooling Our Children, Unschooling Ourselves, by Alison McKee
How Children Fail, by John Holt
How Children Learn, by John Holt
In Defense of Childhood: Protecting Kids' Inner Wildness, by Chris Mercogliano
Learning All the Time, by John Holt
Like Water, by Mark McCaig
The Lives of Children, by George Dennison
The Modern School Movement, by Paul Avrich
Passion-Driven Education, by Connor Boyack
Pedagogy of the Oppressed, by Paulo Freire
Radical Unschooling, by Dayna Martin
Summerhill School: A New View of Childhood, by A. S. Neill
Schools on Trial: How Freedom and Creativity Can Fix Our Educational Malpractice, by Nikhil Goyal
School Free, by Wendy Priesnitz
School's Over: How to Have Freedom and Democracy in Education, by Jerry Mintz
Starting a Sudbury School, by Daniel Greenberg and Mimsy Sadofsky
The Teacher Liberation Handbook: How to Leave School and Create a Place Where You and Young People Can Thrive, by Joel Hammon
Teen 2.0: Saving Our Children and Families from the Torment of Adolescence, by Robert Epstein
The Teenage Liberation Handbook, by Grace Llewellyn
Teaching the Restless: One School's No-Ritalin Approach to Helping Children Learn and Succeed, by Chris Mercogliano
Teach Your Own, by John Holt and Patrick Farenga
The Unschooling Handbook, by Mary Griffith
The Unschooling Unmanual, by Jan Hunt
Weapons of Mass Instruction, by John Taylor Gatto

Films

Class Dismissed, Jeremy Stuart
On Being and Becoming, Clara Bellar
Self-Taught, Jeremy Stuart
Schooling the World: The White Man's Last Burden, Carol Black
The War on Kids, Cevin Soling

Websites

African American Unschooling (http://scwalton0.tripod.com)

Agile Learning Centers (http://agilelearningcenters.org)

Alliance for Self-Directed Education (http://www.self-directed.org)

Alternative Education Resource Organization (http://www.educationrevolution.org)

Alternatives to School (http://www.alternativestoschool.com)

Camp Stomping Ground (http://campstompingground.org)

Christian Unschooling (http://www.christianunschooling.com)

The Classical Unschooler (http://www.purvabrown.com)

Confessions of a Muslim Mom (http://www.confessionsofamuslimmommaholic.com)

CottageClass (http://cottageclass.com)

Eclectic Learning Network (http://www.eclecticlearningnetwork.com)

European Democratic Education Community (http://www.eudec.org)

Fare of the Free Child (http://www.akilahsrichards.com)

Freedom to Learn (http://www.psychologytoday.com/us/blog/freedom-learn)

Free Range Kids (http://www.freerangekids.com)

Growing Minds (http://www.growingminds.co.za)

Happiness Is Here (http://happinessishereblog.com)

I'm Unschooled. Yes, I Can Write. (http://www.yes-i-can-write.blogspot.com)

International Democratic Education Network (http://www.idenetwork.org)

John Holt/Growing Without Schooling (http://www.johnholtgws.com)

Joyfully Rejoicing (http://www.joyfullyrejoycing.com)

Let Grow (http://letgrow.org)

Liberated Learners (http://www.liberatedlearners.net)

Life Learning Magazine (http://www.lifelearningmagazine.com)

Living Joyfully (http://livingjoyfully.ca)

Natural Child Project (http://www.naturalchild.org)

Not-Back-to-School Camp (http://www.nbtsc.org)

Peer Unschooling Network (http://peerunschooling.net)

Praxis (http://discoverpraxis.com)

Project World School (http://projectworldschool.com)

Secular Homeschool (http://www.secularhomeschool.com)

School Sucks Project (http://schoolsucksproject.com)

UnCollege (http://www.uncollege.org)

Unschool Adventures (http://www.unschooladventures.com)

Unschooling Dads (http://www.unschoolingdads.com)

Unschooling Mom2Mom (http://unschoolingmom2mom.com)

Worldschooling Central (http://www.worldschoolingcentral.com)

Notes

Introduction

1. Albert Einstein, *Autobiographical Notes*, trans. Paul Arthur Schlipp (La Salle: Open Court, 1979), 17.

2. John Holt, *How Children Learn*, rev. (New York: Da Capo Press, 2017), xi.

3. Peter Gray, *Free to Learn: Why Unleashing the Instinct to Play Will Make Our Children Happier, More Self-Reliant, and Better Learners for Life* (New York: Basic Books, 2013), x–xi.

4. Ivan Illich, *Deschooling Society* (London: Marion Boyars, 1970), 47.

5. John Holt, *Instead of Education* (Boulder, CO: Sentient Publications, 2004), 4.

1. Playing School

1. Henry David Thoreau, *The Writings of Henry David Thoreau, Journal II: 1850–September 15, 1851*, ed. Bradford Torrey (Boston: Houghton, Mifflin & Co., 1906), 83.

2. Robert L. Fried, *The Game of School: Why We All Play It, How It Hurts Kids, and What It Will Take to Change It* (San Francisco: Jossey-Bass, 2005), x.

3. Cevin Soling, "Why Public Schools Must Be Abolished," *Forbes*, February 27, 2012, http://www.forbes.com/sites/jamesmarshallcrotty/2012/02/27/why-public-schools-must-be-abolished/#d99c7732e377.

4. The Film Archives, "Education Is a System of Indoctrination of the Young - Noam Chomsky," YouTube video, June 1, 2012, 7:35, https://youtu.be/JvqMAlgAnlo.

5. Film Archives, "Education Is a System of Indoctrination."

6. Kirsten Olson, *Wounded by School: Recapturing the Joy in Learning and Standing Up to Old School Culture* (New York: Teachers College Press, 2009), xv.

7. Milton Gaither, *Homeschool: An American History* (New York: Palgrave MacMillan, 2008), 9.

8. Sheldon S. Cohen, *A History of Colonial Education; 1607–1776* (New York: John Wiley & Sons, 1974), 46.

9. Eric R. Eberling, "Massachusetts Education Laws of 1642, 1647, and 1648," *Historical Dictionary of American Education*, ed. Richard J. Altenbaugh (Westport, CT: Greenwood Press, 1999), 225–26.

10. Samuel Bowles and Herbert Gintis, "The Origins of Mass Public Education," *History of Education: Major Themes, Volume II: Education in Its Social Context*, ed. Roy Lowe (London: RoutledgeFlamer, 2000), 62–63.

11. Carl Kaestle, *Pillars of the Republic: Common Schools and American Society, 1780–1860* (New York: Hill and Wang, 1983), xi.

12. Thomas Jefferson, Letter to Charles Yancy, January 6, 1816, http://tjrs.monti cello.org/letter/327.

13. Thomas Jefferson, *The Writings of Thomas Jefferson*, ed. Andrew A. Lipscomb (Thomas Jefferson Memorial Association, 1904), 423.

14. Bob Pepperman Taylor, *Horace Mann's Troubling Legacy: The Education of Democratic Citizens* (Lawrence: University Press of Kansas, 2010), 8.

15. Charles Leslie Glenn, *The Myth of the Common School* (Amherst: University of Massachusetts Press, 1988), 107.

16. Glenn, *Myth of the Common School*, 79.

17. Heather Andrea Williams, *Self-Taught: African American Education in Slavery and Freedom* (Chapel Hill: University of North Carolina Press, 2005).

18. Bowles and Gintis, "Origins of Mass Public Education," 78.

19. US Bureau of the Census, *Education of the American Population, A 1960 Census Monograph*, by John K. Folger and Charles B. Nam (Washington, DC: US Government Printing Office, 1967), 113.

20. Maris A. Vinovskis, *Education, Society, and Economic Opportunity: A Historical Perspective on Persistent Issues* (New Haven, CT: Yale University Press, 1995), 109.

21. David B. Tyack, *The One Best System: A History of American Urban Education* (Cambridge, MA: Harvard University Press, 1974), 30.

22. Paul E. Peterson, *Saving Schools: From Horace Mann to Virtual Learning* (Cambridge, MA: Belknap Press, 2010), 26.

23. Taylor, *Horace Mann's Troubling Legacy*, 33.

24. Jonathan Messerli, *Horace Mann: A Biography* (New York: Alfred A. Knopf, 1972), 429.

25. Michael S. Katz, "A History of Compulsory Education Laws," *Phi Beta Kappa* (Fastback Series No. 75, 1976), 17.

26. James G. Carter, Essays upon Popular Education: Containing a Particular Examination of the Schools of Massachusetts, and an Outline of an Institution for the Education of Teachers. (Boston: Bowles & Dearborn, 1826), 48–49.

27. Messerli, *Horace Mann*, 429.

28. Pierce v. Society of Sisters, 268 U.S. 510 (1925).

29. Charles Leslie Glenn, *The Myth of the Common School* (Amherst: University of Massachusetts Press, 1988), 76.

30. Carla Shalaby, *Troublemakers: Lessons in Freedom from Young Children at School* (New York: New Press, 2017), xx.

31. John Taylor Gatto, "I Quit, I Think," *Wall Street Journal*, Op-Ed, July 25, 1991.

32. John Taylor Gatto, *Dumbing Us Down: The Hidden Curriculum of Compulsory Schooling* (BC, Canada: New Society Publishers, 1992), 7–8.

33. Raymond S. Moore and Dorothy N. Moore, *Better Late Than Early: A New Approach to Your Child's Education* (Camas, WA: Reader's Digest Press, 1976), 52.

34. Margaret L. Kern and Howard S. Friedman, "Early Educational Milestones as Predictors of Lifelong Academic Achievement, Midlife Adjustment, and Longevity," *Journal of Applied Developmental Psychology* 30, no.4 (2008): 419–430.

35. Graeme Paton, "Bright Children Should Start School at Six, Says Academic," *Telegraph*, May 16, 2012, http://www.telegraph.co.uk/education/educationnews /9266592/Bright-children-should-start-school-at-six-says-academic.html.

36. Nancy Wallace, *Better Than School* (Burdett, NY: Larson Publications, 1983), 33.

37. US Department of Education, National Center for Educational Statistics, *Homeschooling in the United States: 2012*, by Jeremy Redford, Danielle Battle, Stacey Bielick, and Sarah Grady, Open-file report 2016-096.rev, National

Center for Education Statistics (Washington, DC, 2017), https://nces.ed.gov
/pubs2016/2016096rev.pdf.

38. Brian Ray, "Research Facts on Homeschooling," National Home Education
Research Institute, January 13, 2018, https://www.nheri.org/research-facts
-on-homeschooling/; US Department of Education, National Center
for Education Statistics, "The Condition of Education 2017," Open-file
report 2017-144, J. McFarland, B. Hussar, C. de Brey, T. Snyder, X. Wang,
S. Wilkinson-Flicker, S. Gebrekristos, J. Zhang, A. Rathbun, A. Barmer,
F. Bullock Mann, and S. Hinz, National Center for Education Statistics
(Washington, DC, March 2017), https://nces.ed.gov/pubs2017/2017144.pdf.

39. William Heuer and William Donovan, "Homeschooling: The Ultimate
School Choice," Pioneer Institute for Public Policy Research, white paper
no. 170, June 2017, https://pioneerinstitute.org/featured/study-states-provide
-parents-information-homeschooling-options.

40. US Department of Education, National Center for Education Statistics, "Parent and Family Involvement in Education: Results from the National Household Education Surveys Program of 2016," September 2017, https://nces
.ed.gov/pubsearch/pubsinfo.asp?pubid=2017102.

41. Tara Bahrampour, "Muslims Turning to Home Schooling in Increasing Numbers," *Washington Post*, February 21, 2010, http://www.washingtonpost.com
/wp-dyn/content/article/2010/02/20/AR2010022001235.html.

42. Jaweed Kaleem, "Homeschooling Without God," *The Atlantic*, March 30, 2016,
https://www.theatlantic.com/education/archive/2016/03/homeschooling
-without-god/475953.

43. Richard G. Medlin, "Homeschooling and the Question of Socialization Revis-
ited," *Peabody Journal of Education* 88, no. 3 (2013): 284–297.

44. Wallace, *Better Than School*, 237.

45. Wendy Priesnitz, *School Free: The Home Schooling Handbook* (St. George,
ON: Alternate Press, 1987), 17,19.

46. Laura Grace Weldon, *Free Range Learning: How Homeschooling Changes
Everything* (Prescott, AZ: Hohm Press, 2010).

2. What Is Unschooling?

1. Akilah S. Richards, "The Freedom of Unschooling: Raising Liberated Black Children Without the Restrictions of School," *Student Voices*, February 21, 2016, https://mystudentvoices.com/the-freedom-of-unschooling-raising -liberated-black-children-without-the-restrictions-of-school-58347bf5919.

2. J. Gary Knowles, Stacey Marlow, and James Muchmore, "From Pedagogy to Ideology: Origins and Phases of Home Education in the United States, 1970– 1990," *American Journal of Education* 100, no. 2 (1992): 195–235.

3. Wendy Priesnitz, "The Words We Use: Living as if School Doesn't Exist," *Life Learning Magazine*, http://www.lifelearningmagazine.com/definitions /the-words-we-use-living-as-if-school-doesnt-exist.htm.

4. Karl F. Wheatley, "Unschooling: A Growing Oasis for Development and Democracy," *Encounter: Education for Meaning and Social Justice* 22, no. 2 (2009): 27–32.

5. Franklin Bobbitt, *The Curriculum* (Boston: Houghton Mifflin, 1918), 42.

6. David Hamilton, *Towards a Theory of Schooling* (London: Falmer Press, 1989), 45.

7. Karl F. Wheatley, "Questioning the Instruction Assumption: Implications for Education Policy and Practice," *Journal of Education and Human Development* 4, no. 1 (March 2015): 27–39.

8. Wheatley, "Questioning the Instruction Assumption."

9. M. G. Siegler, "Eric Schmidt: Every 2 Days We Create as Much Information as Did up to 2003," *TechCrunch*, August 4, 2010, http://techcrunch .com/2010/08/04/schmidt-data.

10. Charlie Magee, "The Age of Imagination: Coming Soon to a Civilization Near You," Second International Symposium: National Security and National Competitiveness: Open Source Solutions, 1993, http://www.oss.net/dynamaster /file_archive/040320/4a32a59dcdc168eced6517b5e6041cda/OSS1993-01-21.pdf.

11. Drew Hansen, "Imagination: What You Need to Thrive in the Future Economy," *Forbes*, August 6, 2012, https://www.forbes.com/sites/drewhansen /2012/08/06/imagination-future-economy/#2718867356dc.

12. Harry Bahrick and Lynda Hall, "Lifetime Maintenance of High School Mathematics Content," *Journal of Experimental Psychology: General* 120, no.1 (March 1991): 20–33.

13. Ansel Adams, *An Autobiography*, with Mary Street Alinder (New York: Little, Brown, 1985).

14. Ronald Swartz, *From Socrates to Summerhill and Beyond* (Charlotte, NC: Information Age Publishing, 2016), 174.

15. John Holt, *How Children Learn*, rev. (New York: Da Capo Press, 2017), xii–xiii.

16. Herbert R. Kohl, *The Open Classroom: A Practical Guide to a New Way of Teaching* (New York: New York Review, 1969), 12.

17. Rebecca M. Ryan, Ariel Kalil, Kathleen M. Ziol-Guest, and Christina Padilla, "Socioeconomic Gaps in Parents' Discipline Strategies from 1988 to 2011," *Pediatrics* 138, no. 6 (December 2016), http://pediatrics.aappublications.org/content/early/2016/11/10/peds.2016-0720.

3. The Roots of Unschooling

1. John Dewey, "My Pedagogic Creed," *School Journal* LIV, no. 3 (January 16, 1897): 77–80.

2. Matthew Josephson, *Edison: A Biography* (New York: John Wiley & Sons, 1992), 21.

3. Josephson, *Edison*, 22.

4. Josephson, *Edison*, 412

5. John Locke, *Some Thoughts Concerning Education 2nd ed*, (London: Cambridge University Press, 1889), 53.

6. Jean-Jacques Rousseau, *Emile, or, On Education: Includes Emile and Sophie, or, The Solitaries*, trans. and ed. Christopher Kelly and Allan Bloom (Hanover, NH: University Press of New England, 2010).

7. Ann Taylor Allen, "Spiritual Motherhood: German Feminists and the Kindergarten Movement, 1848–1911," *History of Education Quarterly* 22, no. 3 (1982): 319–339.

8. Richard Bailey, *A. S. Neill* (London: Bloomsbury, 2013), 24.

9. Ronald Swartz, *From Socrates to Summerhill and Beyond* (Charlotte, NC: Information Age Publishing, 2016), 14; Bailey, *A. S. Neill*, 26–27.

10. Sidney Hook, "John Dewey and His Betrayers," *Change* 3, no. 7 (1971): 26.

11. Paul Goodman, *Compulsory Miseducation and the Community of Scholars* (New York: Vintage Books, 1962), 44.

12. Bailey, *A. S. Neill*, 24–25.

13. Bailey, *A. S. Neill*, 26–27.

14. Homer Lane, *Talks to Parents and Teachers* (New York: Schocken Books, 1969), 177.

15. Lane, *Talks to Parents*, 13.

16. A. S. Neill, *Summerhill School: A New View of Childhood*, rev. (New York: St. Martin's Griffin, 1992), 9.

17. Neill, *Summerhill School*, 15.

18. Paul Goodman, *New Reformation: Notes of a Neolithic Conservative* (New York: Random House, 1970), 67–68.

19. Ivan Illich, *Deschooling Society* (London: Marion Boyars, 1970), 1, 2.

20. John Holt and Patrick Farenga, *Teach Your Own: The John Holt Book of Homeschooling*, rev. (New York: Da Capo Press, 2003), 279.

21. Patrick Farenga, "Homeschooling Summarized in the Congressional Quarterly Researcher," *John Holt GWS*, March 18, 2014, https://www.johnholtgws .com/pat-farengas-blog/2014/3/18/homeschooling-summarized-in-the -congressional-quarterly-researcher.

22. US Department of Education, National Center for Education Statistics, "Parent and Family Involvement in Education: Results from the National Household Education Surveys Program of 2016," Codebook, September 2017, https://nces.ed.gov/nhes/data/2016/cbook_ecpp_pu.pdf.

23. Peter Gray and Gina Riley, "The Challenges and Benefits of Unschooling, According to 232 Families Who Have Chosen that Route," *Journal of Unschooling and Alternative Learning* 7, no. 14 (2013), https://jual.nipissingu.ca /wp-content/uploads/sites/25/2014/06/v72141.pdf.

24. Peter Gray, "Survey of Grown Unschoolers I: Overview of the Results," *Freedom to Learn* (*Psychology Today* blog), June 7, 2014, https://www .psychologytoday.com/blog/freedom-learn/201406/survey-grown -unschoolers-i-overview-findings.

25. Peter Gray, "Survey of Grown Unschoolers II: Going on to College, *Freedom to Learn* (*Psychology Today* blog), June 17, 2014, https://www .psychologytoday.com/blog/freedom-learn/201406/survey-grown -unschoolers-ii-going-college.

26. Herbert R. Kohl, *The Open Classroom: A Practical Guide to a New Way of Teaching* (New York: New York Review, 1969), 15.

27. A. S. Neill, *Freedom—Not License!* (New York: Hart Publishing Company, 1966), 7.

28. Neill, *Summerhill School*, 36.

29. Grace Llewellyn and Amy Silver, *Guerrilla Learning: How to Give Your Kids a Real Education With or Without School* (New York: John Wiley & Sons, 2001), 11.

4. Childhood Isn't What It Used to Be

1. Jay Griffiths, *A Country Called Childhood: Children and the Exuberant World* (Berkeley, CA: Counterpoint, 2014), ix.

2. Michael Pollan, *In Defense of Food: An Eater's Manifesto* (New York: Penguin, 2008), 1.

3. Felix Gussone, MD, "America's Obesity Epidemics Reaches Record High, New Report Says," *NBC News*, October 13, 2017, https://www .nbcnews.com/health/health-news/america-s-obesity-epidemic-reaches -record-high-new-report-says-n810231.

4. F. Thomas Juster, Hiromi Ono, and Frank P. Stafford, "Changing Times of American Youth: 1981–2003," Institute for Social Research (Ann Arbor: University of Michigan, 2004), http://ns.umich.edu/Releases/2004/Nov04 /teen_time_report.pdf.

5. Teresa Morisi, "Teen Labor Force Participation Before and After the Great Recession and Beyond," US Bureau of Labor Statistics, February 2017, https://www.bls.gov/opub/mlr/2017/article/teen-labor-force-participation -before-and-after-the-great-recession.htm.

6. Sandra L. Hofferth and John F. Sandberg, "Changes in American Children's Time, 1981–1997," *Advances in Life Course Research* 6 (2001): 193–229.

7. Peter Gray, "The Decline of Play and the Rise of Psychopathology in Children and Adolescents," *American Journal of Play* 3, no. 4 (2011).

8. Angela Hanscom, *Balanced and Barefoot* (Oakland, CA: New Harbinger Publications, 2016), 30.

9. Jane E. Barker, Andrei D. Semenov, Laura Michaelson, Lindsay S. Provan, Hannah R. Snyder, Yuko Munakata, "Less-Structured Time in Children's Daily Lives Predicts Self-Directed Executive Functioning," *Frontiers in Psychology* 7 (June 17, 2014): 593.

10. "Time to Play, a Study on Children's Free Time: How It Is Spent, Prioritized and Valued," Gallup, August 2017, http://news.gallup.com/reports /214766/7.aspx?ays=n#aspnetForm.

11. Po Bronson and Ashley Merryman, "The Creativity Crisis," *Newsweek*, July 10, 2010, http://www.newsweek.com/creativity-crisis-74665.

12. K. H. Kim, *The Creativity Challenge: How We Can Recapture American Innovation*. (New York: Prometheus Books, 2016), 20.

13. Associated Press, "U.S. Education Spending Tops Global List, Study Shows," *CBS News*, June 25, 2013, https://www.cbsnews.com/news/us-education-spending-tops-global-list-study-shows.

14. Drew Desilver, "U.S. Students' Academic Achievement Still Lags That of Their Peers in Many Other Countries," Pew Research Center, February 15, 2017, http://www.pewresearch.org/fact-tank/2017/02/15/u-s-students-internationally-math-science.

15. Lauren Camera, "Student Scores in Reading and Math Drop," *U.S. News & World Report*, October 28, 2015, https://www.usnews.com/news/articles/2015/10/28/student-scores-in-reading-and-math-drop.

16. Erika Christakis, "The New Preschool Is Crushing Kids," *Atlantic*, January/February 2016, http://www.theatlantic.com/magazine/archive/2016/01/the-new-preschool-is-crushing-kids/419139.

17. Elizabeth Bonawitz, Patrick Shafto, Hyowon Gweon, Noah D. Goodman, Elisabeth Spelke, and Laura Schultz, "The Double-Edged Sword of Pedagogy: Instruction Limits Spontaneous Exploration and Discovery," *Cognition* 120, no. 3 (September 2011): 322–30.

18. Daphna Buchsbaum, Alison Gopnik, Thomas L. Griffiths, and Patrick Shafto, "Children's Imitation of Causal Action Sequences Is Influenced by Statistical and Pedagogical Evidence," *Cognition* 120, no. 3 (September 2011): 331–40.

19. Alison Gopnik, "Why Preschool Shouldn't Be Like School," *Slate*, March 16, 2011, http://www.slate.com/articles/double_x/doublex/2011/03/why_preschool_shouldnt_be_like_school.html#cx.

20. Cory Turner, "Why Preschool Suspensions Still Happen and How to Stop Them," NPR, June 20, 2016, http://www.npr.org/sections/ed/2016/06/20/482472535/why-preschool-suspensions-still-happen-and-how-to-stop-them.

21. US Department of Education, National Center for Educational Statistics, *Status and Trends in the Education of Racial and Ethnic Groups*, by Susan Aud, Mary Ann Fox, and Angelina KewalRamani, Open-file report 2010-015, National Center for Education Statistics (Washington, DC, 2010),https://nces.ed.gov/pubs2010/2010015.pdf.

22. Ama Mazama and Garvey Lundy, "African American Homeschooling as Racial Protectionism," *Journal of Black Studies* 43, no.7 (October 2012): 723–48.

23. Jessica Huseman, "The Rise of Homeschooling Among Black Families," *Atlantic*, February 17, 2015, https://www.theatlantic.com/education/archive /2015/02/the-rise-of-homeschooling-among-black-families/385543.

24. US Department of Health and Human Services, Centers for Disease Control and Prevention, *Diagnostic Experiences of Children with Attention-Deficit/Hyperactivity Disorder*, by Susanna N. Visser, Benjamin Zablotsky, Joseph R. Holbrook, Melissa L. Danielson, and Rebecca H. Bitsko, National Health Statistics Report 81 (September 3, 2015), https://www.cdc.gov/nchs/data/nhsr/nhsr081.pdf.

25. Enrico Gnaulati, *Back to Normal: Why Ordinary Childhood Behavior Is Mistaken for ADHD, Bipolar Disorder, and Autism Spectrum Disorder* (Boston: Beacon Press, 2013), 32.

26. Brent Fulton, Richard Scheffler, and Stephen Hinshaw, "State Variation in Increased ADHD Prevalence: Links to NCLB School Accountability and State Medication Laws," *Psychiatric Services* 66, no. 10 (October 2015): 1074–82, https://ps.psychiatryonline.org/doi/pdf/10.1176/appi.ps .201400145?code=ps-site.

27. Peter Gray, "Experiences of ADHD-Labeled Kids Who Leave Typical Schooling," *Freedom to Learn* (*Psychology Today* blog), September 9, 2010, https://www.psychologytoday.com/blog/freedom-learn/201009 /experiences-adhd-labeled-kids-who-leave-typical-schooling.

28. Peter Gray, "ADHD & School: Assessing Normalcy in an Abnormal Environment," *Freedom To Learn* (*Psychology Today* blog), July 7, 2010, https://www.psychologytoday.com/blog/freedom-learn/201007/adhd -school-assessing-normalcy-in-abnormal-environment.

29. Tracy Ventola, "A Solution to ADHD and Other School-Based Disorders," *OFF KLTR!* (blog), October 2, 2014, https://offkltr.com/2014/10/02 /a-solution-to-adhd-and-other-school-based-disorders.

30. Valerie J. Calderon and Daniela Yu, "Student Enthusiasm Falls as High School Graduation Nears," Gallup, June 1, 2017, http://news.gallup.com /opinion/gallup/211631/student-enthusiasm-falls-high-school-graduation -nears.aspx.

31. Ethan Yazzie-Mintz, "Charting the Path from Engagement to Achievement: A Report on the 2009 High School Survey of Student Engagement," Center

for Evaluation and Education Policy (Bloomington, IN: 2010), https://www
.wisconsinpbisnetwork.org/assets/files/2013%20Conference/Session%20
Material/HighSchoolSurveyStudentEngagement.pdf.

32. Mihaly Csikszentmihalyi and Jeremy Hunter, *Journal of Happiness Studies* 4
(2003): 185–99.

33. Adam Grant, *Originals: How Non-Conformists Move the World* (New York:
Viking, 2016), 7.

5. Natural Literacy and Numeracy

1. Madeleine L'Engle, *A Circle Of Quiet* (New York: HarperCollins, 1972), 54–55.

2. Daphna Bassok, Scott Latham, and Anna Rorem, "Is Kindergarten the New
First Grade?" *AERA Open* 1, no. 4 (January–March 2016): 1–31.

3. John Taylor Gatto, "I Quit, I Think," *Wall Street Journal*, Op-Ed, July 25, 1991.

4. Jane W. Torrey, "Learning to Read Without a Teacher: A Case Study," *Elementary English* 46 (1969): 550–556, 658.

5. William Teale, "Toward a Theory of How Children Learn to Read and Write
Naturally," *Language Arts* 59, no. 6 (1982): 558.

6. Jane W. Torrey, "Reading That Comes Naturally: The Early Reader," *Reading
Research: Advances in Theory and Practice. Vol. I*, ed. T. G. Waller and C. E.
MacKinnon (New York: Academic Press, 1979): 123.

7. Alan Thomas and Harriet Pattison, "The Informal Acquisition and Development of Literacy," *International Perspectives on Home Education*, ed.
P. Rothermel (London: Palgrave Macmillan, 2015): 57–73.

8. Annie Murphy Paul, "Why Third Grade Is So Important: The Matthew
Effect," *Time*, September 26, 2012, http://ideas.time.com/2012/09/26/why
-third-grade-is-so-important-the-matthew-effect.

9. Harriet Pattison, *Rethinking Learning to Read* (Shrewsbury, UK: Educational
Heretics Press, 2016): 138–39.

10. Peter Gray, "Children Teach Themselves to Read," *Freedom to Learn* (*Psychology Today* blog), February 24, 2010, https://www.psychologytoday.com/blog
/freedom-learn/201002/children-teach-themselves-read.

11. Nancy Carlsson-Paige, Geralyn Bywater McLaughlin, and Joan Wolfsheimer
Almon, "Reading Instruction in Kindergarten: Little to Gain and Much
to Lose," Defending the Early Years (2015): https://www.deyproject.org
/uploads/1/5/5/7/15571834/readinginkindergarten_online-1__1_.pdf.

12. Arthur M. Pittis, "Literacy, Not Just Reading," *Waldorf Education: A Family Guide*, eds. Pamela Johnson Fenner and Karen L. Rivers (Amesbury, MA: Michaelmas Press, 1995), 73.

13. Sebastian Suggate, Elizabeth Schaughency, and Elaine Reese, "Children Learning to Read Later Catch up to Children Reading Earlier," *Early Childhood Research Quarterly* 28, no. 1 (October 2013): 33–48.

14. Daniel Greenberg, *Free at Last: The Sudbury Valley School* (Framingham, MA: Sudbury Valley School Press, 1987), 31, 35.

15. Karl F. Wheatley, "How Unschoolers Can Help to End Traditional Reading Instruction," *Journal of Unschooling and Alternative Learning* 7, no. 13 (2013), http://jual.nipissingu.ca/wp-content/uploads/sites/25/2014/06/v71131.pdf.

16. Andrew Perrin, "Who Doesn't Read Books in America?," Pew Research Center, November 23, 2016, http://www.pewresearch.org/fact-tank/2016/11/23/who-doesnt-read-books-in-america.

17. "The U.S. Illiteracy Rate Hasn't Changed in 10 Years," *Huffington Post*, September 6, 2013, https://www.huffingtonpost.com/2013/09/06/illiteracy-rate_n_3880355.html.

18. William Teale, "Toward a Theory of How Children Learn to Read and Write Naturally," *Language Arts* 59, no. 6 (1982): 558.

19. Andrew Hacker, *The Math Myth: And Other STEM Delusions* (New York: The New Press, 2016), 138.

20. Barbara Oakley, *Mindshift: Break Through Obstacles to Learning and Discover Your Hidden Potential* (New York: Tarcher Perigee, 2017), 3.

21. L. P. Benezet, "The Teaching of Arithmetic I: The Story of an Experiment," *Journal of the National Education Association* 24, no 8 (November 1935): 241–44.

22. Hassler Whitney, "Coming Alive in School Math and Beyond," *Educational Studies in Mathematics* 18, no. 3 (August 1987): 229–42.

23. Daniel Greenberg, *Free at Last: The Sudbury Valley School* (Framingham, MA: Sudbury Valley School Press, 1987), 18.

24. Whitney, "Coming Alive in School Math," 229–42.

25. Carlo Ricci, "Emergent, Self-Directed, and Self-Organized Learning: Literacy, Numeracy, and the iPod Touch," *International Review of Research in Open and Distributed Learning* 12, no. 7 (2011): 135–46.

26. "Thinking about Math in Terms of Literacy, not Levels," *PBS News Hour*, August 2, 2016, audio transcript, https://www.pbs.org/newshour/show /thinking-math-terms-literacy-not-levels.

6. Tech-Enabled Unschooling

1. Jeff Goodell, "Steve Jobs in 1994: The *Rolling Stone* Interview," *Rolling Stone*, June 16, 1994, https://www.rollingstone.com/culture/news/steve -jobs-in-1994-the-rolling-stone-interview-20110117.

2. Seymour Papert, *Mindstorms: Children, Computers, and Powerful Ideas*, 2nd ed. (New York: Basic Books, 1993), 7.

3. Papert, *Mindstorms*, 8, 9.

4. Mitchel Resnick, *Lifelong Kindergarten: Cultivating Creativity through Projects, Passion, Peers, and Play* (Cambridge, MA: MIT Press, 2017), 13.

5. Marc Parry, "Online, Bigger Classes May Be Better Classes," *Chronicle of Higher Education*, August 29, 2010, https://www.chronicle.com/article/Open -Teaching-When-the/124170.

6. Laura Pappano, "The Year of the MOOC," *New York Times*, November 2, 2012, https://mobile.nytimes.com/2012/11/04/education/edlife/massive -open-online-courses-are-multiplying-at-a-rapid-pace.html?mcubz=1.

7. Meltem Huri Baturay, "An Overview of the World of MOOCs," *Procedia— Social and Behavioral Sciences* 147 (February 12, 2015): 427–433.

8. Chris Parr, "Mooc Creators Criticize Courses' Lack of Creativity," *Times Higher Education*, October 17, 2013, https://www.timeshighereducation .com/news/mooc-creators-criticise-courses-lack-of-creativity/2008180 .article.

9. Philipp Schmidt, Mitchel Resnick, and Natalie Rusk, "Learning Creative Learning: How We Tinkered with MOOCs," P2P online report, http://reports .p2pu.org/learning-creative-learning.

10. Sugata Mitra, R. Dangwal, S. Chatterjee, S. Jha, RS Bisht, and P. Kapur, "Acquisition of Computer Literacy on Shared Public Computers: Children and the 'Hole in the Wall'," *Australasian Journal of Educational Technology* 21, no. 3 (2005): 407–26. http://eprint.ncl.ac.uk/file_store /production/24094/3344F368-A39A-415F-9F96-E6F101EAA8C6.pdf.

11. Sugata Mitra, "Build a School in the Cloud," TED Talk, February 2013, https://www.ted.com/talks/sugata_mitra_build_a_school_in_the_cloud.

12. John Greathouse, "The Future of Learning: Why Skateboarders Suddenly Became Crazy Good in the Mid-80s," *Forbes*, February 25, 2017, https://www .forbes.com/sites/johngreathouse/2017/02/25/the-future-of-learning-why -skateboarders-suddenly-became-crazy-good-in-the-mid-90s/#352ba03a2c91.

13. Ivan Illich, *Deschooling Society* (London: Marion Boyars, 1970), vii.

14. Ken Robinson, "Do Schools Kill Creativity?," TED Talk, February 2006, https://www.ted.com/talks/ken_robinson_says_schools_kill_creativity.

15. Samuel Levin and Susan Engel, *A School of Our Own: The Story of the First Student-Run High School and a New Vision for American Education* (New York: New Press, 2016), 59.

16. Vasilis Kostakis, Vasilis Niaros, and Christos Giotitsas, "Production and Governance in Hackerspaces: A Manifestation of Commons-Based Peer Production in the Physical Realm?" *International Journal of Cultural Studies* 18, no. 5 (February 13, 2014): 555–73.

17. Neil Gershenfeld, "How to Make Almost Anything: The Digital Fabrication Revolution," *Foreign Affairs* 91, no. 6 (Nov/Dec 2012), http://cba.mit.edu /docs/papers/12.09.FA.pdf.

18. Deborah Fallows, "The Library Card," *Atlantic*, March 2016, http://www .theatlantic.com/magazine/archive/2016/03/the-library-card/426888.

19. Neil Gershenfeld, *Fab: The Coming Revolution on Your Desktop—From Personal Computers to Personal Fabrications* (New York: Basic Books, 2005), 7.

20. Clive Thompson, "Texting Isn't the First Technology Thought to Impair Social Skills," *Smithsonian Magazine*, March 2016, http://www.smithsonianmag .com/innovation/texting-isnt-first-new-technology-thought-impair-social -skills-180958091/#RyYV2qBULE6F0h0R.99.

21. Frank Rose, "*The Art of Immersion* Excerpt: Fear of Fiction," *Wired*, March 10, 2011, https://www.wired.com/2011/03/immersion-fear-of-fiction.

22. Bob Pepperman Taylor, *Horace Mann's Troubling Legacy: The Education of Democratic Citizens* (Lawrence: University Press of Kansas, 2010), 19.

23. Joe Clement and Matt Miles, *Screen Schooled: Two Veteran Teachers Expose How Technology Overload Is Making Our Kids Dumber* (Chicago: Chicago Review Press, 2017), 5.

24. danah boyd, *It's Complicated: The Social Lives of Networked Teens* (New Haven: Yale University Press, 2014), 18.

25. Andrew K. Przybylski, Netta Weinstein, and Kou Murayama, "Internet Gaming Disorder: Investigating the Clinical Relevance of a New Phenomenon," *American Journal of Psychiatry* 174, no. 3 (March 1, 2017): 230–36.

26. Cheryl K. Olson, "Children's Motivations for Video Game Play in the Context of Normal Development," *Review of General Psychology* 14, no. 2 (2010): 180–87.

27. Peter Gray, "The Many Benefits, for Kids, of Playing Video Games," *Freedom to Learn* (*Psychology Today* blog), January 7, 2012, https://www.psychologytoday.com/blog/freedom-learn/201201/the-many-benefits-kids-playing-video-games.

28. Peter Gray, "The Human Nature of Teaching II: What Can We Learn from Hunter-Gatherers?.," *Freedom to Learn* (*Psychology Today* blog), May 2, 2012, https://www.psychologytoday.com/blog/freedom-learn/201105/the-human-nature-teaching-ii-what-can-we-learn-hunter-gatherers.

29. Philipp Schmidt, Mitchel Resnick, and Natalie Rusk, "Learning Creative Learning: How We Tinkered with MOOCs," P2PU online report, http://reports.p2pu.org/learning-creative-learning.

7. Unschooling Resource Centers

1. Harper Lee, *To Kill a Mockingbird* (New York: Grand Central Publishing, 1960), 43–44.

2. John Holt, *Learning All the Time*, rev. (New York: Da Capo Books, 1990), 162.

8. Unschooling Schools

1. Jerry Large, "Astrophysicist Has Plan for Drawing Kids into Science," *Seattle Times*, May 15, 2011, https://www.seattletimes.com/seattle-news/astrophysicist-has-plan-for-drawing-kids-into-science.

2. Daniel Greenberg, *Free at Last: The Sudbury Valley School* (Framingham, MA: Sudbury Valley School Press, 1987), 8.

3. William K. Stevens, "Students Flock to Philadelphia 'School Without Walls,'" *New York Times*, January 23, 1970, http://www.nytimes.com/1970/01/23/archives/students-flock-to-philadelphia-school-without-walls.html?_r=0.

4. Lynne Blumberg, "Out of the Mainstream: Staying There Isn't Easy," *Education Next* 10, no. 3 (Summer 2010), http://educationnext.org/out-of-the-mainstream.

5. Ron Miller, *Free Schools, Free People: Education and Democracy after the 1960s* (Albany: State University of New York Press, 2002), 130.

6. Jonathan Kozol, *Free Schools* (Boston: Houghton Mifflin Company, 1972), 11.

7. Daniel Greenberg, *Free at Last: The Sudbury Valley School* (Framingham, MA: Sudbury Valley School Press, 1987), 184.

8. Peter Gray and David Chanoff, "Democratic Schooling: What Happens to Young People Who Have Charge of Their Own Education?," *American Journal of Education* 94 (1986): 182–213.

9. Daniel Greenberg and Mimsy Sadofsky, *Legacy of Trust: Life after the Sudbury Valley School Experience* (Framingham, MA: Sudbury Valley School Press, 1992); Daniel Greenberg, Mimsy Sadofsky, and Jason Lempka, *The Pursuit of Happiness: The Lives of Sudbury Valley Alumni* (Framingham, MA: Sudbury Valley School Press, 2005).

10. Kirsten Olson, "The Shadow Side of Schooling," *Education Week*, April 21, 2008, https://www.edweek.org/ew/articles/2008/04/23/34olson_web.h27.html.

11. Peter Gray, "School Bullying: A Tragic Cost to Undemocratic Schools," *Freedom to Learn* (*Psychology Today* blog), May 12, 2010, https://www.psychologytoday.com/blog/freedom-learn/201005/school-bullying-tragic-cost-undemocratic-schools.

12. Mark McCaig, *Like Water: The Extraordinary Approach to Education at the Fairhaven School* (Upper Marlboro, MD: Fairhaven School Press, 2008), 5.

9. Unschooled Teens

1. Carol Black, "A Thousand Rivers: What the Modern World Has Forgotten About Children and Learning," CarolBlack.org, http://carolblack.org/a-thousand-rivers.

2. Robert Epstein, *Teen 2.0: Saving Our Children and Families from the Torment of Adolescence* (Fresno, CA: Quill Driver Books, 2010), 21.

3. Perri Klass, "Kids' Suicide-Related Hospital Visits Rise Sharply," *New York Times*, May 16, 2018, https://www.nytimes.com/2018/05/16/well/family/suicide-adolescents-hospital.html.

4. Gregory Plemmons, et al., "Hospitalization for Suicide Ideation or Attempt: 2008–2015," *Pediatrics*, May 2018.

5. CDC QuickStats, "Suicide Rates for Teens Aged 15–19 Years, by Sex — United States, 1975–2015," *MMWR Morb Mortal Wkly Rep* 2017;66:816. DOI: http://dx.doi.org/10.15585/mmwr.mm6630a6.

6. CDC QuickStats, "Death Rates for Motor Vehicle Traffic Injury, Suicide, and Homicide Among Children and Adolescents aged 10–14 Years — United

States, 1999–2014," *MMWR Morb Mortal Wkly Rep* 2016;65:1203. DOI: http://dx.doi.org/10.15585/mmwr.mm6543a8.

7. Margaret Shapiro, "Stressed-Out Teens, with School a Main Cause," *Washington Post*, February 17, 2014, https://www.washingtonpost.com/national /health-science/stressed-out-teens-with-school-a-main-cause/2014/02/14/d3b 8ab56-9425-11e3-84e1-27626c5ef5fb_story.html?utm_term=.e8719bda42c6.

8. Epstein, *Teen 2.0*, 4.

9. Thomas Hine, "The Rise and Decline of the Teenager," *American Heritage* 50, no. 5 (September 1999), https://www.americanheritage.com/content /rise-and-decline-teenager.

10. Grace Llewellyn, *The Teenage Liberation Handbook: How to Quit School and Get a Real Life and Education*, 2nd ed. (Eugene, OR: Lowry House Publishers, 1998), 38.

11. John Hagel III and Jeff Schwartz, "A Framework for Understanding the Future of Work," *Deloitte HR Times* blog, September 27, 2017, https://hrtimesblog .com/2017/09/27/a-framework-for-understanding-the-future-of-work.

12. Paul Goodman, *New Reformation: Notes of a Neolithic Conservative* (New York: Random House, 1970), 87.

13. Paul Goodman, *Compulsory Miseducation and the Community of Scholars* (New York: Vintage Books, 1962), 61.

14. Robert Epstein, *Teen 2.0: Saving Our Children and Families from the Torment of Adolescence* (Fresno, CA: Quill Driver Books, 2010), 320.

15. Teresa Morisi, "Teen Labor Force Participation Before and After the Great Recession and Beyond," US Bureau of Labor Statistics, February 2017, https://www .bls.gov/opub/mlr/2017/article/teen-labor-force-participation-before-and -after-the-great-recession.htm.

16. Bryan Caplan, *The Case Against Education: Why the Education System Is a Waste of Time and Money* (Princeton, NJ: Princeton University Press, 2018), 3.

17. Robert Halpern, *The Means to Grow Up: Reinventing Apprenticeship as a Developmental Support in Adolescence* (New York: Routledge, 2009), xiv.

10. Out-of-School Unschooling

1. Heidi Moore, "Why Play Is the Work of Childhood," Fred Rogers Center, September 23, 2014, http://www.fredrogerscenter.org/2014/09/why -play-is-the-work-of-childhood.

2. Donna St. George, "'Free Range' Parents Cleared in Second Neglect Case After Kids Walked Alone," *Washington Post*, June 22, 2015, https://www.washingtonpost.com/local/education/free-range-parents-cleared-in-second-neglect-case-after-children-walked-alone/2015/06/22/82283c24-188c-11e5-bd7f-4611a60dd8e5_story.html?utm_term=.cda931cd6d6b.

3. Lenore Skenazy, *Free-Range Kids: How to Raise Safe, Self-Reliant Children—Without Going Nuts with Worry* (San Francisco, CA: Jossey-Bass, 2009), 8.

11. An Unschooled Future

1. Ta-Nehisi Coates, *Between the World and Me* (New York: Spiegel and Grau, 2015), 48.

2. Cathy N. Davidson, *Now You See It: How Technology and Brain Science Will Transform Schools and Business for the 21st Century* (New York: Viking, 2011), 18, 12.

3. World Economic Forum, "The Future of Jobs: Employment, Skills and Workforce Strategy for the Fourth Industrial Revolution," January 2016, http://www3.weforum.org/docs/WEF_Future_of_Jobs.pdf.

4. Sonia Smith, "Big-Box Store Has New Life as an Airy Public Library," *New York Times*, September 1, 2012, http://www.nytimes.com/2012/09/02/us/former-walmart-in-mcallen-is-now-an-airy-public-library.html.

5. Patricia Lee Brown, "These Public Libraries are for Snowshoes and Ukuleles." *The New York Times*, September 14, 2015, http://www.nytimes.com/2015/09/15/us/these-public-libraries-are-for-snowshoes-and-ukuleles.html.

6. Joseph Frazier Wall, *Andrew Carnegie* (New York: Oxford University Press, 1970), 818–19.

7. David Nasaw, *Andrew Carnegie* (New York: Penguin, 2006), 45.

8. Nasaw, *Andrew Carnegie*, 42–43.

9. Deborah Fallows, "The Library Card," *Atlantic*, March 2016, retrieved from web May 5, 2016: http://www.theatlantic.com/magazine/archive/2016/03/the-library-card/426888.

10. Andrew Carnegie, *The Autobiography of Andrew Carnegie* (Boston: Houghton Mifflin, 1920), 45.

11. Paul Goodman, *Compulsory Miseducation and the Community of Scholars* (New York: Vintage Books, 1962), 61.

Selected Bibliography

Caplan, Bryan. *The Case Against Education: Why the Education System Is a Waste of Time and Money.* Princeton, NJ: Princeton University Press, 2018.

Epstein, Robert. *Teen 2.0: Saving Our Children and Families from the Torment of Adolescence.* Fresno, CA: Quill Driver Books, 2010.

Gatto, John Taylor. *Dumbing Us Down: The Hidden Curriculum of Compulsory Schooling.* BC, Canada: New Society Publishers, 1992.

Gnaulati, Enrico. *Back to Normal: Why Ordinary Childhood Behavior Is Mistaken for ADHD, Bipolar Disorder, and Autism Spectrum Disorder.* Boston: Beacon Press, 2013.

Goodman, Paul. *Compulsory Miseducation and the Community of Scholars.* New York: Vintage Books, 1962.

Gray, Peter. *Free to Learn: Why Unleashing the Instinct to Play Will Make Our Children Happier, More Self-Reliant, and Better Learners for Life.* New York: Basic Books, 2013.

Greenberg, Daniel. *Free at Last: The Sudbury Valley School.* Framingham, MA: Sudbury Valley School Press, 1987.

Hanscom, Angela J. *Balanced and Barefoot: How Unrestricted Outdoor Play Makes for Strong, Confident, and Capable Children.* Oakland, CA: New Harbinger Publications, 2016.

Holt, John. *How Children Learn,* rev. New York: Da Capo Press, 2017.

Holt, John. *Instead of Education.* Boulder, CO: Sentient Publications, 2004.

Holt, John. *Learning All the Time.* Rev. ed. New York: Da Capo Books, 1990.

Holt, John, and Patrick Farenga. *Teach Your Own: The John Holt Book of Homeschooling.* Rev. ed. New York: Da Capo Press, 2003.

Illich, Ivan. *Deschooling Society*. London: Marion Boyars, 1970.

Kozol, Jonathan. *Free Schools*. Boston: Houghton Mifflin Company, 1972.

Llewellyn, Grace, and Amy Silver. *Guerrilla Learning: How to Give Your Kids a Real Education With or Without School*. New York: John Wiley & Sons, 2001.

Llewellyn, Grace. *The Teenage Liberation Handbook: How to Quit School and Get a Real Life and Education*. 2nd ed. Eugene, OR: Lowry House Publishers, 1998.

Miller, Ron. *Free Schools, Free People: Education and Democracy After the 1960s*. Albany, NY: State University of New York Press, 2002.

Neill, A. S. *Summerhill School: A New View of Childhood*. Rev. ed. New York: St. Martin's Griffin, 1992.

Priesnitz, Wendy. *School Free: The Home Schooling Handbook*. St. George, ON: Alternate Press, 1987.

Shalaby, Carla. *Troublemakers: Lessons in Freedom from Young Children at School*. New York: New Press, 2017.

Skenazy, Lenore. *Free-Range Kids: How to Raise Safe, Self-Reliant Children— Without Going Nuts with Worry*. San Francisco, CA: Jossey-Bass, 2009.

Weldon, Laura Grace. *Free Range Learning: How Homeschooling Changes Everything*. Prescott, AZ: Hohm Press, 2010.

Index

About the Author

KERRY MCDONALD IS AN EDUCATION policy writer whose articles have appeared at *Forbes*, *Newsweek*, NPR, *Reason*, *Education Next*, and *Natural Mother* magazine, among others. She has a BA in economics from Bowdoin College, a master's degree in education from Harvard University, and is a board member at the Alliance for Self-Directed Education. The mother of four never-been-schooled children, Kerry lives in Cambridge, Massachusetts, and blogs at WholeFamilyLearning.com